Your
iPad 2 ™
at Work

Jason R. Rich

que®

800 East 96th Street,
Indianapolis, Indiana 46240 USA

YOUR iPAD™ 2 AT WORK

COPYRIGHT © 2012 BY QUE PUBLISHING

ISBN-13: 978-0-7897-4937-6

ISBN-10: 0-7897-4937-8

Library of Congress Cataloging-in-Publication data is on file.

Printed in the United States of America

First Printing: September 2011

TRADEMARKS

WARNING AND DISCLAIMER

BULK SALES

Que Publishing offers excellent discounts on this book when ordered in quantity for bulk purchases or special sales. For more information, please contact

U.S. Corporate and Government Sales
1-800-382-3419
corpsales@pearsontechgroup.com

For sales outside of the U.S., please contact

International Sales
international@pearson.com

EDITOR-IN-CHIEF
Greg Wiegand

ACQUISITIONS EDITOR
Laura Norman

DEVELOPMENT EDITOR
Robin Drake

MANAGING EDITOR
Sandra Schroeder

SENIOR PROJECT EDITOR
Tonya Simpson

COPY EDITOR
Charlotte Kughen

INDEXER
Heather McNeill

PROOFREADER
Megan Wade

TECHNICAL EDITOR
Greg Kettell

PUBLISHING COORDINATOR
Cindy Teeters

BOOK DESIGNER
Anne Jones

COMPOSITOR
Bumpy Design

CONTENTS AT A GLANCE

TABLE OF CONTENTS

ABOUT THE AUTHOR

Jason R. Rich (www.JasonRich.com) is the bestselling author of more than 49 books, as well as a frequent contributor to a handful of major daily newspapers, national magazines, and popular websites. He's also an accomplished photographer and an avid Apple iPad 2, iPhone, and Mac user.

You can read more than 40 free, feature-length "how-to" articles by Jason R. Rich covering the Apple iPhone and iPad, online at the Que Publishing website. Visit www.iOSArticles.com and click the Articles tab. You can also follow Jason R. Rich on Twitter (@JasonRich7).

ACKNOWLEDGMENTS

Thanks to Laura Norman at Que Publishing for inviting me to work on this book and for all of her guidance as I've worked on this project. My gratitude also goes out to Greg Wiegand, Tonya Simpson, Robin Drake, Cindy Teeters, Todd Brakke, Greg Kettell, and Paul Boger, as well as everyone else at Que Publishing and Pearson who contributed their expertise, hard work, and creativity to the creation of *Your iPad 2 at Work*.

I'd also like to acknowledge the amazing talent of Steve Jobs—and everyone at Apple—and congratulate them on the incredible success of the iPad 2.

Thanks to my friends and family for their ongoing support. Finally, thanks to you, the reader. I hope this book helps you take full advantage of the power and capabilities of this amazing tablet device so that you're able to fully utilize your iPad 2 in every aspect of your life.

WE WANT TO HEAR FROM YOU!

As the reader of this book, *you* are our most important critic and commentator. We value your opinion and want to know what we're doing right, what we could do better, what areas you'd like to see us publish in, and any other words of wisdom you're willing to pass our way.

As an editor-in-chief for Que Publishing, I welcome your comments. You can email or write me directly to let me know what you did or didn't like about this book—as well as what we can do to make our books better.

Please note that I cannot help you with technical problems related to the topic of this book. We do have a User Services group, however, where I will forward specific technical questions related to the book.

When you write, please be sure to include this book's title and author as well as your name, email address, and phone number. I will carefully review your comments and share them with the author and editors who worked on the book.

Email: feedback@quepublishing.com

Mail: Greg Wiegand
Editor-in-Chief
Que Publishing
800 East 96th Street
Indianapolis, IN 46240 USA

READER SERVICES

Visit our website and register this book at quepublishing.com/register for convenient access to any updates, downloads, or errata that might be available for this book.

Introduction

When Apple announced the original iPad, and later the iPad 2, company CEO Steve Jobs referred to the tablet device as "magical." Within a year, more than 15 million people were caught in the iPad's spell, and millions more immediately sought out the iPad 2 when it was released in March 2011. By June 2011, Apple reported sales of more than 25 million iPads.

While this might not be a "magical" device that a fictional wizard like Harry Potter would use, it is a powerful tool that millions of real-life business professionals, consultants, and freelancers have added to their proverbial bag of tricks to stay better organized, be more productive, and become a better communicator.

In addition to the core preinstalled apps that come with the iPad 2, more than 100,000 iPad-specific apps are available from Apple's App Store. Plus, more than 350,000 Apple iPhone apps work flawlessly on the iPad 2 tablet. By customizing your iPad 2 with apps, you can give the device extra features and functionality that make it work better for your specific needs.

Along with apps, hundreds of accessory products, ranging from screen covers and iPad 2 cases, to wireless keyboards, external speakers, headsets, docking stations, and cable or adapters for connecting the iPad 2 to other devices, are readily available, and more are being introduced each week.

Combine the iPad 2 with the right collection of apps and accessories, and it becomes the perfect tool for anyone who needs advanced computer power while on the go but who doesn't want to carry around a bulky laptop or netbook computer.

With its 10-hour battery life, the iPad 2 keeps the information you need literally at your fingertips throughout your workday. In addition to sending and receiving email from virtually anywhere, you can stay informed by using your iPad 2 to access a wide range of websites, streaming Internet content, eBooks, and digital editions of newspapers and magazines. Plus, you can keep in touch with friends, family, co-workers, or clients by participating in videoconferencing or using Twitter.

If you're a business professional, consultant, salesperson, or freelancer or work in a specialized field, throughout this book you discover hundreds of ways you can use your iPad 2 on the job, regardless of what industry or field you work in.

Aside from general-interest work-related apps, the App Store has many vertical market apps that are designed to give the iPad 2 specialized functionality that caters to specific work-related tasks for a variety of fields, including the medical, real estate, construction, engineering, scientific, and financial fields.

There are also specialized apps for people in many other specialized professions or fields including, but not limited to, these professions: professional photographers, writers, public speakers, lawyers, inventors, mathematicians, teachers, architects, professional bloggers, website designers, scientists, programmers, meeting/party planners, and graphic artists.

WHAT YOU CAN EXPECT FROM THIS BOOK

Your iPad 2 at Work provides step-by-step instructions, plus hundreds of tips and strategies for incorporating the iPad 2 into your personal and professional life with the shortest learning curve possible—even if you don't consider yourself to be technologically savvy or adept at using the latest high-tech gadgets.

Later in this book, you discover how to utilize your tablet with your main computer and smartphone (such as an Apple iPhone), including how to easily transfer and synchronize data between these devices using the iTunes software. You will also discover how to wirelessly sync or transfer data using Apple's iCloud service.

Because we could not include everything in this printed book that we would like to cover, an extended version is available through Safari Books Online (www.safaribooksonline.com) that you can access using your free 30-day trial offered with this book.

If your iPad is running iOS 5, connecting it to your primary computer is no longer a requirement—it's an option. You can now set up and install your iPad without connecting it to a computer, plus you can back up your tablet and transfer data between devices (or other users working on other devices) wirelessly, assuming your tablet has access to the Web.

However, if you opt to use the iTunes sync process to link your computer to your tablet via a USB cable connection, whether your primary computer is a Mac or a PC running Windows, you must have the latest version of iTunes installed on the computer. To download the latest version of iTunes, use your primary computer to visit www.apple.com/itunes/download/.

> **TIP** As you read *Your iPad 2 at Work*, keep your eye out for the Tips, Notes, and Caution icons. Each of these icons has short tidbits of information that are particularly important and directly relevant to the chapter you're reading.

WHAT'S NEW WITH THE iPAD 2 AND APPLE'S iOS 5

Between the time that Apple first introduced the original iPad and the iPad 2 was released in March 2011, Apple made several major advancements to the device. In addition to making the iPad 2 faster, thinner, and lighter than the original iPad, the iPad 2 now offers both a front- and back-facing camera, which makes it capable of handling tasks such as videoconferencing via the Web.

In conjunction with the iPad 2, Apple also released Smart Covers, which serve as both a screen protector and a stand for the tablet. Even if you're planning to purchase another type of case for your iPad 2 (some of which are shown in Chapter 19), investing in a Smart Cover is definitely worthwhile because the iPad 2 hardware was designed to work seamlessly with this accessory.

In Fall 2011, Apple released the most significant improvement yet to the iOS operating system, which operates the iPad as well as other Apple mobile devices, including the iPhone and iPod touch.

> **NOTE** iOS is the operating system that makes your iPad 2 function, just like many PCs run using the Microsoft Windows operating system, and Apple Macs use the Mac OS X operating system. The iOS 5 operating system now comes preinstalled on all new iPad 2 units but will need to be updated periodically with a new version. Or, if you purchased an iPad 2 prior to Fall 2011, you will need to upgrade (for free) from iOS 4.4.4 to iOS 5 as soon as possible.

Using iOS 5, your iPad becomes more powerful and is no longer reliant on your primary computer. Plus, this new operating system is designed to work seamlessly with Apple's iCloud online-based file sharing service, so transferring files and documents between your iPad, primary computer, other Apple devices (such as your iPhone), as well as with other users has become a much easier and more straightforward process (as long as your iPad has access to the Web).

The iOS 5 upgrade, which comes preinstalled on all new iPad 2 units as of Fall 2011, also introduces the new Notification Center, which keeps you up to date on all incoming messages, alarms, and other time-sensitive information from a single, easy-to-access screen. See Chapter 5 for more information on how to use the Notification Center.

Another new feature offered through the iOS 5 upgrade is the iMessage app, which enables you to use the Internet to send and receive text messages to other iOS devices for free. This service is similar to text messaging on a cellular phone.

Using the new Newsstand app, you can subscribe to the digital editions of your favorite newspapers and magazines and have the latest issues of those publications automatically download to your iPad as soon as they're published.

For business people who are constantly juggling multiple deadlines and tasks, the new Reminders app enables you to create and manage multiple to-do lists and keep track of an unlimited number of upcoming deadlines. You'll read about other to-do list management apps within *Your iPad 2 at Work*, but this one automatically integrates with other core iPad apps, plus it offers unique features that will help keep you better organized. You learn more about this app in Chapter 9.

NOTE   All the information in this book addresses updates made to the iPad 2 through the iOS 5 operating system upgrade and includes information on how to utilize Apple's iCloud service for a variety of purposes.

TIP   Available on the quepublishing.com website are dozens of feature-length "how-to" articles and app reviews targeted to iPad 2 business users. From quepublishing.com's home page, click the Browse By Format tab at the top of the screen, and then select the Articles and Chapters option. To read more than 40 free how-to articles by Jason R. Rich, the author of this book, on the quepublishing.com website, simply visit www.iOSArticles.com and click the Articles tab.

THE ANATOMY OF THE iPAD 2

It measures 9.5 inches tall by 7.31 inches wide and is just .34 inches thick. When you look at the front of the iPad 2, what you see is the main screen. The front-facing camera is located at the top center, and you can find the iPad 2's Home button at the bottom center of the iPad 2's front, as well as the other physical ports and buttons found on the body of the iPad 2 (shown in Figure I.1).

Aside from these few buttons and ports, you do everything while using your iPad 2 via the tablet's touch screen. To properly navigate around your tablet via this touch screen, you need to utilize several simple finger movements.

FIGURE I.1

The front of the iPad 2 features a 7-inch, full-color, multitouch screen; the Home button; and the device's front-facing camera. On the back of the iPad 2 unit, in the upper-left corner, you see the back-facing camera.

TURNING YOUR iPAD 2 ON AND OFF

Your iPad 2 has four main states: On, Off, Sleep mode, and Airplane mode:

■ **Power On:** To turn on your iPad 2 when it's been powered off, press the Power button located on the top right of the tablet. It takes up to 15 seconds for the unit to fully power up. The Apple logo displays first on the screen, followed shortly thereafter by the Lock screen. When powered on, your iPad 2 is fully operational and the touch screen is on and active.

■ **Power Off:** When the iPad 2 is powered off, all apps are shut down and the tablet is not capable of sending or receiving data from the Web. To turn off the iPad 2, press and hold down the Power button for three to five seconds. The Home screen goes black, but at the top of the screen a slider switch with a red arrow and a Slide to Power Off message displays. Touch the red slider icon with your finger and slide it to the right to turn off the iPad 2.

■ **Sleep Mode:** You can place the iPad 2 in Sleep mode at any time when the iPad 2 is not in use. Press the Power button or place a Smart Cover over the iPad's screen. When put into Sleep mode, the iPad's screen goes dark; however, any apps currently running continue running in the background, and your iPad is still able to access the Web on its own. It's also able to receive alerts. In addition, if you have set any alarms, the iPad 2 wakes up on its own to display the alarm message or sound the alert tone you selected. To "wake up" your iPad when it's in Sleep mode, remove the Smart Cover from the screen and press the Home button once, or press the Power button once. The screen immediately turns on and your iPad's Lock screen, followed by the Home screen, displays.

> **TIP** Most of the time, when your iPad 2 is not in use (such as when it's being transported), putting it in Sleep mode is sufficient. Sleep mode is convenient because the wake-up process takes just a second or two, and you can keep apps running in the background.

■ **Airplane Mode (3G Models Only):** Putting your iPad 2 in Airplane mode shuts down its capability to access the 3G wireless web and keeps the unit from sending or receiving wireless transmissions, which is a perfect state when you're on an airplane or traveling overseas. All the iPad's other features and functions remain fully operational. You can place the tablet in Airplane mode by accessing the Settings app (described in Chapter 2). When the iPad is in Airplane mode, a small airplane icon displays in the upper-left corner of the screen, as shown in Figure I.2.

Even in Airplane mode, you can still turn on Wi-Fi mode or Bluetooth, enabling the iPad 2 to access the Web via a Wi-Fi hotspot (to utilize the wireless web access available on some commercial aircrafts, for example) and also communicate with a Bluetooth-enabled wireless keyboard.

FIGURE I.2

In Airplane mode, a small airplane icon displays in the upper-left corner of your iPad 2's screen.

USING THE TOUCH SCREEN

From the moment you turn on your iPad 2 (or take it out of Sleep mode), aside from pressing the Home button to return to the Home screen at any time, virtually all of your interaction with the tablet is through finger movements and taps on the iPad's highly sensitive touch screen:

- **Tapping:** Tapping an icon or link that's displayed on your iPad's screen serves the same purpose as clicking the mouse when you use your main computer. And, just as when you use a computer, you can single-tap or double-tap, which is equivalent to a single- or double-click of the mouse.

- **Hold:** Instead of a quick tap, in some cases, it is necessary to press and hold your finger on an icon or onscreen command option. When a hold action is required, place your finger on the appropriate icon or command option and hold it there. There's never a need to press down hard on the tablet's screen.

- **Swipe:** A swipe refers to quickly moving a finger along the screen from right to left, left to right, top to bottom, or bottom to top to scroll to the left, right, down, or up, respectively, depending on which app you're using.

- **Pinch:** Using your thumb and index finger (the finger next to your thumb), perform a pinch motion on the touch screen to zoom out when using certain apps. Or, unpinch (moving your fingers apart quickly) to zoom in on what you're looking at on the screen when using most apps.

> **TIP** Another way to zoom in or out when looking at the iPad 2's screen is to double-tap the area of the screen you want to zoom in on. This works in Safari when surfing the Web, when looking at photos using the Photos app, as well as within most other apps that support the zoom in/out feature.

However, you cannot delete from the iPad the icons for the core apps that came preinstalled on your iPad 2, such as Safari, Mail, Photos, App Store, Settings, Notes, FaceTime, Contacts, Calendar, Music, iTunes, Maps, Game Center, Photo Booth, Camera, YouTube, Reminders, Newsstands, and Videos.

When you finish moving the icons around, press the Home button on your iPad 2 to exit out of this mode and save your changes. The icons stop shaking, and you can return to the normal use of your tablet.

CREATING FOLDERS TO ORGANIZE ICONS

Just as you can on your main computer, you can create onscreen folders on your iPad's Home screen that can store multiple app icons within them. You can use folders to help organize your Home screen, group apps based on their category, and remove clutter from your Home screen by consolidating the app icons that are displayed.

To create a folder, from the Home screen press and hold down any app icon for 2–3 seconds. When all the app icons start to shake, pick one app icon that you want to place in a new folder. Place your finger on that app icon, and drag it directly on top of a second app icon that you want to include in the folder you're creating.

When the two app icons overlap, a folder is automatically created, as shown in Figure I.5. As soon as this happens, the other app icons on the Home screen fade slightly and a window containing the two apps within the newly created folder appears.

At the top of this window is a text field that contains the default name of the folder. (Your iPad 2 gives the folder an appropriate default name based on the category into which the two apps fall.) You can keep this name by tapping anywhere on the screen outside the folder window. Alternatively, you can change the name of the folder by tapping the circular X icon that's displayed to the extreme right of the folder name field.

To save your folder, tap anywhere outside the folder window. You now see the newly created folder appear among your app icons on the Home screen. In Figure I.6, the folder labeled Games currently contains five apps.

FIGURE I.5

A window appears on the Home screen as you're creating a folder. Enter the folder's name and see which app icons have already been placed in the folder.

FIGURE I.6

When a folder appears on the Home screen, it displays among the app icons but looks slightly different. Thumbnails of the apps that are stored within the folder are shown within the folder icon.

After you initially create a folder, it contains two app icons. You can add more icons to it whenever all the app icons on the Home screen are shaking. Simply place your finger on the app icon you want to move into the folder and drag that icon on top of the folder icon.

When you're finished adding app icons to the folder, you can move the folder around on the Home screen just as you would move any app icon, or press the Home button on the iPad to save your changes and return the Home screen to its normal appearance (causing the app icons to stop shaking).

To launch an app that's stored in a folder, from the Home screen tap the folder icon. When the folder window appears on the iPad's screen (as shown in Figure I.7), it displays all the app icons stored within the folder. Tap the icon for the app you want to use. To close the folder window on the Home screen, tap anywhere on the screen outside the folder window.

FIGURE I.7

An open folder and its folder window (which in this example contains five game apps) on the iPad's Home screen.

To remove an app icon from within a folder, from the Home screen tap the folder icon representing the folder in which the app is stored. When the folder window appears, hold your finger on the app icon that you want to move for two or three seconds. When the app icons start to shake, drag the app icon out of the folder window and back onto the main Home screen. When you're done, press the Home button to save your changes and return the Home screen to normal.

If you want to delete an app from a folder and from the iPad 2, when the icons are shaking tap the black-and-white X icon in the icon's upper-left corner. If you've synced your iPad 2 with your computer via iTunes, a copy of that app remains on your primary computer. Also, after you've initially purchased an app, you can freely download it again from the App Store or from your iCloud account.

> **TIP**   In addition to app icons and folders, you can set Safari bookmark icons to be displayed on your Home screen. Step-by-step directions for creating a Safari bookmark icon are provided in Chapter 4.

THE iPAD 2'S VIRTUAL KEYBOARD

Whenever you need to enter data into your iPad 2, you almost always use the virtual keyboard that pops up on the bottom portion of the screen when it's needed. The virtual keyboard typically resembles a typewriter or computer keyboard; however, certain onscreen keys have different purposes, depending on which app you're using.

For example, when you access the iPad 2's main Search screen, as shown in Figure I.8, notice the large Search key on the right side of the keyboard. However, when you use the Pages word processor app, the Search key becomes the Return key. When you surf the Web using the Safari web browser app, the Search key becomes the Go key in certain situations.

When using an app that involves numeric data entry, such as Numbers (see Figure I.9), the layout and design of the virtual keyboard changes dramatically.

As part of the iOS 5 upgrade, using your index fingers on your right and left hand simultaneously, if you place them in the center of the virtual keyboard and move them apart quickly, this will divide the iPad's onscreen keyboard into two sections, as shown in Figure I.10. Some people find this virtual keyboard format more convenient for typing while they're holding their tablet.

FIGURE 1.8
Your iPad 2's virtual keyboard when accessed from the main Search screen.

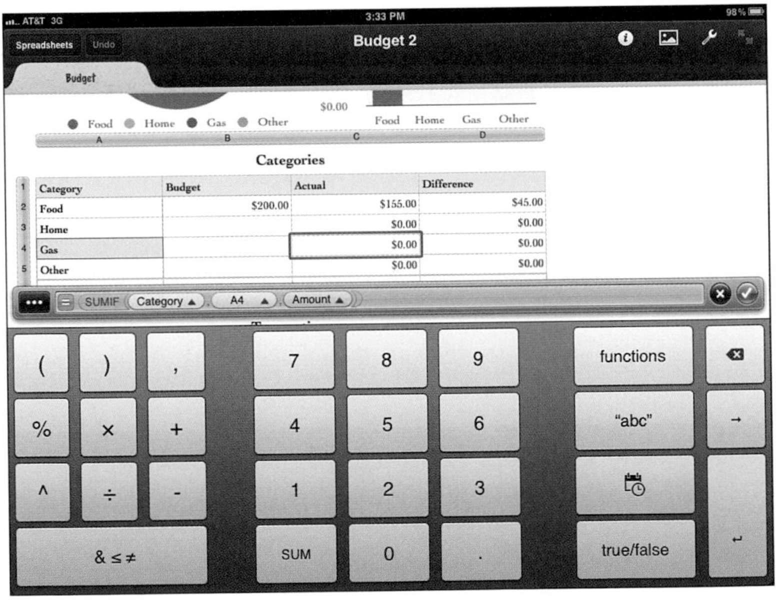

FIGURE I.9
The appearance of the virtual keyboard changes based on which app you're using and the type of data you need to enter.

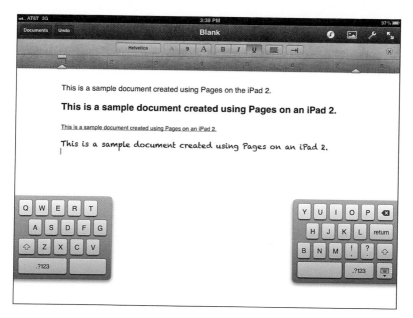

FIGURE I.10

Splitting the virtual keyboard in half is a new iOS 5 option.

When the virtual keyboard appears, use your fingers to tap the keys and type. From the Settings app, you can turn off the keyboard click noise that's otherwise heard when you're tapping the virtual keyboard keys. You also can turn off the Auto-Capitalization, Auto-Correction, Check Spelling, and Enable Caps Lock features that, when turned on, automatically fix what you're typing when the iOS deems it appropriate.

To make the keyboard disappear, you can often tap anywhere on the screen except on the virtual keyboard itself, or you can tap the Hide Keyboard key, which is always located in the lower-right corner of the virtual keyboard.

Whenever data entry is required when using an app, the virtual keyboard automatically displays as it's needed. However, if you need to fill in a data field when using a particular app, for example, and the virtual keyboard is not visible, simply tap the blank onscreen field where data needs to be entered, and the virtual keyboard displays.

1

ACTIVATING YOUR iPAD

When you first purchase your iPad 2, take it out of the box, and turn it on, you see a black screen that displays the iPad 2 logo. Before you can begin using your tablet, it must be initialized and set up for the first time. When prompted, swipe your finger on the onscreen switch to begin this setup procedure.

TIP The new wireless setup procedure that's built in to iOS 5 is used to initially set up your iPad 2. To do this, your tablet will need access to a Wi-Fi network. Or, you can connect your tablet to your primary computer via the supplied USB cable and then use iTunes on your primary computer to initially set up your tablet. This setup procedure is mandatory, but it needs to be done only once.

iPAD 2 WIRELESS SETUP

If you're setting up a brand-new iPad 2 that comes with iOS 5 installed and you're within a Wi-Fi hotspot, you can use the wireless setup procedure called PC Free. However, if you're using an iPad 2 that has iOS version 4.4.4 (or earlier) installed, it will be necessary to initially set up your tablet by connecting it to your primary computer and using iTunes.

The very first time you turn on a brand-new iPad 2, you see a black screen with the word *iPad* displayed near the center of the screen. Near the bottom-center of this screen is a virtual switch that says Slide to Set Up. Using your finger, slide this switch from left to right.

When the Welcome screen appears (shown in Figure 1.1), select your language (the default option is English), and then tap the right-pointing arrow icon that's displayed near the upper-right corner of the screen.

FIGURE 1.1

Select your language preference, and then tap the arrow icon to continue with the initial setup procedure.

Next, select your country or region. If you purchased the iPad within the United States, the default option will be United States. Again, tap on the right-pointing arrow icon displayed near the top-right corner of the screen to continue.

From the Wi-Fi Networks screen (shown in Figure 1.2), select the Wi-Fi network to which you want your tablet to connect. The available Wi-Fi networks display on the screen. When you tap your finger on the network you want to choose, a small checkmark appears next to the Wi-Fi network's name. Tap the Next icon that's displayed near the upper-right corner of the screen to continue.

FIGURE 1.2

To continue with the wireless setup, your tablet must be within a Wi-Fi hotspot.

The Set Up iPad screen displays next. From this screen, you can set up your iPad from scratch or restore the tablet from a previous backup. Near the bottom-center of this screen will be the following three command icons:

- Set Up As New iPad
- Restore from iCloud Backup
- Restore from iTunes

If you're upgrading from an original iPad to the iPad 2 and want to load all your apps, iPad customizations, and data, select the Restore from iTunes option, connect your tablet to your primary computer via the supplied USB cable, and follow the onscreen prompts. However, if you're setting up a brand-new iPad 2, tap the Set Up As New iPad option, and then tap the Next icon that appears near the upper-right corner of the screen to continue.

When the Apple ID screen appears (shown in Figure 1.3), you see a handful of enlarged app icons scrolling across the screen. Near the bottom center of this screen are two command icons:

- Sign In with an Apple ID
- Create a Free Apple ID

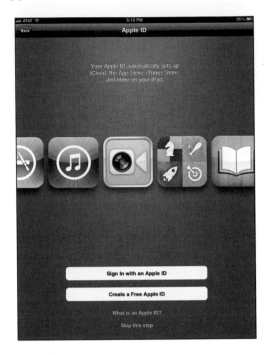

FIGURE 1.3

A valid Apple ID is required to initially set up an iPad 2. You can use an existing Apple ID account or create a free account from this screen.

NOTE   To use Apple's iCloud service, purchase apps, purchase content from iTunes, purchase eBooks from Apple's iBookstore, and do other things related to Apple, you must set up a free Apple ID account and associate a major credit card to that account. More information about Apple ID accounts is provided later.

If you already own any other Apple computer or iOS device, chances are you already have an Apple ID account set up. Tap the Sign In with an Apple ID command icon to continue. When the next screen appears, use the iPad's virtual keyboard to enter your Apple ID username and password.

> **NOTE** If you don't have an Apple ID, tap the Create a Free Apple ID command icon, and then follow the screen prompts to create your Apple ID. After you have your Apple ID, you can continue with the setup procedure for your iPad 2.

Next, you'll be able to set up iCloud services from the Set Up iCloud screen (shown in Figure 1.4). Near the bottom center of this screen, you can turn on or off the iCloud service. When you've made your selection, tap the Next icon that's displayed in the upper-right corner of the screen.

FIGURE 1.4

To use Apple's online-based file sharing service, called iCloud, it must be set up on your iPad 2.

Setting up iCloud is free, and because many of the apps enable you to share data and sync files using this online-based file sharing service, this is something you should do now. However, you will have the opportunity to set up iCloud later via the Settings app.

You now have the option to turn on and activate Apple's free Find My iPad service, which helps you locate your tablet if it gets lost or stolen. To activate this feature now (which is recommended), leave the Find My iPad switch, which is displayed near the bottom center of the Find My iPad screen, turned on. Then, tap the Next icon that appears near the top-right corner of the screen. You learn more about Find My iPad later.

Within a few seconds, the Thank You screen appears. On the screen is a message that states, "Your iPad is now set up. You're ready to start using the most advanced iOS ever." Near the bottom center of the screen, tap the Start Using iPad command icon.

Now that your iPad 2 has been set up, the tablet's Home screen is displayed (shown in Figure 1.5). On the Home Screen are the app icons for all the core apps that come preinstalled on your tablet, including Messages, Calendar, Notes, and so on.

> **TIP** When you're ready, one of the first apps you should download from the App Store is iBooks. This free app enables you to access Apple's online-based eBook store to find, purchase, and download eBooks, as well as read eBooks on the iPad. This app can also be used for reading PDF files.

FIGURE 1.5

After the setup procedure is finished, the iPad displays its default Home screen.

PREINSTALLED APPS ON YOUR iPAD 2

At this point, the default Home screen of your iPad 2 displays. On this screen are app icons for 20 core apps that come preinstalled under iOS 5 on your tablet, including the following:

- **Messages:** If you're already familiar with text messaging on your cell phone, the Messages app is similar. It enables you to use Apple's iMessage text messaging service to send and receive text messages. This service is compatible with all devices running iOS 5 (iPad 2, iPhone, iPod touch, and so on) and enables you to send/receive unlimited messages from fellow iOS 5 device users for free. Your tablet must be connected to the Internet to use this app and the service.

- **Calendar:** A powerful scheduling, time-management, and calendar app that can sync data with the scheduling software used on your primary computer, as well as with your iPhone. This includes iCal on a Mac or Microsoft Outlook on a PC running Windows. You learn more about the Calendar app in Chapter 5, "Using the Calendar App and Notification Center."

- **Notes:** Use this app to quickly jot notes and memos or maintain to-do lists, which can later be synced with your primary computer or shared with others via email. It's a basic text editor, as opposed to a full-featured word processor.

- **Reminders:** Introduced as part of iOS 5, Reminders is a feature-packed to-do list manager that enables you to juggle an unlimited number of lists and deadlines. As you'll discover in Chapter 10, "Finding Other Useful Business Apps," this app has some very unique and useful features for staying organized.

- **Maps:** When your iPad is connected to the Web, this app utilizes data from Google Maps to provide detailed onscreen maps and turn-by-turn directions. It also enables you to find specific addresses of companies.

- **YouTube:** This app is designed specifically to enable you to stream YouTube videos on your iPad 2 when the tablet has ongoing access to the Internet.

- **Videos:** Use this app to watch video content that's stored on your iPad 2, such as TV shows or movies you've purchased and downloaded from iTunes.

- **Contacts:** A comprehensive contact management app that maintains a detailed database of your contacts' information, such as multiple addresses, phone numbers, email addresses, and notes. This app can sync with the contacts management software on your primary computer or iPhone. You learn more about the Contacts app from Chapter 6, "Working with the Contacts App."

- **Game Center:** This is an interactive, online-based community for participating in multiplayer games on your iPad 2. You can compete against and communicate with other players from around the world and experience a variety of Game Center–compatible games. You learn more about Game Center in Chapter 16, "Relaxing with Games."

- **iTunes:** Similar to the iTunes software on your primary computer, this iTunes app is used to find, purchase, and download music, movies, and other content from the online-based iTunes Store. Your iPad must have access to the Internet to utilize this app. Downloading large files sometimes requires a Wi-Fi connection, as opposed to a 3G Internet connection.

- **App Store:** Use this app to access the online-based App Store to find, purchase, and download additional apps for your iPad 2. (This includes downloading free apps available from the App Store.) An Internet connection must be available to do this. For details, see Chapter 7, "Finding and Installing Apps from the App Store."

- **Newsstand:** New to iOS 5, this app enables you to subscribe to the digital editions of newspapers and magazines. Most of these digital publications require a paid subscription. Once you subscribe, however, new issues are automatically downloaded to your iPad as soon as they're published. You learn more about this app from Chapter 14, "Finding and Using News and Information Apps."

- **FaceTime:** When your iPad 2 is connected to the Web via a Wi-Fi connection, you have the ability to do real-time videoconferencing with other iPad 2, iPhone 4 (or later), and Mac users who also have the FaceTime app or software. This is a free service. You learn more about videoconferencing with your iPad 2 in Chapter 13, "Conducting Videoconferences and Virtual Meetings."

- **Camera:** Your iPad 2 has two built-in cameras that are capable of shooting digital photos or video. The Camera app is used to take pictures or shoot video using your tablet.

- **Photo Booth:** Like Camera, this app enables you to take and share photos using the cameras built in to your iPad 2. However, this app takes a more whimsical approach to picture taking and enables you to add comical special effects to your photos.

- **Settings:** Your iPad 2 is an extremely customizable device. Using the Settings app, you can personalize the tablet's settings, as well as settings related to certain apps. You can find more information on how to use the Settings app in Chapter 2, "Customizing iPad Settings."

- **Safari:** Many of the apps you use on your iPad 2 automatically connect to the Internet to utilize data or gather and share information. Safari is a full-featured web browser used to surf the Internet when your iPad 2 is connected to the Internet via Wi-Fi or 3G connection. You learn all about how to surf the Web using Safari on your iPad in Chapter 4, "Surfing the Web."

- **Mail:** Use this app to manage your existing email accounts, as well as access, read, write, and send email messages. Mail is capable of managing multiple email accounts simultaneously after you set up the app, which you learn to do in Chapter 3, "Working with Email."

- **Photos:** Use this app to view, edit, and share digital photos and images stored on your iPad 2. It works very much like iPhoto on the Mac.

- **Music:** If you transfer or load digital music, podcasts, or audio books into your iPad 2, use this app to experience your audio content. The iPod app transforms your iPad 2 into a full-featured iPod. If you already own an iPod, iPod touch, or iPhone, you should have no trouble using this app to enjoy your favorite music or audio that's stored on your tablet.

> TIP   To utilize the iTunes, Newsstand, FaceTime, Game Center, iBooks, and App Store apps, you must have an Apple ID account established and have a major credit card associated with that account to pay for online purchases. You have the opportunity to create a free Apple ID account, if you don't already have one, the first time you try to make an online purchase using one of these apps. In the meantime, to learn more about how Apple ID accounts work, visit www.apple.com/support/appleid/.

ACTIVATING YOUR iPAD'S DATA SERVICES

Now that you have activated your iPad 2, if you have an iPad 2 Wi-Fi + 3G model, you can activate a wireless data plan. To do this, make sure your iPad 2 is not in Airplane mode. You should see the 3G connection signal bars and your wireless data provider's 3G label in the upper-left corner of the screen. Next, tap the Safari icon.

Before you're allowed to gain access to the wireless web via a 3G connection, you must activate an account with your wireless data provider, depending on which iPad 2 Wi-Fi + 3G model you've purchased. This account setup procedure takes just a few minutes but requires a major credit card to activate.

When you tap the Safari icon for the first time, follow the onscreen prompts when asked if you want to set up a wireless data provider 3G account. You must choose a monthly service plan that costs between $14.99 and $80.00 per month depending on the plan you choose. This is a month-to-month plan that you can cancel or change any time. No long-term service agreement is required.

> **TIP**   Your iPad 2 is now fully activated and ready to be used; however, you might want to plug it in to charge the battery. You can see the level of battery life remaining by looking at the battery icon located in the upper-right corner of the tablet's screen. You can use the iPad 2 while it is charging. A lightning bolt graphic appears within the onscreen battery icon to indicate the tablet is currently charging.

CUSTOMIZING iPAD SETTINGS

Along with adding apps to your iPad to customize the tablet's features and functionality, you can use the built-in Settings app to personalize a wide range of options that affect your interaction with the tablet, how it connects to the Internet, and how your apps function.

Regardless of what you use your iPad 2 for, you occasionally need to access the Settings app. Think of the Settings app as the control center for the tablet's operating system. For example, it's from here that you can put your tablet into Airplane Mode, find and connect to a Wi-Fi hotspot, set up your email accounts, and customize your tablet's wallpapers. In fact, there are dozens of options available from the various Settings menus and submenus that directly affect how your iPad 2 operates.

Begin exploring the Settings app by launching it. From your tablet's Home screen, which is shown in Figure 2.1, tap the Settings app icon.

NOTE   The location of the Settings app icon varies based on whether you personalize your tablet's Home screen by moving app icons around or creating folders, for example.

Settings app icon

FIGURE 2.1

From the Home screen, launch the Settings app to customize a wide range of the tablet's settings and options.

Upon launching the Settings app, you see the screen is divided into two sections. On the left are the main categories offered within the Settings app, starting with the virtual Airplane Mode (on/off) switch that's located near the top-left corner of the screen.

On the right side of the screen are the various options available to you based on the highlighted category on the left side of the screen. If you hold your iPad 2 vertically (in portrait mode), as shown in Figure 2.2, you can see the entire main Settings screen at once. As you can see, the General option on the left is high-lighted (in blue on your screen), and the specific options you can adjust on your iPad 2 under the General option are displayed on the right side of the screen.

FIGURE 2.2

Displayed in portrait mode, the main Settings screen is shown, with the General option on the left highlighted.

To select a different Settings category, tap on its heading that's listed within the left column of the screen.

SWITCHING TO AIRPLANE MODE

The first option found under the Settings heading, within the left column of the main Settings app screen, is the virtual Airplane Mode on/off switch. This option enables you to turn off the iPad's capability to communicate with the Internet using a 3G or Wi-Fi connection. To switch Airplane Mode to the ON or OFF position, simply tap the virtual switch that's displayed near the upper-left corner of the main settings screen.

When Airplane Mode is turned OFF, and you're using an iPad 2 with 3G, the tablet automatically connects to the wireless data network to which you've subscribed. The signal bars for this wireless data connection display in the upper-left corner of the screen (as seen previously in Figure 2.1).

If you turn ON Airplane Mode, the tablet's wireless data connection shuts down and your existing Wi-Fi connection also turns off. Everything else on your tablet

■ Using a Wi-Fi connection, you can use the FaceTime app for video conferencing, plus download movies and TV show episodes from iTunes directly onto your tablet.

CONFIGURING NOTIFICATIONS SETTINGS

From the Notifications option within Settings, you can customize the Notification Center, which is continuously operational when your iPad is turned on. Notification Center is a single window that displays all current calendar appointments and alarms, all alerts from the Reminders app, alerts generated by Game Center, incoming missed call notifications from FaceTime, new incoming email alerts, and new text messages from the Messages app.

When Notifications is selected on the left side of the Settings screen, you can turn on or off the apps from which you want to receive notifications, and customize how those notifications will be seen and heard, by adjusting the options under the In Notification Center heading, as shown in Figure 2.4.

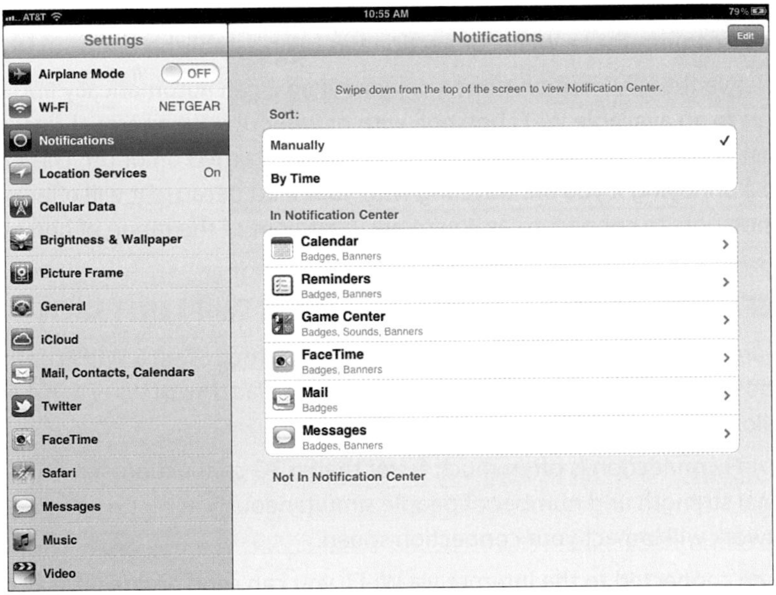

FIGURE 2.4

You can customize how the Notification Center continuously performs when your iPad is turned on or in Sleep Mode by adjusting the Notifications options in the Settings app.

Tap on each of the app names under the In Notification Center heading to customize the text-based alerts and audible alarms for that particular app. For example, you can do the following:

- Choose whether the alerts pertaining to the app will appear in the Notification Center window.
- Set how many alerts from that app can be generated simultaneously.
- Determine whether alerts will be visible on the Lock Screen.
- Customize the Alert Style. A banner alert will be displayed at the top of the screen but will disappear automatically. Alerts require you to manually acknowledge it with a tap of an icon.
- Turn Home Screen Badge App icons on or off.

A Home Screen Badge is a small circular graphic that can appear in the upper-right corner of an app icon on your tablet's Home screen. The Home Screen Badge can be a number or an exclamation point, for example. These badges are used to graphically show you that something relating to that specific app has changed and needs your attention. For example, a number appears as a Home Screen Badge on your Mail app icon if you've received new email messages. Likewise, a number appears as a Home Screen Badge on the App Store icon if any of your apps require you to download updates. You can see a sample Home Screen Badge on the Mail icon in Figure 2.5. This badge disappears when the messages are read.

FIGURE 2.5

The badge that's displayed in the upper-right corner of the Mail app shows how many new incoming email messages have been received.

SETTING LOCATION SERVICES OPTIONS

The third option displayed on the left side of the Settings screen is labeled Location Services. When this option is turned on, the iPad can automatically utilize the GPS functionality built in to the device in conjunction with various apps. Certain apps and services, such as Maps or Find My iPad, rely on knowing your exact location to function properly.

When Location Services is selected in the left column menu, a virtual ON/OFF switch that completely enables or disables this feature is displayed on the right.

Below that is a listing of all apps stored on your iPad 2 that can use Location Services. Thus, you can turn on the master Location Services switch but turn off the feature in conjunction with specific apps that would otherwise utilize it.

When the Location Services option is set to ON, your iPad 2 can fully utilize its GPS capabilities. When the option is set to OFF, your tablet is not able to determine (or broadcast) your exact location.

Some apps automatically track your whereabouts and add that geographic information to files. For example, if Location Services is turned on, when you snap a photo using the Camera app, the exact location where the photo was shot is automatically saved. Likewise, when posting a Tweet, you can set the Twitter app to automatically display your exact location within that Tweet message if Location Services is turned on. And, theoretically, your boss, spouse, or someone else who knows your Apple ID could track your whereabouts using the Find My iPad service from any computer.

If you don't want the iPad tracking your whereabouts in real time, set this feature to OFF. When using Maps, for example, if the feature is turned off, you will need to manually enter your location each time the app is used.

NOTE Your ability to customize the Location Services feature within each app stored on your iPad 2 was enhanced with the release of the iOS 4.3.3 operating system in early May 2011, due to concerns people were having about third parties being able to track their whereabouts. To learn more about how Location Services operates and determine for yourself whether it impedes on your privacy, visit http://support.apple.com/kb/HT4084.

CONFIGURING CELLULAR DATA OPTIONS

When you select the Cellular Data option, a virtual ON/OFF switch appears on the right side of the screen (see Figure 2.6). The Data Roaming option also appears.

The Cellular Data option of the Settings app applies to the iPad 2 with 3G models only. When the option is set to ON, your tablet can access your wireless data provider's data network, depending on the 3G model that you own. When set to OFF, your iPad 2 can access the Internet only via a Wi-Fi connection, assuming a Wi-Fi hotspot is present.

When set to ON, the Data Roaming option enables your iPad to connect to a 3G network outside the one you subscribe to. The ability to tap in to another wireless data network might be useful if you must connect to the Internet, there's no Wi-Fi hotspot present, and you're outside your wireless data provider's 3G coverage area (such as when you're traveling abroad).

CHAPTER 2 | Customizing iPad Settings

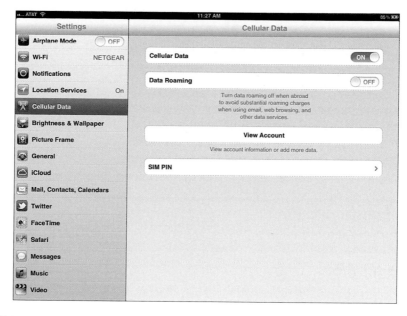

FIGURE 2.6

From the Cellular Data option, you can control whether your iPad 2 can connect to the 3G wireless network to which you subscribe. You can also give your tablet the ability to roam to other networks for 3G Internet access.

CAUTION When your iPad 2 is permitted to roam and tap in to another 3G wireless data network abroad, you might incur hefty roaming charges, often as high as $20.00 per megabyte (MB). Refrain from using this feature unless you've secured a 3G data roaming plan in advance through your service provider or you're prepared to pay a fortune to access the Web.

You can view or modify your 3G wireless data plan account details by tapping the View Account option. After you log in with the username and password you created when you set up the account with your wireless data provider, you can do things such as change your credit card billing information or modify your monthly plan.

TIP Unless specifically instructed by a technical support person representing Apple or your 3G wireless data service provider, avoid changing the SIM PIN option that's displayed at the bottom of the Cellular Data screen. Simply leave this option on its default setting and ignore it.

ADJUSTING THE SCREEN BRIGHTNESS

On the left column displayed within the Settings app is the Brightness & Wallpaper setting. When you tap this setting, the Brightness & Wallpaper options appear on the right side of the Settings screen (see Figure 2.7).

At the top of the screen is a Brightness slider. Place your finger on the white dot on the slider and drag it to the right to make the screen brighter, or drag it to the left to make the screen darker. Manually adjusting the brightness overrides the Auto-Brightness option if you have this feature turned on.

The Auto-Brightness option displayed under the brightness slider has a virtual on/off switch associated with it. When Auto-Brightness is set to ON, your tablet takes into account the surrounding lighting where you're using your iPad and adjusts the screen's brightness accordingly. It's useful for keeping the brightness of the screen at a consistent level if you move between a brightly lit area and a dimly lit one, for example.

The default setting for the Auto-Brightness feature is the ON position. Leave it there unless you consistently have difficulty seeing what's displayed on your iPad's screen based on its brightness setting.

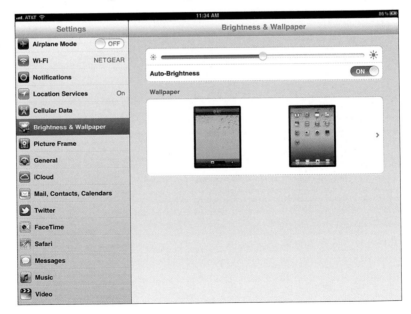

FIGURE 2.7

Use the Brightness slider to control how light or dark your iPad 2's screen appears. You can change this based on the external lighting conditions where you're using your iPad to make what's displayed on the screen easier to view.

CUSTOMIZING THE LOCK SCREEN AND HOME SCREEN WALLPAPERS

One of the ways you can customize the appearance of your iPad 2 is to change the wallpaper displayed on the device's Lock screen and behind your app icons on the Home screen.

CHOOSING A PREINSTALLED WALLPAPER

From the Brightness & Wallpaper option in the Settings app, you can quickly change the wallpapers that are displayed on the tablet. Your iPad 2 has 30 preinstalled wallpaper designs, plus you can use any digital images stored on your iPad (within the Photos app) as your Lock screen or Home screen wallpaper.

As mentioned in the preceding section, the Brightness & Wallpaper options display when you tap the Brightness & Wallpaper option on the Settings screen (refer to Figure 2.7). Below the brightness slider is the Wallpaper option. Here, you see a thumbnail graphic of your iPad's Lock screen on the left and Home screen on the right. Tap either of these thumbnail images to change their appearance. The right side of the Settings screen changes, and two options are listed. The Wallpaper option is on top and the Camera Roll or Photos option is on bottom.

Tap on the Wallpaper option to display thumbnails for the 30 preinstalled wallpaper graphics you can choose from (see Figure 2.8).

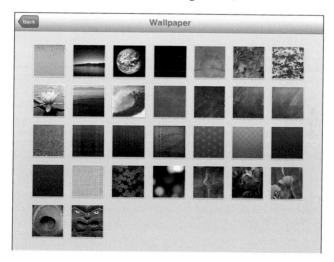

FIGURE 2.8

Choose from 30 preinstalled wallpaper graphics for your iPad 2's Lock screen and Home screen.

When looking at the collection of wallpaper graphics, tap the one you'd like to use, such as the planet earth graphic that's displayed on the top row.

Next, the graphic you select is displayed in full-screen mode. In the upper-right corner of the screen are three command buttons (see Figure 2.9). Choose one of these options by tapping its button:

- **Set Lock Screen:** Tap this icon to change just the wallpaper graphic of your iPad's Lock Screen. As a reminder, this is the screen you see when you first turn on your tablet or wake it from Sleep Mode. From the Lock screen, you must swipe your finger along the Slide to Unlock slider to unlock the tablet and access the Home screen.

- **Set Home Screen:** Tap this icon to change just the wallpaper graphic of your iPad's Home screen. This is the graphic that displays behind your app icons on each of your Home screen pages.

- **Set Both:** Tap this icon to use the same wallpaper graphic as both your Lock screen and your Home screen wallpapers.

After you make your selection, your newly selected wallpaper graphic is displayed when you return to the iPad's Lock screen or Home screen.

FIGURE 2.9
When you select a custom graphic to use as a wallpaper, tap one of these three icons to determine where the graphic is displayed—on your Lock screen, Home screen, or both.

Instead of choosing one of the 30 preinstalled wallpaper graphics, you also have the option to use any of your own digital images. This includes photos you've transferred to your iPad 2 and have stored within the Photos app and photos you've shot using the tablet's Camera app.

DISPLAYING A CUSTOM IMAGE AS A WALLPAPER

To select one of your own photos to use as your Lock screen or Home screen wallpaper, tap the Brightness & Wallpaper option in the Settings app.

On the right side of the screen, tap the thumbnails of your iPad's Lock screen and Home screen. Underneath the Wallpaper option, tap the folder that contains the image you want to use as your wallpaper. This might be a photo you've shot using your iPad (found within the Camera Roll folder) or a photo you've imported into the Photos app of your tablet.

When the image thumbnails appear, tap the image thumbnail you want to use as your wallpaper for your Lock screen or Home screen (or both).

When the photo you selected appears in full-screen mode, tap one of the three command icons that appear in the upper-right corner of the screen. Once again, your options include Set Lock Screen, Set Home Screen, or Set Both.

After you make your selection, your newly selected wallpaper graphic displays on your Lock screen and Home screen, as you can see in Figure 2.10 and Figure 2.11.

FIGURE 2.10

A newly selected Lock Screen graphic, chosen from a photo stored on the iPad within the Photos app. The image was originally imported into the iPad using the iTunes sync process.

FIGURE 2.11

The image selected from the Settings app is displayed as your Home screen wallpaper appearing behind your app icons.

TRANSFORMING YOUR iPAD 2 INTO A DIGITAL PICTURE FRAME

When your iPad 2 isn't in use or on the go with you, it might sit idly on your desk. If this is the case, you could instead transform the device into a digital picture frame and have it display an animated slideshow of your favorite images when it's not otherwise being used. You can set up a slideshow using the Picture Frame option of the Settings app.

To personalize the settings of the Picture Frame app, you need to access the Picture Frame options from the Settings app. Tap the Picture Frame setting listed on the left side of the main Settings screen to display the Picture Frame options on the right side of the screen.

The first option is the animated transition shown in between images. Your choices are Dissolve or Origami.

Moving down this settings screen, you can determine how long each image is displayed (your choices are 2, 3, 5, 10, or 20 seconds) and whether you want the app to automatically zoom in on people's faces as your images are displayed.

In the bottom area of the Picture Frame screen within the Settings app, you can choose which images should be displayed as part of your slideshow. Either choose All Photos or choose a specific Album or Event folder.

You can launch the Picture Frame app from the lower-right corner of the Lock screen using the picture frame icon. Tap the icon (the flower inside the picture frame) to start the slideshow, which is presented based on the settings you personalized using the Settings app.

GENERAL OPTIONS

Several options found under the General heading are things you'll probably never need to tinker with or adjust, such as International or Accessibility, so just leave them at their default settings. Others are things you change often as you use your iPad 2 for different tasks.

The General option of the Settings screen enables you to view and adjust the following options:

■ **About:** Tap the About option to access information about your iPad 2, including its serial number, which version of the iOS is running, the memory capacity, and how much memory is currently available on the device. This is purely an informative screen with no options to customize or adjust.

■ **Software Update:** Periodically, when Apple releases a revision to the iOS operating system, you will need to download and install this update. This can be done wirelessly using the Software Update feature. When you tap Software Update, your iPad will check to see whether a new version of the iOS is available and, if so, prompt you to download and install it. You can also check for new iOS updates and install them using iTunes on your primary computer. See Chapter 8, "Syncing the iPad Using iTunes or iCloud," for details on how to do this.

■ **Usage:** Tap the Usage option to decide whether to display your tablet's battery life as a numeric percentage (such as 73) or only as a battery icon. Also, from this screen you can see how much data the iPad 2 has sent or received using the 3G wireless data network to which it's connected.

Tap the Reset Statistics option to reset the Sent and Received settings. When you add the Sent and Received numbers together, you can determine your total data usage since you last tapped the Reset Statistics icon. This feature is particularly useful if you're overseas and roaming, to determine how much you'll be billed, or for making sure you don't go beyond your monthly allocated data use based on the 3G wireless data plan you have.

swipe your finger from left to right along these icons. The audio control panel appears. Tap the speaker icon that's displayed in the lower-right corner of the screen to mute all iPad sounds. To unmute the sounds, tap this speaker icon again. Press the Home button again to return to the Home Screen.

- **Multitasking Gestures:** iOS5 introduced several new finger and hand motions for use on the touch-screen. When the Multitasking Gestures option is set to ON, these new finger/hand motions are usable. For example, you can start with your fingers spread out and perform a full-hand pinch motion while in any app to return to the Home Screen. Or, you can swipe upward to reveal the multitasking bar (instead of pressing the Home button twice). You can then perform a full hand swipe to switch between apps in multitasking mode. Visit Apple's website to see a video about how to use these new hand gestures on your touch screen (www.apple.com/ios/ios5/features.html#more).

- **Date & Time:** Use the Date & Time setting to switch between a 12- or 24-hour clock and determine whether you want your iPad to automatically set the time or date (when it's connected to the Internet). To ensure the time and date are correct regardless of what time zone you travel to, leave the Set Automatically option set to ON.

- **Keyboard:** You can make certain customizations from the Settings screen that affect how your virtual keyboard responds as you type. The Keyboard option gives you six customizable settings, such as Auto-Capitalization, Auto-Correction, and Check Spelling. You also have the option to turn on or off the Split Keyboard feature, which is new within iOS 5, plus create and edit keyboard shortcuts that are useful when typing text. A keyboard shortcut might include typing "omw," which the iPad will translate into "on my way."

- **International:** By default, if you purchased your iPad 2 in the United States, the default language and keyboard options are for English. However, you can adjust these settings by tapping the International option.

- **Accessibility:** The Accessibility options are designed to make the iPad 2 easier for people with various sight or hearing difficulties to use, as well as physical limitations. Features include VoiceOver or Large Text.

- **Reset:** Every so often, you might run into a problem with your iPad, as when the system crashes or you need to reset specific settings. To restore your iPad 2 to its factory default settings and erase everything stored on it, tap the Reset option, and then tap the Erase All Content and Settings option. In general, you should refrain from using these settings unless you're instructed to use them by an Apple Genius or a technical support person.

CAUTION Before using any of the Reset options, which potentially erase important data from your iPad, be sure to perform an iTunes or iCloud sync to create a reliable backup. See Chapter 8 for step-by-step directions on how to do this.

KEEPING YOUR iPAD 2 PRIVATE WITH THE PASSCODE LOCK FEATURE

There are several simple ways to protect the data stored on your iPad 2 and keep it away from unauthorized users. If you want to keep data on your tablet private, the first thing to do is set up and activate the Passcode Lock feature that's built in to the iOS.

As noted in the previous section, from the Settings app, tap the General setting on the left side of the screen. Next, tap the Passcode Lock option that's listed on the right side of the screen to set the Passcode feature to ON. (By default, the Passcode option is set to OFF.)

When the Passcode Lock screen appears (see Figure 2.12), tap the Turn Passcode On button to activate this security feature.

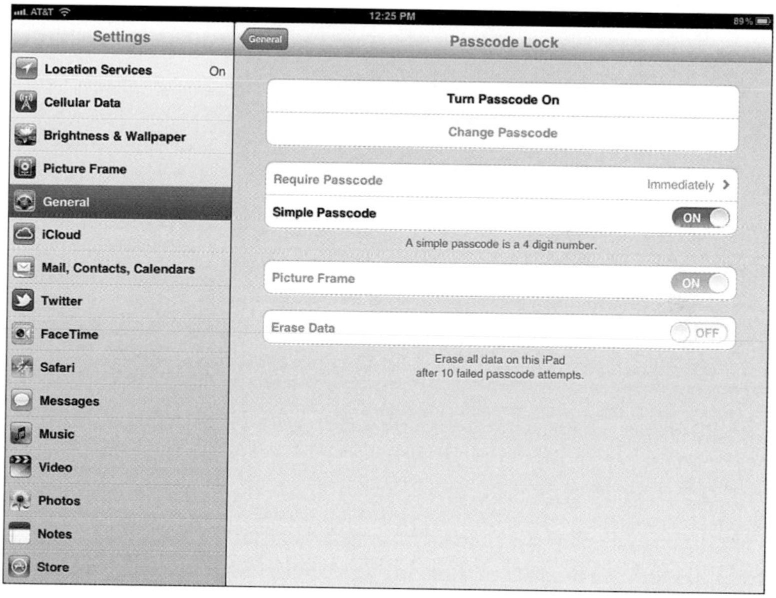

FIGURE 2.12

From the Passcode Lock screen, you can set and then activate the Passcode Lock feature built in to the iPad 2. Use it to keep unauthorized people from using your tablet or accessing your sensitive data.

When the Set Passcode window appears on the tablet's screen (see Figure 2.13), use the virtual numeric keypad to create a four-digit security passcode for your device. You must enter this code every time you turn on the tablet or wake it from Sleep Mode.

You can enter any four-digit code as your passcode. When promoted, type the same code a second time. The Set Passcode window disappears and the feature becomes active.

Now, from the Passcode Lock screen in the Settings app, you can further customize this feature. For example, tap the Require Passcode option to determine when the iPad prompts the user to enter the passcode. The default option is Immediately, meaning each time the tablet is turned on or woken up.

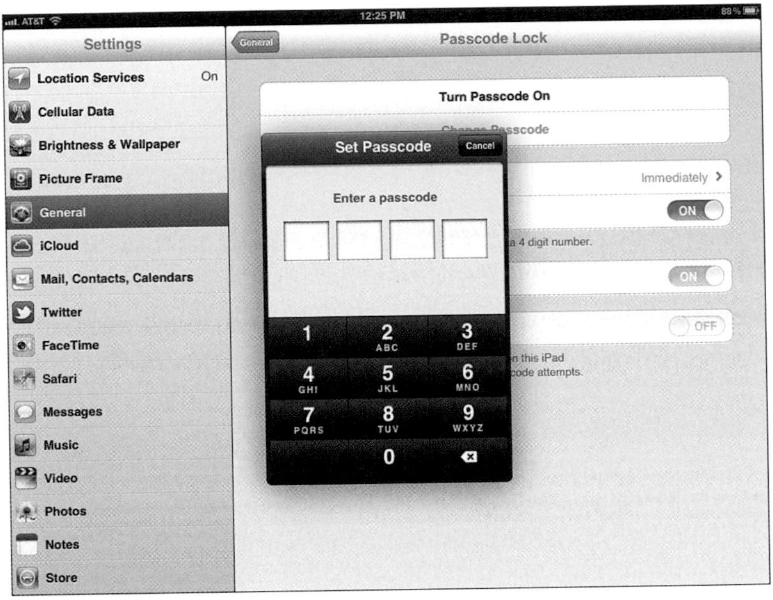

FIGURE 2.13

Create a four-digit numeric passcode for your iPad 2 from this Set Passcode window.

If you don't believe a four-digit passcode is secure enough, turn off the Simple Passcode option, which makes a Change Passcode window appear along with the iPad's full virtual keyboard. You can create a more complicated, alphanumeric passcode to protect your device from unauthorized use.

From the Passcode Lock screen, you can determine whether the Picture Frame app option is displayed on your Lock screen. This option has a virtual on/off switch associated with it. When turned on, the Picture Frame app icon displays on the Lock screen. When turned off, you are not able to turn on the Picture Frame app from the Lock Screen because the icon does not display.

Also on the Passcode Lock screen is the Erase Data option. If an unauthorized user enters the wrong passcode 10 consecutive times, the iPad automatically erases all data stored on it when the feature is turned on.

> **CAUTION** Activating the Erase Data feature gives you an added layer of security if your tablet falls into the wrong hands. However, to recover the data later, you must have a reliable backup created using the iTunes Sync process; otherwise, that data is lost forever.

CUSTOMIZING iCLOUD SETTINGS

From the left side of the Settings screen, tap the iCloud option to customize the settings associated with Apple's online file-sharing and data backup service. You'll learn more about this service in Chapter 8.

From Settings, however, you can adjust what data automatically gets wirelessly backed up and/or synced with the iCloud service, including Mail, Contacts, Calendars, Reminders, (Safari) Bookmarks, Notes, and Photo Stream. You can also turn on or off the Find My iPad service. Your options are shown in Figure 2.14.

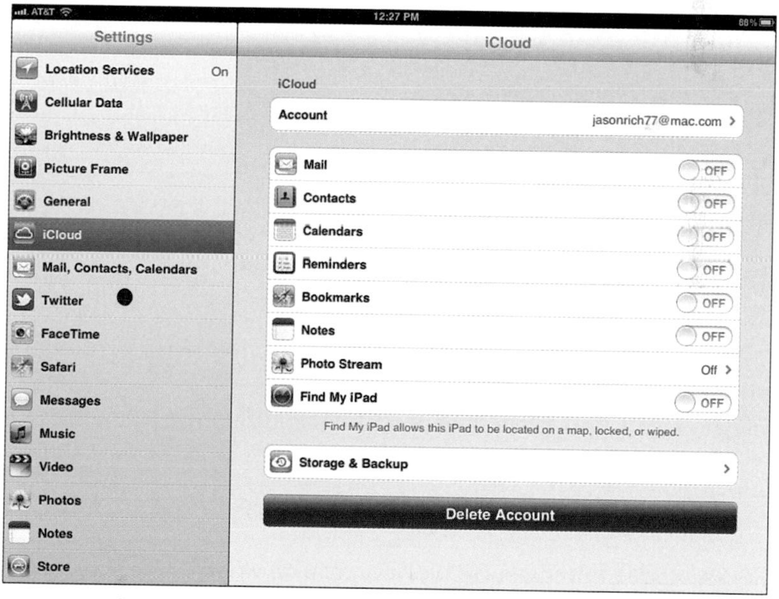

FIGURE 2.14

Being able to back up your iPad and transfer files wirelessly using Apple's iCloud service is a major enhancement to iOS 5. You can customize your iCloud settings from the Settings app.

Your free iCloud account comes with 5GB of online storage space. Tap the Storage & Backup tab near the bottom of the iCloud screen to manage your existing online storage space or purchase additional online storage space. From the Storage & Backup screen within Settings (shown in Figure 2.15), you can also turn on or off the Back Up to iCloud feature. This determines whether your iPad will automatically wirelessly back up your Camera Roll, accounts, documents, and tablet settings using iCloud.

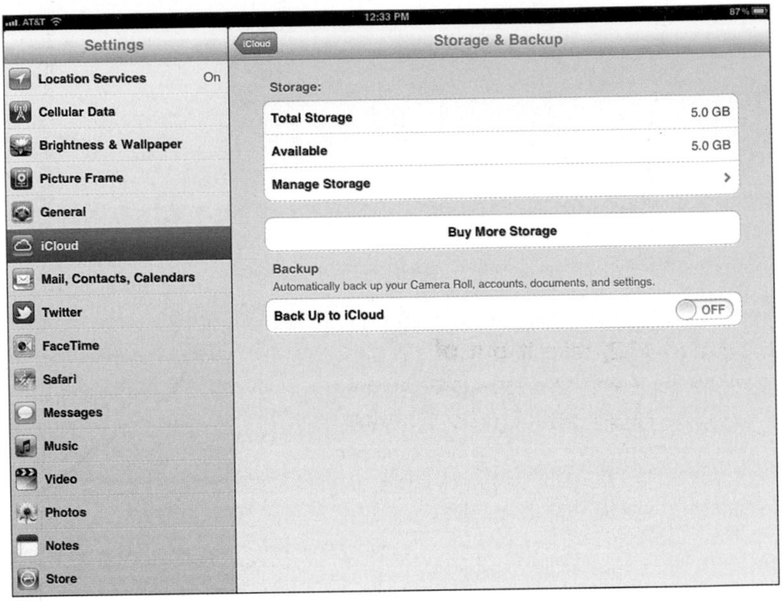

FIGURE 2.15

Manage your free, online-based iCloud account from the Settings app on your iPad.

ADJUSTING THE SETTINGS FOR MAIL, CONTACTS, AND CALENDARS

If you use your iPad 2 on the job, three apps you probably rely heavily on are Mail, Contacts, and Calendars. From the Settings app, you can customize a handful of options pertaining to each of these apps, and you can actually set up your existing email accounts to work with your tablet.

For information about how to use the Settings app to customize the related settings, see Chapter 3, "Working with Email," Chapter 5, "Using the Calendar App," and Chapter 6, "Working with the Contacts App."

SET UP THE TWITTER APP

The Twitter online social networking service has now been fully integrated into iOS 5 and is accessible from within several different iPad core applications, as well as the actual official Twitter app. The Twitter features built in to iOS 5 will work with your existing Twitter account; however, you will need to download the free, official Twitter app to utilize the Twitter integration that's now offered in some of the iPad 2 apps. You can also set up a free Twitter account if you don't already have one. Customize the settings as desired so you can send Tweets from a variety of different iPad core apps, including Photos.

Many third-party apps for the iPad that enable you to access Twitter are available from the App Store. However, only the official Twitter app (that can be downloaded from within the Settings app) enables you to utilize all the Twitter-related features integrated into iOS 5.

CUSTOMIZING YOUR WEB SURFING EXPERIENCE WITH SAFARI

Safari is the web browsing app built in to the iPad 2. It's similar to the Safari web browser available on all Mac computers. The Safari app has a handful of settings you can customize using the Settings, such as which search engine to use, whether to show the Bookmarks Bar, or whether you want to block pop-up ads. These options, as well as the others found in the Safari settings, are explained in Chapter 4, "Surfing the Web."

CUSTOMIZE THE MESSAGES APP

iMessage is a new online-based text messaging service introduced by Apple in conjunction with iOS 5. This service works very much like the text messaging capabilities of your cell phone, but with this service, you can send and receive an unlimited number of messages for free. The service is compatible with all iOS 5–enabled devices, including the iPad, iPad 2, iPhone 3Gs, iPhone 4, and iPod Touch.

The iMessage service must be accessed using the iPad's Messages app, which comes preinstalled with iOS 5. Tap the Messages option within Settings to set up an iMessage account using your Apple ID and manage your account. You learn more about the Messages app and iMessage service in Chapter 12, "iPad Apps for Productivity, Organization, and Brainstorming."

PERSONALIZING MUSIC SETTINGS

One of the apps built in to your iPad 2 is the Music app, which replaced the iPod app that was part of iOS 4.3.3 (and earlier versions of the iOS). Basically, this app transforms your tablet into a full-featured digital music player and enables you to experience the music and audio files you have stored on your tablet. This includes music, podcasts, and audiobooks acquired from iTunes.

Using the Settings app, you can customize a handful of options relating to the Music app. From the left column of the main Settings app screen, tap the Music setting. Then, on the right side of the screen, adjust the Sound Check, EQ, Volume Limit, and Lyrics & Podcast Info options.

When connected to a public Wi-Fi hotspot, to keep your iPad secure, enter your Apple ID and Password into the Home Sharing section of the Music settings.

PERSONALIZING VIDEO SETTINGS

You use the Videos app that comes on your iPad 2 to watch TV show episodes and movies you've purchased or rented. From the Settings app, you can adjust how the Videos app functions by turning on or off various settings.

From the Settings app, tap the Videos setting in the left column. When the Video options appear on the right side of the screen, you can adjust four main options, starting with the Start Playing feature. The default option for this feature is to resume playing a video where you last left off. However, you can change this option so videos always start at the beginning. You can also turn on or off closed captioning, for example.

MAKING APP-SPECIFIC ADJUSTMENTS

You can customize settings for the preinstalled apps, such as the Photos, FaceTime, Notes, and App Store apps. These are all displayed toward the bottom of the main Settings screen's left column. To make adjustments that are specific to any of the apps listed, tap the app name (displayed in the left column of the Settings screen), and then adjust the app-specific settings on the right side of the screen. For each app, the customizations you can make are specific to the app. For example, to set up a FaceTime account, switch the FaceTime option to ON and enter your Apple ID and password.

Apps that have customizable options will also be accessible from the Settings app. When this is the case, those apps are also listed within the left column of the main Settings app screen.

3

WORKING WITH EMAIL

As long as your iPad 2 has access to the Internet via a Wi-Fi or 3G connection, it has the capability to securely access virtually any type of email account. In fact, using the tablet's preinstalled Mail app, you have the ability to manage multiple email accounts simultaneously without having to open and close accounts to switch between them.

Your iPad 2 is also capable of viewing certain types of attachments that accompany emails, including PDF files, photos, and Microsoft Office files. Plus, if you have access to an AirPrint-compatible printer, you can print incoming or outgoing emails directly from the Mail app.

Using your iPad 2, you can easily send and receive email messages and manage personal and work-related email accounts at the same time, yet keep the content of the various accounts totally separate.

Before you can manage one or more existing email accounts from your iPad 2, it's necessary to access the Settings app to configure your tablet to work with your email account(s).

> **NOTE** How to set up your iPad 2 to work with your existing email account(s) is explained in this chapter; however, if you don't yet have an email account, there are several ways to get one. For example, you can get a free account from both Google (mail.google.com) and Yahoo! (http://features.mail.yahoo.com). Both types of accounts are fully compatible with your iPad 2's Mail app.

SETTING UP YOUR iPAD 2 TO WORK WITH EXISTING EMAIL ACCOUNTS

To initially set up your iPad 2 to work with your existing email account(s), you use the Settings app that's accessible from your tablet's Home screen. (For more on the Settings app, see Chapter 2, "Customizing iPad Settings.") The process described here works with virtually all email accounts, including Yahoo! Mail, Google Gmail, AOL Mail, MobileMe Mail, Microsoft Exchange, and other email accounts established using industry-standard POP3 and IMAP email services.

If you have an email account through your employer that doesn't initially work using the setup procedure outlined in this chapter, contact your company's IT department or Apple's technical support for assistance.

> **NOTE** The process for setting up an existing email account to use with your iPad 2 and the Mail app needs to be done only once per account.

Follow these steps to set up your iPad 2 to work with your existing email account:

1. From the Home screen, tap the Settings app icon.

2. On the left side of the main Settings app screen, tap the Mail, Contacts, Calendars option.

3. When the Mail, Contacts, Calendars options display on the right side of the screen (see Figure 3.1), tap the Add Account option that's displayed near the top of the screen, below the Accounts heading. If you've already set up iCloud on your iPad when you initially set up the tablet, the iCloud account will be listed under the Accounts heading, just above the Add Account option.

4. From the Add Account screen, select the type of email account you have: Microsoft Exchange, MobileMe, Gmail, Yahoo! Mail, AOL Mail, or Other. Tap the appropriate option (shown in Figure 3.2). If you have a POP3- or IMAP-compatible email account, tap the Other option and follow the onscreen prompts.

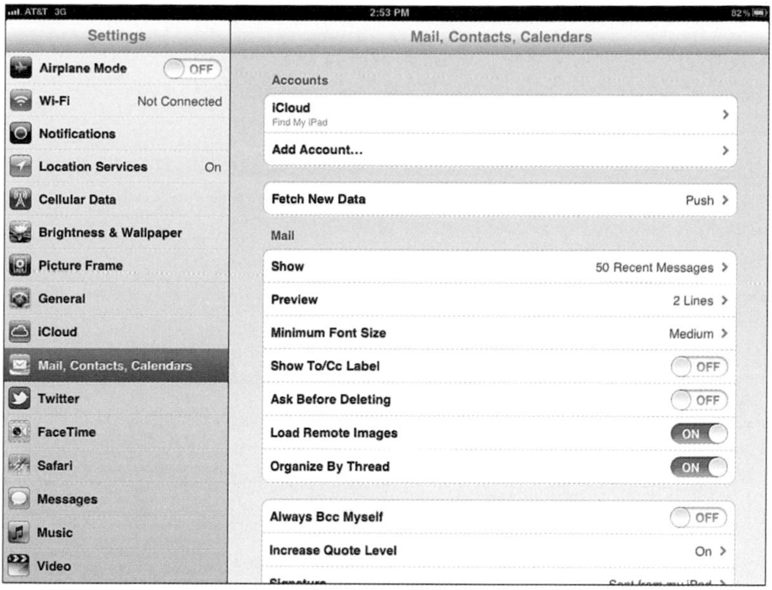

FIGURE 3.1

Tap the Mail, Contacts, Calendars option from within Settings, and then tap the Add Account option.

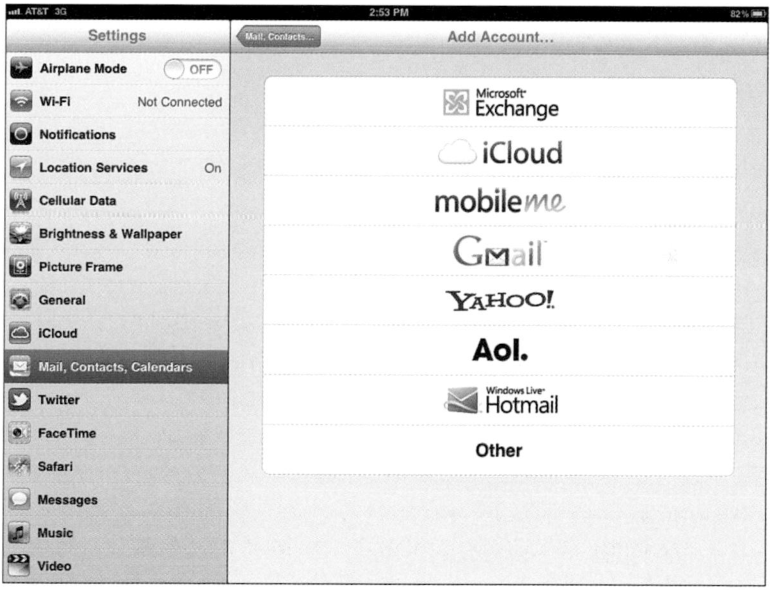

FIGURE 3.2

Select the type of email account you are setting up by tapping the appropriate icon: Microsoft Exchange, MobileMe, Gmail, Yahoo! Mail, AOL, or Other.

If you have an existing Yahoo! Mail account, for example, tap the Yahoo! icon. When the Yahoo! screen appears (shown in Figure 3.3), use the iPad's virtual keyboard to enter the Account Name, Email Address, Password, and a Description for the account.

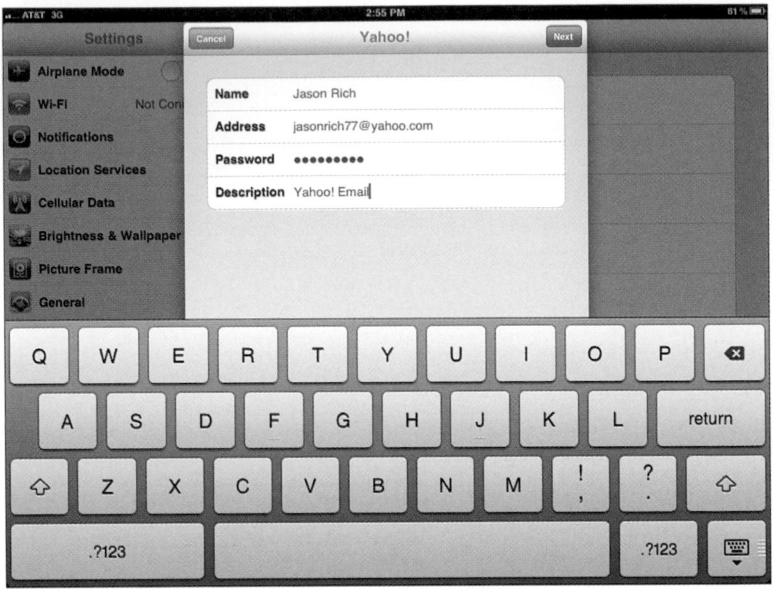

FIGURE 3.3
Using the iPad's virtual keyboard, enter the details pertaining to your existing email account.

5. Tap the Next button that's located in the upper-right corner of the window.

6. Your iPad 2 connects to the email account's server and confirms the account details you entered. You see a Verifying... message on the screen.

7. After the account has been verified, a new window with four options—Mail, Contacts, Calendars, and Notes—is displayed. Each has a virtual on/off switch associated with it. The default for these three options is On.

8. Tap the Save button that's located in the upper-right corner of this window.

9. Details about the email account you just set up are added to your iPad 2 and accessible from the Mail app.

10. If you have another existing email account to set up, from the Mail, Contacts, Calendars screen in the Settings app, again tap the Add Account option, and repeat the preceding steps.

As you're setting up your email account and responding to onscreen prompts within the Settings app, the Name field should include your full name. This is what is displayed within the email messages you send. The Address is your email address, and you should enter it in the *yourname@mailservice*.com format.

The Password is the password you currently use to access your existing email account. For the description, you can enter any text that helps you differentiate the email account from others, such as AOL Mail Account, "Yahoo! Email," or Work Email.

> **TIP** If you're trying to set up a POP3, IMAP, or Exchange IMAP account, for example, and you're prompted for information you don't have, such as your Incoming Mail Server Host Name, Incoming Mail Server Port Number, Outgoing Mail Server, or Outgoing Server Authentication Type, contact your Internet service provider or the company that provides your email account.

Depending on the type of email account you're setting up for use with your iPad, the information you are prompted for varies slightly:

- To set up an existing Microsoft Exchange email account, the prompts you need to fill in during the email setup procedure include Email Address, Domain, Username, Password, and a Description for the account.

- To set up an existing MobileMe email account, you must enter your Apple ID and password. By tapping the MobileMe icon during the email setup procedure, you can actually set up a new MobileMe account from your iPad 2. Apple has announced that with the introduction of iCloud, its MobileMe service will be discontinued in June 2012. However, all existing MobileMe email accounts will continue to work with iCloud.

- To set up a Gmail or AOL Mail account, enter your Name, Email Address, Password, and an account Description.

After you have set up the account, it is listed within the Settings app when you tap the Mail, Contacts, Calendars option. Now, review what's listed under the Accounts heading on the right side of the screen (see Figure 3.4).

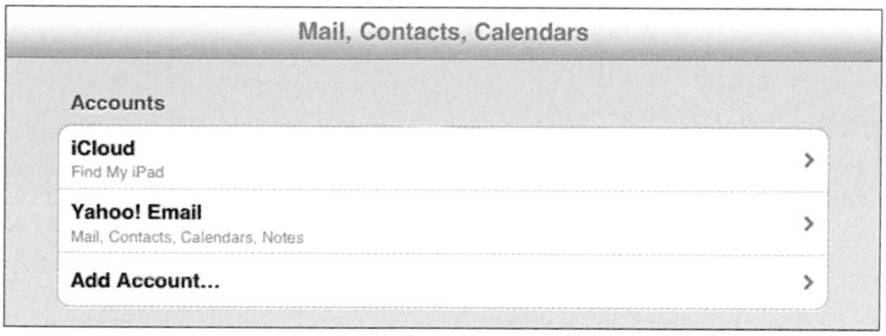

FIGURE 3.4

The existing email account you set up using this procedure is displayed on the Settings screen (listed under the Accounts heading) when you've completed the initial setup process.

TIP   When you purchase a new iPad 2, it comes with free technical support from AppleCare for 90 days. This includes the ability to make an in-person appointment with an Apple Genius at any Apple Store to get help setting up your email accounts on your iPad 2. To schedule a free appointment, visit www.apple.com/retail/geniusbar. Or you can call Apple's toll-free technical support phone number and have someone talk you through the email setup process. Call (800) APL-CARE.

CUSTOMIZING YOUR EMAIL ACCOUNT SETTINGS

From the Settings app, as you look at the Mail, Contacts, Calendars screen, you see a variety of customizable options that pertain to your email accounts. Tap each of these customizable options, one at a time, to personalize the settings based on your preferences and needs.

FETCHING NEW DATA

You can set up your iPad to automatically access the Internet and retrieve new email messages by tapping the Fetch New Data option and adjusting its settings. If you prefer, you can also make sure the Push option, listed at the top of the Fetch New Data screen, is turned on.

If you turn off the Push option, set the Fetch option to check for new emails every 15 minutes, every 30 minutes, hourly, or manually. One reason why you might consider turning off the Push feature and use Fetch to periodically check for emails (or do this manually) is to reduce your 3G wireless data usage.

When you signed up for a 3G wireless data plan with your wireless data provider, you selected a plan with an established wireless data allocation per month. Having your iPad constantly check for new incoming emails can quickly use up this allocation. This is not a concern, however, if you're using a Wi-Fi Internet connection.

CUSTOMIZING MAIL OPTIONS

Under the Mail heading of the Mail, Contacts, Calendars screen (refer to Figure 3.4) are a handful of additional customizable features pertaining to how your iPad 2 handles your email accounts. These options include the following:

■ **Show:** This feature determines how many messages within a particular email account the Mail app downloads from the server and displays at once. Your options include 50 Recent Messages, 100 Recent Messages, 200 Recent Messages, 500 Recent Messages, and 1,000 Recent Messages.

■ **Preview:** As you look at your Inbox using the *I* app, you can determine how much of each email message's body text is visible from the Inbox summary screen, in addition to the From, Date/Time, and Subject lines.

■ **Minimum Font Size:** Regardless of the font size used by the sender, your iPad can automatically adjust the font size so messages are more easily readable on the tablet's display. You can change the default font size for emails to be Small, Medium, Large, Extra Large, or Giant. The default option is Medium, which is acceptable to most iPad 2 users.

■ **Show To/Cc Label:** To save space on your screen as you're reading emails, you can decide to turn off the To and CC label within each email message by tapping the virtual switch associated with this option.

■ **Ask Before Deleting:** This option serves as a safety net to ensure you don't accidently delete an important email message. When this feature is turned on, you are asked to confirm your message deletion request before an email message is actually deleted. It's a good idea to leave this feature turned on at least until you become comfortable using the Mail app on your iPad. Keep in mind that, by default, you cannot delete email messages stored on your email account's server. When you delete a message, it is only deleted from your iPad 2.

■ **Load Remote Images:** When an email message has a photo or graphic embedded with it, this option determines whether that photo or graphic is automatically downloaded and displayed in conjunction with the email message. You can opt to have your iPad refrain from automatically loading graphics in conjunction with email messages. This reduces the amount of data transferred to your tablet and provides an additional level of security from email spammers and scammers. You always have the option to tap an icon within the email message to download the graphic content of that message, including photos.

■ **Organize By Thread:** This feature enables you to review messages in reverse chronological order if a single message turns into a back-and-forth email conversation, where multiple parties keep hitting Reply to respond to messages with the same topic. When turned on, this makes keeping track of email conversations much easier, especially if you're managing several email accounts on your iPad. If turned off, messages in your Inbox are displayed in reverse chronological order, as they're received, and are not grouped together by subject.

■ **Always Bcc Myself:** To ensure you keep a copy of every outgoing email you send, turn on this feature. A copy of every outgoing email is sent to your Inbox if this feature is turned on. After a while, however, the copies of your emails will start to use up a lot of storage space, so you'll eventually want to delete or archive them if you opt to turn on this feature.

■ **Signature:** For every outgoing email that you compose, you can automatically add an email signature. The default signature is "Sent from my iPad." By tapping on this option, you can use the tablet's virtual keyboard to create a customized signature. A signature might include your name, mailing address, email address, phone number(s), and so on.

After you make whatever adjustments you want to the Mail app-related options from within the Settings app, exit the Settings app by pressing the Home button on your iPad 2 to return to the Home screen. You're now ready to begin using the Mail app to access and manage your email account(s).

MANAGING YOUR EMAIL ACCOUNTS WITH THE MAIL APP

The Mail app that is preinstalled on your iPad 2 is loaded with features to make managing multiple email accounts a straightforward process when you're on the go.

NOTE If you've recently upgraded your iPad to iOS 5, you'll discover a handful of new features built in to the Mail app, including the ability to boldface, italicize, and underline text within emails you're composing; rearrange names in the address fields of email messages; flag important email; and create custom folders in which you can manually sort and store email messages.

When you use the Search feature within Mail, you can now opt to search the From, To, or Subject field or the entire body of the message stored within the Mail app.

Using iCloud, you can also sign up for a free *username*@me.com email address that will automatically remain synchronized between your iPad 2, Mac, and other iOS devices, such as your iPhone.

If you need to manage multiple email accounts with your iPad, it's important to understand that although the Mail app enables you to view email messages in all of your accounts simultaneously, the app actually keeps messages from your different accounts separate.

As you view your incoming email messages, by default, the app groups emails together by message thread, enabling you to follow an email-based conversation that extends through multiple messages and replies. When turned on, this feature displays emails within the same thread in reverse chronological order, with the newest message first.

TIP To send and receive emails from your iPad 2 using the Mail app, your tablet must be connected to the Internet via a Wi-Fi or 3G connection. If you're connected using a 3G connection, each time you check your email and download new incoming messages or send messages, some of your monthly wireless data allocation is used. Keep in mind, emails with large attachments, such as photos, Microsoft Office, or PDF files, deplete your monthly wireless data allocation from your wireless data provider much faster, as does having your iPad 2 check for new emails often.

After you've initially set up your existing email accounts to work with your iPad 2 and the Mail app, you can use this app to manage your email accounts from anywhere. You can launch the Mail app from the Home Screen. Its app icon is blue and white and looks like an envelope with clouds in the background, as shown in earlier figures.

To alert you of incoming messages without having the Mail app running, you can access the Settings app to add an app icon badge on the Mail app icon displayed on the Home Screen as new emails arrive. Plus, you can set the Notification Center to list incoming emails. To access the Notification Center while using any app (or from the Home Screen), slide your finger from the top of the screen in a downward motion.

If the Notification Center window displays an incoming message alert (shown in Figure 3.5), tap it to automatically open the Mail app and display that new message. You learn more about the Notification Center in Chapter 5, "Using the Calendar App and Notification Center."

FIGURE 3.5

This is what the Notification Center window looks like when just one incoming email message alert is displayed.

Upon launching the Mail app, you can access the Inbox for one or more of your existing email accounts, compose new emails, or manage your email accounts. Just like the Inbox on your main computer's email software, the Inbox of the Mail app (see Figure 3.6) displays your incoming emails.

FIGURE 3.6

The Mail app's inbox screen. In this example, just one email account is set up to work with the app.

WORKING WITH THE INBOX

On the left side of the Mail app's Inbox screen is a list of the individual emails within your Inbox (refer to Figure 3.5). A blue dot to the left of a message indicates the message has not yet been read.

As you can see, based on the customizations that you made from within the Settings app that pertain to the Mail app, the Sender, Subject, Date/Time, and five lines of the message's body text are displayed for each incoming message.

The email message that's highlighted in blue on the left side of the screen is the one that's currently being displayed, in its entirety, on the right side of the screen. Tap any email item on the left side of the screen to view the entire message on the right side of the screen.

At the bottom of the Inbox message listing that's located on the left side of the screen is a circular arrow icon. Tap this icon to refresh your Inbox and manually check for new incoming emails. The Updated message, accompanied by the date and time, indicates the last time your Inbox was refreshed.

At the top of the Inbox message listing are two buttons labeled Mailboxes and Edit. Between these two icons is the Inbox heading, along with a number that's displayed in parentheses. This number indicates how many new, unread messages are currently stored in your inbox.

Just below the Inbox heading is a Search field. Tap this Search field to make the iPad's virtual keyboard appear so that you can enter a search phrase and quickly find a particular email message. You can search the content of the Mail app using any keyword, sender's name, or email subject, for example.

NOTE   If your email account is associated with MobileMe/iCloud, Exchange, or some IMAP email account servers, when you perform a search, you also are able to search your mail server, not just the messages and content that are stored on your iPad.

ORGANIZING MAILBOX ACTIONS WITH THE MAILBOXES BUTTON

When looking at your Inbox, the Mailboxes button is displayed in the upper-left corner of the screen. If you're managing just one email account with the Mail app, when you tap on this icon, you can immediately switch from your Inbox to your Drafts folder, Sent Message folder, Trash folder, Bulk Mail folder (see Figure 3.7), or other folders associated with your email account.

However, if you're managing multiple email accounts using the Mail app, when you tap the Mailboxes button, you see a listing of each mail account's Inbox, as well as each email account, displayed on the left side of the screen.

If you look on the left side of this Mailboxes screen, you see tabs for each email account's Inbox displayed to the upper left. At the top of this listing is an All Inboxes tab. Tap this icon to view a listing of all your incoming emails, from all your accounts, on a single screen. (These messages are displayed together but are actually kept separate by the Mail app.)

When you're managing multiple accounts, you can also tap the Mailboxes tab to switch between individual email account Inboxes or, under the Accounts heading, access the Inbox, Drafts, Sent, Trash, Bulk Mail, or other folders for each account separately.

Depending on the email account, from your main computer's email program or from the Web, you can typically create custom folders based on your work habits and needs. For example, you can associate folders labeled Personal, Urgent, Work, or Clients, with each email account. For example, from the Yahoo! Mail website, I created folders labeled Personal, Urgent, and Work. When the iPad 2 accessed the email account, these folders automatically became available from the Mail app.

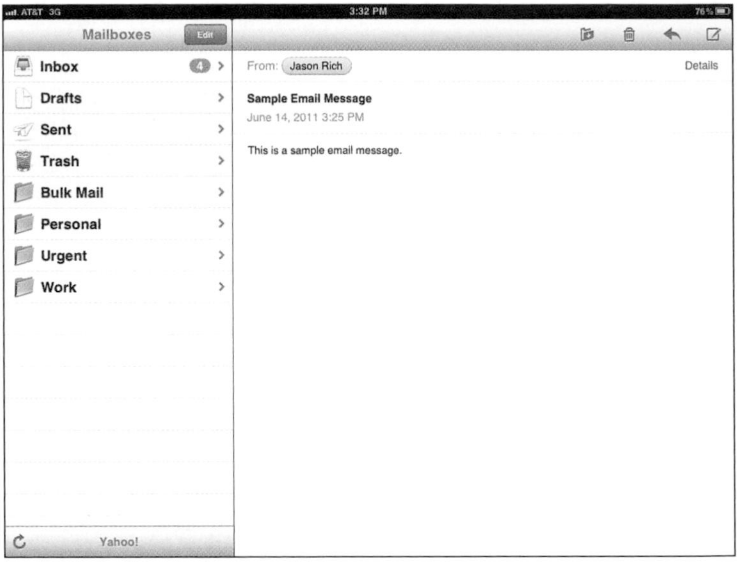

FIGURE 3.7

Tap the Mailboxes button in the upper-left corner of the screen to switch between the Inbox, Drafts, Send, Trash, Bulk Mail folders, or other folders.

From the Mail app, you can also add new folders for storing email messages on your iPad. As you're looking at the current list of folders associated with one email account, tap the Edit icon that's displayed at the top of the screen next to the Mailboxes heading. Now, at the bottom of the screen, in the lower-right corner of the left mailbox folder column, you will see a new icon appear labeled New Mailbox (shown in Figure 3.8).

Tap this icon to manually enter the name of a new folder, and decide under which email account (Mailbox Location) the folder will be displayed (as shown in Figure 3.9).

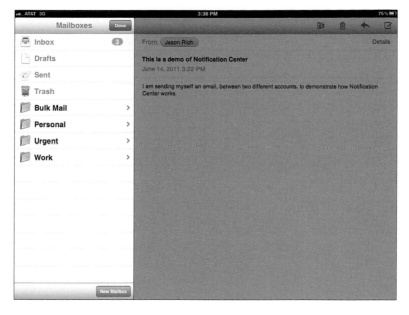

FIGURE 3.8

In the iOS 5 version of Mail, you can now create an unlimited number of mailbox folders (each with a custom name) on your iPad for organizing email messages.

FIGURE 3.9

Create as many email folders as you need, and give each of them a customized name.

SELECTING MESSAGES FOR USE WITH AN EDIT BUTTON

Located on top of the Inbox message listing (to the right of the Inbox heading) is an Edit button. When you tap this button, you can quickly select multiple messages from your Inbox to delete or move to another folder (see Figure 3.10).

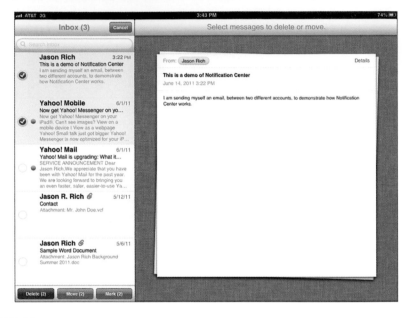

FIGURE 3.10

Tap the Edit command icon to quickly delete or move multiple email messages currently stored in your Inbox.

After you tap the Edit button, an empty circle icon displays to the left of each email message summary. To move or delete one or more messages from this Inbox listing, tap the empty circle icon for that message. A red-and-white checkmark fills the empty circle icon when you do this, and the Delete and Move buttons displayed at the bottom of the screen become active.

After you've selected one or more messages, tap the Delete button to quickly delete the messages from your Inbox (which sends them to the Trash folder) or tap the blue-and-white Move button, and then select which folder you want to move those email messages to.

To exit out of this option without doing anything, tap the blue-and-white Cancel button displayed at the top of the Inbox listing.

DELETING INDIVIDUAL INCOMING MESSAGES

As you're looking at the listing of messages in your Inbox, you can delete individual messages, one at a time, in several ways. Swipe your finger from left to right over a message listing on the left side of the screen. A red-and-white Delete button displays on the right side of that email message listing (shown in Figure 3.11). Tap this Delete button to delete the message.

FIGURE 3.11

Swipe your finger from left to right over a single email message listing to display the Delete icon, which enables you to delete the message from your Inbox and send it to the Trash folder.

Another way to delete a message from your Inbox or any folder is to tap the message listing that's displayed on the left side of the screen, highlighting the message in blue. At the same time, the entire message is displayed on the right side of the screen. To then delete the message, tap the Trash Can icon displayed in the upper-right corner of the screen. Doing this immediately sends the message to the Trash folder and removes it from its current folder.

NOTE   When you delete any email message on your iPad 2, the message is removed from your Inbox or from your iPad, but by default it is not deleted from your email server. So, if you also manage the same email account from your primary computer or another device, the message you delete on your iPad is still present on those other computers or devices. You can change this default option, however, so that your actions also affect email messages stored on the server. To do this, contact your company's IT department or your email service provider.

VIEWING YOUR EMAIL

When a single email message is highlighted on the left side of the Inbox screen, that message is displayed, in its entirety, on the right side of the screen. At the top of the message, you see the From, To, Cc, Bcc, Subject, and Date/Time lines.

In the upper-right corner of the email message is a blue Hide command. If you tap this, some of the message header information is no longer displayed. Hiding some of the header info enables you to display more of that email's message on the tablet's screen. To make this information reappear, tap the Details command that appears in the upper-right corner of the message.

Located to the right of the Date and Time the email was received is a blue Mark command. When you tap this Mark tab, two new command icons appear, labeled Flag and Mark As Unread. If you Flag a message, a small orange flag appears next to its listing on the left side of the screen (as shown in Figure 3.12), which indicates the message is urgent. If you tap the Mark As Unread option, that message remains in your Inbox with a blue dot next to it, indicating that it's a new message that has not yet been read.

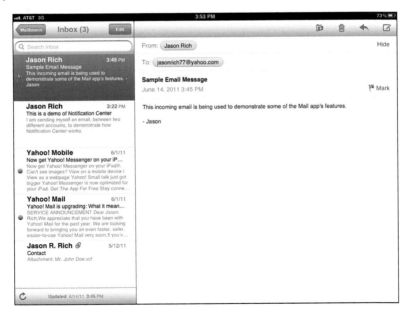

FIGURE 3.12

As you're reading any incoming email message on your iPad, you can flag it to indicate to yourself that the message is urgent.

> **TIP** The Mail app enables you to access certain types of attachment files that accompany an incoming email message. You can view and access the following files from the iPad using the Mail app: photos (in the .JPEG, .GIF, and .TIFF formats), audio files (in the .MP3, .AAC, .WAV, and .AIFF formats), PDF files, as well as Pages, Keynote, Numbers, Microsoft Word, Microsoft Excel, and Microsoft PowerPoint files.
>
> If an incoming email message contains an attachment that is not compatible or accessible from your iPad, you see that an attachment is present but you can't open or access it. In this case, you must access this content from another app or your primary computer.
>
> To open an attached file using another app, within the incoming email message tap and hold down the attachment icon for one to three seconds. If the attachment is compatible with an app that's installed on your iPad, you are given the option to transfer the file to that app or directly open or access the file using that app.

TRANSFERRING MESSAGES TO OTHER FOLDERS

As you're viewing an email message on the right side of the screen, you can move it from your Inbox to another folder in one of two ways. First, you can tap the Edit button, or you can tap the file folder-shaped icon that's displayed in the upper-right corner of the screen. When you tap this icon (see Figure 3.13), the various folders available for that email account are displayed on the left side of the screen. Tap the folder to which you want to move the message. In this case, you can send it to the Sent or Trash folder. The folders available vary for different types of email accounts.

FORWARDING, REPLYING, AND PRINTING

From within the Mail app, you can reply to the message, forward any incoming message to someone else, or print the email by tapping the left-pointing arrow icon that's displayed in the upper-right corner of the main Inbox screen (next to the Trash Can icon).

When you tap this icon as you're reading any email message, a menu is displayed in the upper-right corner of the screen (see Figure 3.14).

FIGURE 3.13

To move a file, tap the folder icon and then tap the folder name (displayed on the left side of the screen) where you want to move the message. The message is transferred from your Inbox to that other folder.

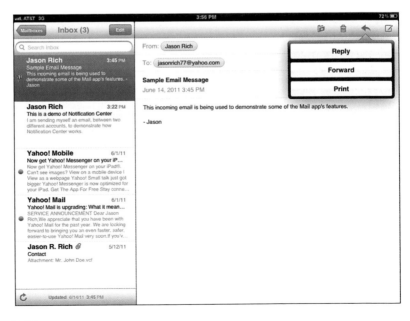

FIGURE 3.14

As you're reading any email message, tap the left-pointing arrow icon to Reply To, Forward, Save/Open Attachments, or Print that message.

To reply to the message you're reading, tap the Reply button. A blank email message template appears on the screen. See the "Composing Messages" section later in this chapter for details on how to write and send an email message from the Mail app.

To forward the email you're reading to another recipient, tap the Forward button. If there's an attachment associated with this email, you are asked if you want to include the attachments from the original email and you see two buttons labeled Include and Don't Include. Choose the appropriate response.

When you opt to forward an email, a new message template displays. However, within the body of the email message are the contents of the message you're forwarding (see Figure 3.15). Start the message forwarding process by filling in the To field. You can also modify the Subject field (or leave the message's original Subject) and then add to the body of the email message with your own text. The newly added text displays above the forwarded message's content.

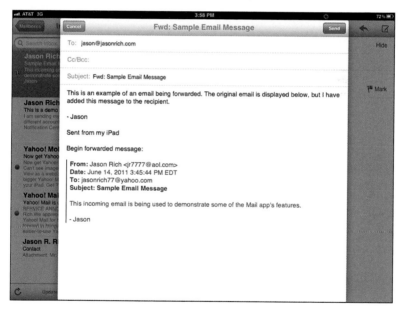

FIGURE 3.15

To forward an email message to one or more recipients, tap the Forward command and fill in the To field of the new outgoing message that contains the email message you're forwarding.

TIP   To forward an email to multiple recipients, enter each person's email address in the To field of the outgoing message, but separate each address with a comma (,). Thus, you'd type Jason@JasonRich.com, JasonRich77@yahoo.com in the To field to forward or send the message to these two recipients simultaneously. You can also tap the plus icon (+) that appears to the right of the To field to add more recipients.

When you're ready to forward the message to one or more recipients, tap the blue-and-white Send button that appears in the upper-right corner of the email message window. Or tap the Cancel button (located in the upper-left corner of the message window) to abort the message forwarding process.

WORKING WITH EMAIL ATTACHMENTS

If an incoming email message contains photos or other types of files that your iPad 2 can view or save (such as PDF files, Word documents, Excel spreadsheets, and so on), you have the option of storing these attachments on your tablet or view them, depending on the file type.

When an email contains an attachment, a thumbnail of that attachment appears at the bottom of the message, below its text. To download the attachment, tap it. Then, after it's download, hold your finger on the attachment icon. A menu appears giving you options related to what you can do with the attachment. These menu options will vary based on the type of file it is. For example, if it's a Word document, a Quick Look icon appears when you tap the thumbnail for the attachment, allowing you to view the document. However, if you have Pages installed on your iPad, you'll have the option of opening the file within Pages to read, edit, print, and/or share it.

If you receive a PDF file, the Quick Look option appears when you hold your finger on its thumbnail within the email. However, if you have iBooks or another PDF reader app installed on your tablet, you'll have the option to open the PDF file within that app.

If the attachment is a photo, after you download the photo by tapping its attachment icon, you can hold your finger on the photo that's now displayed within the email message (shown in Figure 3.16), and then choose to save the image or copy it to your iPad's virtual clipboard (which will allow you to paste it directly into certain apps).

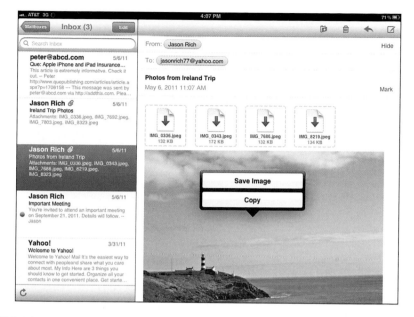

FIGURE 3.16

When you hold your finger on an email attachment after it has been downloaded, command icons appear giving you the available options for what you can do with that particular type of attachment. This varies based on what apps you have installed on your iPad that are compatible with that file type.

Chapter 9, "Using Pages, Numbers, Keynote, and Other Must-Have Business Apps," focuses more on managing and viewing Word documents, PDF files, Excel spreadsheet files, and PowerPoint presentation files on your tablet.

If you have a wireless printer set up to work with your iPad 2 (using the AirPrint feature built in to the iOS operating system and some printers), you can tap the Print command that displays on the menu that appears when you tap the left-pointing arrow command icon as you're reading an email.

TIP As you're reading emails, you'll discover that all the touch screen finger motions you've learned work on the section of the iPad's screen that's displaying the actual email messages; you can scroll and zoom. Plus, you can use the Select, Cut, Copy, and Paste features built in to the iOS operating system to manipulate the contents of an email message and utilize that content in other apps. You can also select, cut, and paste a portion of one email and insert it into another email message you're composing.

COMPOSING MESSAGES

From within the Mail app, you can easily compose an email from scratch and send it to one or more recipients. To compose a new email, tap the Compose icon that's displayed in the upper-right corner of the main Inbox screen. The Compose icon looks like a square with a pencil on it.

When you tap the Compose icon, a blank email message template (shown in Figure 3.17) displays. Using the virtual keyboard, fill in the To, Cc, Bcc, and Subject fields. At the very least, you must fill in the To field with a valid email address for at least one recipient. The other fields are optional.

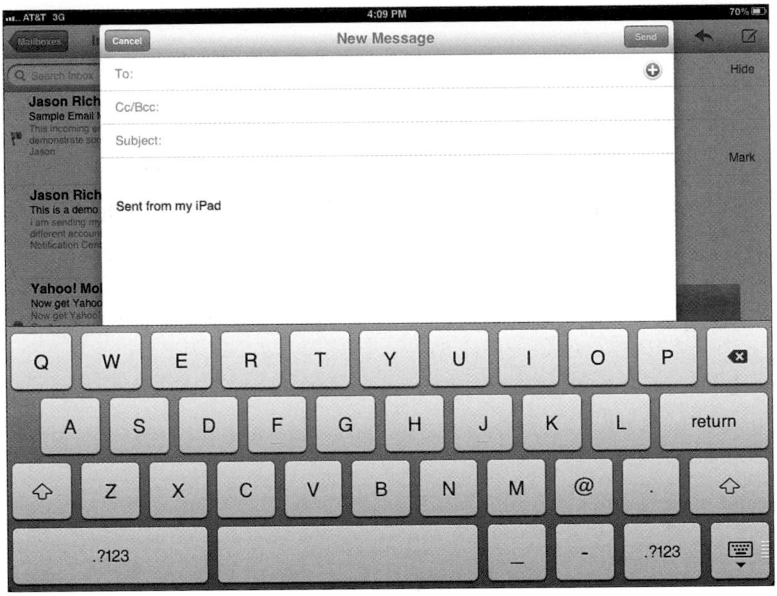

FIGURE 3.17

Tap the Compose icon to create an email from scratch and send it from your iPad 2.

You can send the same email to multiple recipients by either adding multiple email addresses to the To field or adding additional email addresses to the Cc or Bcc fields.

If you're managing just one email address from your iPad 2, the From field automatically fills with your email address and will not be displayed. However, if you're managing multiple email addresses from the tablet, tap the From field to select the email address from which you want to send the message.

Tap the Subject field and use the virtual keyboard to enter the Subject for your message. As you do this, the Subject displays in the title bar of the Compose window.

To begin creating the main body of the outgoing email message, tap in the main body area of the message template and use the virtual keyboard (or the external keyboard you're using with your iPad 2) to compose your message.

CAUTION If you have the Auto-Correction or Spell Check feature turned on (both of which are adjustable from the Settings app) as you type, the iPad automatically corrects anything that it perceives as a typo or misspelled word.

Be very careful when using these features because they are notorious for plugging the wrong word into a sentence. Especially if you're creating important business documents and emails, make sure you proofread whatever you type on your iPad carefully before sending it. Typically, these features are helpful, but they do have quirks that can lead to embarrassing and unprofessional mistakes.

The Signature you set up in the Settings app is displayed automatically at the bottom of the newly composed message. You can return to the Settings app to turn off the Signature feature, or you can change the signature that appears.

When your email is fully written and ready to be sent, tap the blue-and-white Send button in the upper-right corner of the Compose window. Within a few seconds, the message is sent from your iPad 2, assuming the tablet is connected to the Internet. A copy of the message goes to your Sent or Outbox folder.

As a message is being sent, a Sending notification displays in the lower-left corner of the screen.

SAVING UNSENT DRAFTS OF AN EMAIL MESSAGE

If you want to save a draft of an email (within your Draft folder, for example), without sending it, as you're composing the email message tap the Cancel icon that appears in the upper-left corner of the Compose message window. The Delete Draft and Save Draft buttons display. To save the unsent draft, tap Save Draft. This draft will permanently be saved in your Drafts folder until you either send it or delete it.

TIP To send an email message that contains an attachment, such as a Pages document or a photo, those attachments must be sent from within a specific app, not from the Mail app. So you must send a Pages, Word, or PDF document from within Pages; a Numbers or Excel (spreadsheet) file from within Numbers; and a photo from within the Photos app.

Currently, attachments cannot be added to outgoing messages composed using the Mail app, but this could change as new versions of the app are released. Other apps also enable you to attach app-specific files to outgoing emails that are composed and sent from within that app.

USING THE WEB TO ACCESS EMAIL

In addition to using the Mail app to access your email, for some types of email accounts, you can also use the Safari web browser to access your email account directly from the server.

For example, the same Yahoo! Mail account that was used to demonstrate the Mail app throughout this chapter was accessed directly from the Yahoo! website, using the Safari web browser on the iPad.

IN THIS CHAPTER

- An introduction to the Safari app
- Customizing your web surfing experience
- Creating and syncing bookmarks
- Accessing the online social networks—Facebook, Twitter, and LinkedIn

4

SURFING THE WEB

Back in the sixteenth century, long before people even dreamed of iPads and the Internet, Sir Francis Bacon stated, "Knowledge is power." In today's cut-throat business world, this statement is truer than ever.

People who possess knowledge, and who consistently stay up to date and in the know, have a distinct advantage over the masses who don't keep their skill set, knowledge, and education current. With the iPad 2's ability to access the Internet from virtually anywhere there's a Wi-Fi or 3G signal, your tablet is a powerful tool that can help you stay informed. The iPad can place a vast amount of information at your fingertips exactly when you need it. Like never before, the iPad is a tool that can keep you in the know, and provide the knowledge you need to be a powerful force in the business world.

Your iPad 2 can provide you with breaking news, keep you informed about what's happening on Wall Street, or enable you to exchange time-sensitive files or data with co-workers.

It also gives you the tools you need to quickly research virtually any topic, gather facts fast, and use that information to your advantage as you juggle day-to-day responsibilities.

You already know that the iPad 2 enables you to manage your email accounts while you're on the go. However, it also offers unprecedented access to the World Wide Web.

Many apps available for your tablet automatically tap into the Web to gather or share information and data. However, using the Safari web browser, you can easily visit any website using your iPad 2.

NOTE If you've recently upgraded to iOS 5 on your iPad 2 that was previously running iOS 4.33 (or earlier), you'll discover a handful of powerful new features incorporated into the Safari web browser, such as tabbed browsing and reading lists, that make web surfing even more efficient. You learn more about these new features shortly.

TIP Your iPad 2 enables you to visit virtually any website and navigate around the World Wide Web with ease using now-familiar finger motions on the tablet's touch-screen.

As you visit web pages using Safari, you can utilize hyperlinks or activate command icons with the tap of the finger, scroll up or down on a web page with a finger swipe, perform a reverse pinch or double-tap to zoom in on specific areas of a web page, or flick your finger to scroll left or right.

If you're already familiar with how to surf the Web on your primary computer using a web browser such as Microsoft Internet Explorer, Firefox, Google Chrome, or the Mac version of Safari, you should have little trouble surfing the Web on your iPad 2. The iPad's version of Safari was custom-designed specifically for your tablet to give you the most authentic and robust web surfing experience possible from a mobile device.

USING THE SAFARI WEB BROWSER

The Safari web browser comes with your tablet, and you can launch it from the Home screen. The app's red, white, and blue app icon looks like a compass dial. Obviously, to surf the Web, your tablet must be connected to the Internet via a 3G or Wi-Fi connection.

CUSTOMIZING SAFARI SETTINGS

The Safari app offers a handful of user-customizable settings that you can adjust from the Settings app on your iPad 2. Several of these settings relate to security and privacy.

TIP Adjusting the settings for Safari isn't required before you can begin using the browser. If you like, you can skip directly to the section "You're Ready to Begin Surfing" to start web surfing immediately. However, before you hit the Web, seriously consider adjusting some of the default Safari settings as discussed in this section, to ensure a safer and more pleasant online experience when visiting websites, doing research, and so on.

To access and personalize the settings for Safari, tap the Settings app icon that's displayed on your tablet's Home screen, and then tap the Safari option listed on the left side of the screen under the Settings heading. On the right side of the screen, a handful of Safari-specific options are displayed (see Figure 4.1).

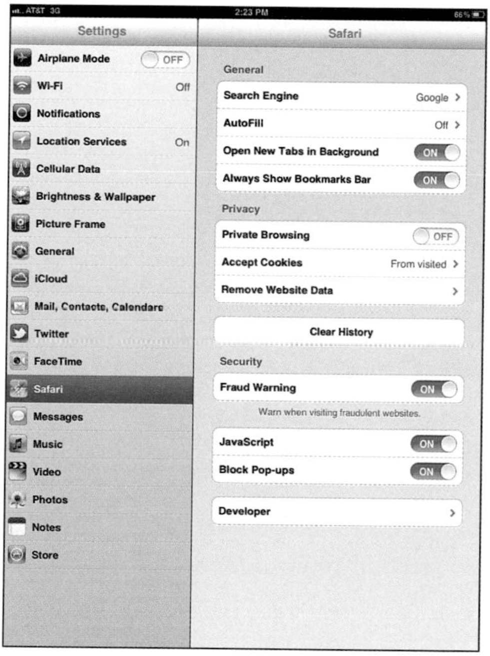

FIGURE 4.1

You can customize your web surfing experience by first accessing the Settings app, and then tapping the Safari option on the left (which will then be highlighted in blue).

At the top of the Settings screen (on the right), when the Safari option is selected (on the left), you see a General heading with four options below it: Search Engine, AutoFill, Open New Tabs in Background, and Always Show Bookmarks Bar.

As you're actually surfing the Web using Safari and looking at the main Safari screen (see Figure 4.2), note the Search field in the upper-right corner of the screen just below the battery icon. From the Settings app, you can determine whether your default search engine should be Google, Yahoo!, or Bing. This determines which search engine Safari utilizes when you perform a keyword search as you surf the Web. Your selection is displayed in the Search field. After you make a default search engine selection for Safari's Search field, it is saved and remains in effect until you change it.

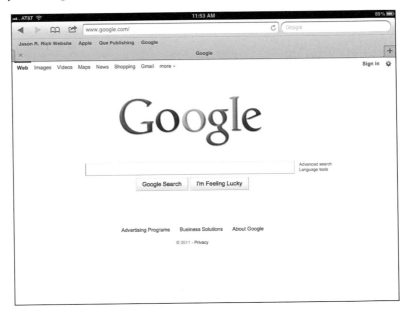

FIGURE 4.2

The main Safari browser screen contains a Search field in the upper-right corner. In the Settings app, you can control with search engine is set as your default.

The AutoFill option has two main uses when it's activated. First, as you're surfing the Web, whenever you're asked to enter your personal information—such as your name, address, phone number, or email address—Safari automatically inserts the information into the appropriate fields on the website.

To use AutoFill, make sure the virtual switch that's associated with the Use Contact Info option is turned on (as shown in Figure 4.3). You also need to tap the My Info option and select your own contact entry from your Contacts database.

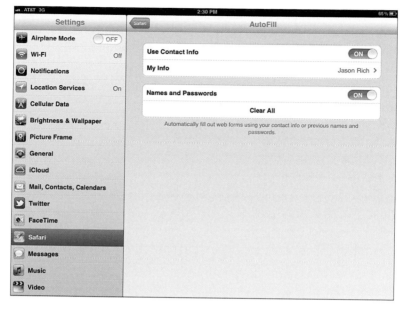

FIGURE 4.3

When turned on, the Use Contact Info option automatically fills in your personal contact info on websites you visit.

Farther down on the AutoFill screen is the Names and Passwords option (refer to Figure 4.3). This is the second main use for AutoFill. When it's turned on, this feature remembers your usernames and passwords for the websites you visit and automatically enters them whenever you revisit websites that require you to otherwise manually enter a username or password.

> **CAUTION** If you're concerned about security and other people accessing personal information about you from the Web when they use your iPad 2, make sure you keep the Names and Passwords option turned off. This prevents other users from accessing your account(s) or signing in to websites as you.

The Clear All option at the bottom of the AutoFill screen (refer to Figure 4.3) resets all the names and passwords data from websites you've visited and deletes this information from your tablet.

To exit the AutoFill screen while in Settings, tap the Safari button at the top of the screen in the upper-left corner.

The next option found under the General heading (refer to Figure 4.1) is the Open New Tabs in Background feature. The iOS 5 version of Safari enables you to open multiple web pages at once using tabs and instantly switch between them with a tap of the finger. With this feature turned on, when a new web page is opened automatically (and a new tab is created), that page will not take precedence over the web page you're currently viewing. You'll need to tap on the new page's tab to access it.

Also under the General heading, you'll discover the Always Show Bookmarks Bar option. This option is accompanied by a virtual on/off switch on the right. As you're surfing the Web using Safari, under the Title Bar command icons at the top of the screen, you can opt to display your personalized Bookmarks Bar, which offers links to commonly visited websites that you assign to appear within this portion of the display.

When the Always Show Bookmarks Bar option is turned on, the bookmarks bar is displayed at all times below the title bar in Safari (see Figure 4.4), giving you one-tap access to your favorite websites. You can assign which websites appear along your bookmarks bar, or you can sync this information with the browser you use on your primary computer.

FIGURE 4.4

The bookmarks bar is one way to create one-tap shortcuts to your favorite websites. In Safari, you can assign which websites appear along your bookmarks bar, or you can sync this information with the browser you use on your primary computer.

When the Always Show Bookmarks Bar option is turned off, one line of onscreen real estate is conserved, which enables you to see more of the websites you're visiting. The bookmarks bar, however, is displayed automatically whenever you use the Search field within Safari to perform a search, or when you tap on the address bar.

Under the Privacy heading of the Safari screen within Settings, you can customize a handful of security-related options. For example, you can turn on or off the Private Browsing option. By default, this option is turned off. This option will keep Safari from storing cookies or other data pertaining to the websites you visit. You can also opt to keep Safari from saving cookies related to the websites you visit or delete cookies that have already been stored by Safari (by tapping on the Remove Website Data option that's found under the Privacy heading).

The Accept Cookies option allows Safari to store certain information relating to specific websites you visit so that those sites remember you on subsequent visits. By selecting the From Visited option, only information that relates to websites you have chosen to visit is saved.

Safari automatically keeps a detailed listing of every website you visit. By tapping the Clear History command icon, this listing will be reset and deleted.

Under the Security heading of the Safari screen with Settings, you can turn on or off the Fraud Warning option. By default, this option is turned on and should remain on for your protection. This option will help prevent you from accidentally surfing to imposter or fraudulent websites, for example.

Don't mess with the default settings for the next two options, JavaScript (on/off) and Block Pop-ups (on/off), unless you know what you're doing or are instructed by a specialist to change these settings. The JavaScript option enables you to visit and access websites that utilize JavaScript programming. The Block Pop-ups option prevents those annoying pop-up windows (which are usually ads) from cluttering your screen as you're surfing the Web.

Unless you have a programming background or you're told to do so by an AppleCare technical support specialist, refrain from changing any settings found under the Developer or Databases submenus, if and when these options are displayed on the Safari screen within Settings. Simply leave the default settings as is.

To exit the Settings app and automatically save your changes, press the Home button on your iPad 2. This returns you to the Home screen. From here, you can launch Safari and begin surfing the Web.

WHERE'S THE FLASH?

The one main drawback to surfing the Web using Safari on your iPad 2 is the web browser's inability to display Adobe Flash-based graphics and animations. This limitation is not due to lack of technological capability of your tablet, however. It's the result of ongoing disagreements between Apple and Adobe in regard to offering Flash compatibility through the iOS operating system.

Unfortunately, websites that rely heavily on Flash are not accessible from your iPad 2. Some websites that contain some Flash-based animations might be visible, but certain elements or aspects of those sites are inaccessible. In these situations, either an error message is displayed, or you see a non-animated graphic in place of the Flash-based animation.

With tens of millions of iOS-based iPhones and iPads in use, many website developers and operators have created mobile versions of their sites that are fully compatible with the iPad 2. These sites automatically detect that you're accessing the site using your tablet and adjust the content accordingly, insuring everything is visible on your iPad's screen.

In the future, hopefully the Safari web browser for iPad 2 will be made compatible with Adobe Flash or an emulator will be approved and released, allowing you to access any website, regardless of the programming language used to create it.

YOU'RE READY TO BEGIN SURFING

To access the Web using your iPad, make sure it's connected to the Internet, and then tap the Safari app icon that's displayed on the tablet's Home screen. The main Safari web browser screen appears.

USING SAFARI'S TITLE BAR FEATURES

Located along the top of the Safari screen is the title bar, which includes a handful of command icons that you use to navigate around the Web. Although the icons might look different than what you're used to when surfing the Web using the browser installed on your primary computer, their features and functions are similar.

> **TIP** As you surf the Web using Safari, you can hold your tablet in portrait or landscape mode. Landscape mode makes the portion of the websites you're viewing appear larger on the screen, but portrait mode enables you to see more of the web page vertically. When visiting a website, you can always switch between viewing perspectives by rotating your tablet. You can also zoom in on particular areas of a website to make content appear larger on the screen.

Located in the upper-left corner of the Safari screen are the Back and Forward arrow-shaped icons used for jumping to a previous web page you've visited.

The open book-shaped icon displayed on the title bar (shown in Figure 4.5) enables you to access your reading list, history, bookmarks bar, and the bookmarks you've added to your bookmarks list. Later in this chapter, you learn how to sync your bookmarks between Safari on your iPad 2 with the bookmarks stored on your primary computer's web browser software.

When you're visiting any website, you can tap the rectangular icon with a right-pointing arrow sticking out of it (the Share icon) that's located to the immediate left of the address field to access a submenu with the following five options (see Figure 4.6): Add Bookmark, Add to Reading List, Add to Home Screen, Mail Link to This Page, and Print.

> **NOTE** If you have Twitter set up on your iPad (from within the Settings app), a sixth option, labeled Tweet, will be displayed within the Share menu, allowing you to send a tweet to your followers, containing your 140-character message and a link to the website you're viewing. The Share menu offered in other apps, such as Photos, YouTube, Camera, and Maps, will also display a Tweet option if you have Twitter turned on and you're signed in to your Twitter account from within the Settings app.

FIGURE 4.5

Tap the open book-shaped icon to access your reading list (which is explained shortly), as well as your history, bookmarks bar listing, and saved bookmarks.

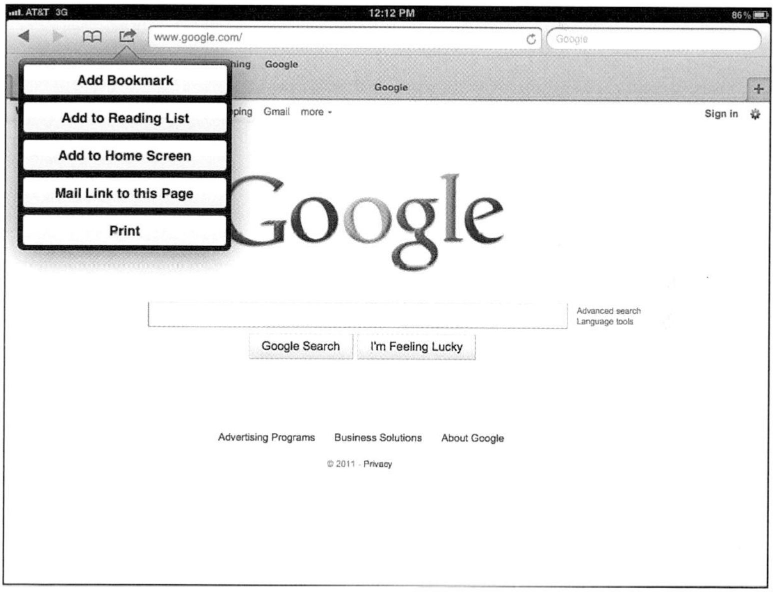

FIGURE 4.6

This submenu offers several useful web surfing options.

The Add Bookmark command adds the website URL for the page you're currently viewing to your Bookmarks menu or bookmarks bar. When you tap the Add Bookmark command, the Add Bookmark window (shown in Figure 4.7) displays. Using the virtual keyboard, enter the title for this web page—or use the default title—and then choose whether you want to store the bookmark within your Bookmarks menu or display it on your bookmarks bar.

The Bookmarks menu is a pull-down menu that lists your favorite bookmarks. It is a listing you can create and maintain as you're surfing the Web. You can access it by tapping on the open book-shaped icon at the top of the Safari screen.

The bookmarks bar can be constantly displayed below the title bar. It offers one-tap access to the bookmarked web pages listed on it.

Be sure to tap the blue-and-white Save button in the upper-right corner of the Add Bookmark window to save your changes before returning to the main Safari screen.

The Add to Reading List option immediately stores the web page you're viewing in the iPad's memory and enables you to access it later (even if you're offline). When you add a website to your reading list, you can access it by tapping the open book-shaped icon, and then tapping the Reading List option. This feature is particularly useful if you find an interesting article or blog entry that you don't have time to read at the moment, but you know you want to refer to later.

FIGURE 4.7

The Add Bookmark window enables you to add a bookmark for the web page you're viewing to either Safari's Bookmark menu or the bookmarks bar.

Instead of adding a bookmark to the Bookmark menu or the bookmarks bar, both of which are only visible when Safari is running and you're surfing the Web, you can create a bookmark icon for a specific web page on your Home screen using the Add to Home Screen command. When you tap a Home screen bookmark icon, the Safari browser launches and automatically loads the bookmarked web page. This enables you to access your favorite websites directly from the iPad 2's Home screen. Home screen bookmark icons (see the Jason R. Rich, Que Publishing, and Google icons in Figure 4.8) look similar to app icons on your Home screen. However, instead of launching an app when you tap one, Safari launches and opens the specific web page the icon is associated with.

FIGURE 4.8

You can create and display Bookmark icons on your Home screen, which enables you to launch Safari and access a specific web page with a single tap. The icon that's displayed includes a thumbnail of the web page.

When you tap the Add to Home Screen command, an Add to Home window displays (see Figure 4.9). Using the virtual keyboard, enter the title of the bookmark in the displayed field, and then tap the blue-and-white Add button displayed in the upper-right corner of the window. After doing this, when you access your Home Screen, the new Home Screen Bookmark icon will appear.

After you added a Home screen bookmark icon, you can treat it like any Home screen app icon, which means you can tap it to launch the website, move It around on the Home screen, or place it into a folder.

> **TIP** As you're surfing, some websites that cater specifically to iOS users have custom icons associated with their site that look great when added to your iPad's Home Screen. CNN.com is an example of this. If your company has a web presence that caters to iPad and iPhone users, you might want to build a custom icon into your site's programming.

When you tap the Mail Link to This Page command, an email message screen displays. Fill in the To field to specify who should receive the email. A link to the website you're currently viewing is automatically placed in the body of the email. You can add additional text to the body of the email before tapping the Send button.

> **TIP** The address field of Safari does not distinguish between capitalized and lowercase letters as you enter website URLs. Thus, entering either www.*YourWebsiteName*.com or www.*yourwebsitename*.com takes you to the same location on the Web. If you're accessing a subdirectory within a website (www.yourwebsitename.com/subdirectory); however, the subdirectory portion of a website's URL might be case sensitive.

USING THE SEARCH FIELD

Located in the upper-right corner of the screen is Safari's Search field. Here, you can enter any keyword or search phrase to perform a web search using Google, Yahoo!, or Bing, depending on which default search engine you previously selected from the Settings app.

USING TABS

Tabs enable you to load multiple web pages within Safari simultaneously and then instantly switch between them. The tab bar is displayed below the bookmarks bar, near the top of the Safari screen. When you first load Safari, only one tab will be open. However, at any time, you can tap the plus (+) icon that's displayed to the extreme right of the tab bar to open a new browser window and create a new tab.

You can have multiple tabs displayed at the top of the Safari screen. When multiple tabs are open, tap any of them to switch to the website to which the tab corresponds. Displayed in Figure 4.13 are five tabs representing the Que Publishing, Apple, Jason R. Rich, CNN.com, and Weather.com websites (going from left to right).

The website that's actually displayed on the iPad's screen is the active tab. To the left of the active tab's title is an X icon. Tap this X to delete the tab and close the web page associated with it. To keep the web page open but view a different web page, tap on another displayed tab, or open a new tab and manually surf to another website.

The ability to quickly switch between web pages that are open (which is referred to as *tabbed browsing*), makes surfing the Web on the iPad much faster and more convenient. This feature is new to iOS 5.

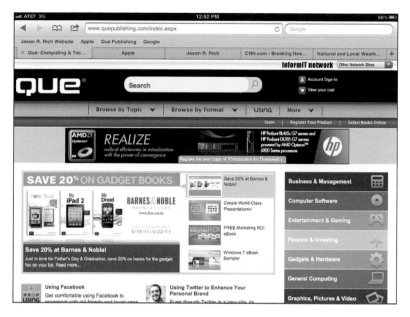

FIGURE 4.13

Here, five tabs are open and displayed near the top of the Safari browser screen.

USING SAFARI'S READER

Sometimes, web pages are cluttered with ads, graphics, menus, and other content that makes reading a text-based article confusing. With the Reader option built in to Safari, the web browser automatically strips away this clutter, allowing you to read the text-based article more easily and with no onscreen distractions. When this option is available, a small Reader icon appears to the left of the website's URL in the Address field of Safari (as shown in Figure 4.14). Tap this icon, and the text-based article displays in a new, clutter-free window. Active links within the article or text remain active.

FIGURE 4.14

When the Reader icon appears in the Address Bar of Safari, you can tap it to read the text-based content on that site on a clutter-free screen.

As you're reading a text-based article in Reader, in the upper-left corner of the screen will be an aA icon. Tap it to increase or decrease the size of the onscreen text.

UNDERSTANDING THE WEB PAGE VIEWING AREA

Getting back to surfing the Web, displayed below the title bar and the bookmarks bar (if you have this option turned on) is the main website viewing area of Safari. As you view website content, you can scroll around on the page using upward, downward, left, or right finger swipes. To instantly jump back to the top of a web page, tap anywhere on the status bar at the top of the iPad's screen (above the title bar). The status bar displays the Internet connection's signal bars, the current time, and the battery life indicator.

To zoom in or out of a particular area of a web page, either double-tap on the area that you want to zoom in on or perform a reverse-pinch finger motion. To zoom out, double-tap on the screen again or perform a pinch finger motion.

If you see a hyperlink or a command button displayed within a web page, tap it to follow the link or activate the button. To see where the link takes you before actually surfing there, hold your finger on the link or button for two to three seconds. The link's URL address is displayed along with a menu containing three commands:

- **Open:** This opens the web page that the link directs you to.
- **Open in New Page:** This opens the web page that the link directs you to but does so within a new Safari browser window.
- **Copy:** This copies the website URL to your iPad's virtual clipboard so you can paste this information elsewhere.

TIP   As you're viewing almost any graphic or photo that's displayed within a website, you can hold your finger on the image to save it on your iPad, where it becomes accessible from the Photos app. After holding your finger on an image for two to three seconds, several command icons appear: Open (which opens just that graphic or photo in the Safari screen or opens the link associated with it), Open in New Tab (the photo is displayed or the link associated with it is displayed, but in a new Safari window that's associated with a new tab), Add to Reading List (the related image or content is saved in your reading list), Save Image (which saves the photo on your iPad), and Copy (which temporarily stores the image in your iPad's virtual clipboard, so you can paste it into another file or document).

If for some reason a web page doesn't fully load or you want to refresh the information displayed on a web page you're currently viewing, tap the circular arrow icon that's displayed to the extreme right of the address bar.

If you want to stop a web page as it is loading, tap the X icon to the extreme right of the address bar during the web page loading process.

To jump back to a web page you just looked at, tap the left-pointing arrow command icon that's displayed in the upper-left corner of the screen on the title bar. Then, to return to the web page you're currently viewing, tap the right-pointing arrow, also displayed in the upper-left corner of the screen.

Any time you need to enter text or numerical data in a field on a website you're viewing, tap the empty field, which causes the iPad's virtual keyboard to display. To move to another field that requires data entry, either tap your finger on the next field or tap the Next or Previous icon that appears on the screen above the virtual keyboard.

To close the virtual keyboard when you no longer need it, tap the Close Keyboard key that's always displayed in the lower-right corner of the virtual keyboard.

SYNCING BOOKMARKS WITH YOUR PRIMARY COMPUTER

To ensure your web surfing experience is similar to when you're exploring the Web using the web browser on your primary computer, you have the option to sync your bookmarks between your computer and your iPad 2.

There are two methods for syncing your Safari bookmarks. One happens automatically using the iCloud service, and the other is done through an iTunes sync procedure when your tablet is connected to your primary computer via a USB cable. This sync process works with Safari for the Mac, Microsoft Internet Explorer on a PC, as well as a variety of other popular web browser applications.

Using the iTunes sync procedure, to sync your Bookmarks menu and bookmarks bar, begin by connecting your iPad 2 to your computer using the USB cable.

When iTunes on your primary computer launches, select your iPad 2 under the devices heading on the left side of the iTunes screen. Next, at the top, near the center of the iTunes screen, click the Info tab. Select the Sync Safari Bookmarks option. Click the Apply button to complete the process.

NOTE If you use the iCloud online service, you can automatically sync your bookmarks wirelessly between your tablet and primary computer (as well as your iPhone). To set this up, after you have an iCloud account, access the Settings app from your tablet's Home Screen and tap the iCloud option that's displayed on the left column. When the iCloud screen appears on the right side of the Settings screen, turn on the Bookmarks option.

ACCESSING SOCIAL NETWORKS ON YOUR iPAD

Whether you use Facebook, Twitter, and LinkedIn to promote your business, a product, or a service; to help position yourself as an expert in your field; to meet new people; or simply to stay in touch with your friends and family, you can fully utilize these online social networking sites using specialized apps available from the App Store.

Online social networking sites are not just for kids and teens. In fact, many companies of all sizes and in all industries are creating a presence on these services to use them as promotional and sales tools and to inexpensively develop an online community around their companies, products, or services.

Many business professionals, top-level executives, and politicians are also using services like Twitter to position themselves as experts in their fields and to communicate directly with customers, clients, constituents, investors, and employees.

The ability to share information on social networks from virtually anywhere using your iPad brings a new level of interactivity to these services. For many businesses, social networking services are also being used as an incredibly useful, inexpensive, and highly targeted advertising medium.

NOTE To learn more about how companies of all sizes and in a wide range of industries are utilizing Twitter, visit http://business.twitter.com. For more information about how your business can benefit from having a presence on Facebook, visit http://www.facebook.com/platform. Or, if you're a public figure, non-profit organization, or small business operator, visit http://www.facebook.com/FacebookPages. For details on working with LinkedIn, go to http://www.linkedin.com.

WORKING WITH FACEBOOK

The official Facebook app is freely available from the App Store. It was designed for the iPhone, but it works flawlessly on the iPad 2. It offers a few features not available from your iPad 2 if you use the Safari web browser to access this immensely popular online social networking service (www.facebook.com), such as the ability to chat in real-time with your friends or upload photos. An iPad-specific official Facebook app is slated for release in the fall of 2011, along with iOS 5. It's designed specifically with the iPad's larger touch screen and offers a variety of new features.

There are also a bunch of other third-party apps that serve as an interface for Facebook that are optimized for the iPad 2 and that give you additional features and functions for managing your Facebook photos and photo albums, for example, or participating in real-time chats with your friends.

TIP   To find third-party apps designed to work with Facebook or Twitter, visit the App Store. Within the Search field, enter either "Facebook" or "Twitter" as your keyword. Although the official Facebook and Twitter apps are free, many of the third-party apps designed to work with these online social networking sites are paid apps.

The benefit to several of these paid apps is that they enable you to manage multiple Facebook or Twitter accounts, which many business professionals who maintain accounts on behalf of their company, find useful.

TWEETING FROM YOUR iPAD 2

For the iPad 2, there is also an official Twitter app, designed specifically for the iPad (free), and dozens of third-party apps that work with Twitter that are either free or are paid apps. The official Twitter app for iPad is shown in Figure 4.15. This app, as well as Twitter functionality, has now been fully integrated into iOS 5, so you can ty of different apps as long as the official Twitter app is loaded

FIGURE 4.15

The official Twitter app for iPad is free. It enables you to send tweets, manage your Twitter feed, and follow others. You can also monitor trending topics, perform searches, and share photos or website URLs within outgoing tweets.

To initially set up Twitter on your iPad, access the Settings app and tap the Twitter option displayed on the left side of the screen (shown in Figure 4.16). On the right side of the screen, you will have the option to install the official Twitter app by tapping the Install Now icon.

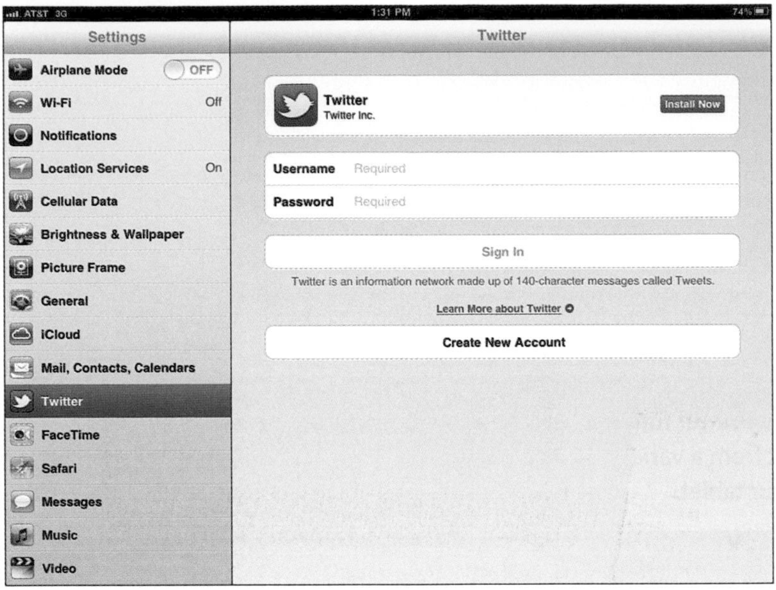

FIGURE 4.16

Load the official Twitter app from within Settings, and then sign in to your Twitter account. You'll discover several apps on your iPad now fully integrate with Twitter, including Photos, Safari, Camera, Contacts, YouTube, and Maps.

Once installed, launch the Twitter app on your iPad. You can then sign in using one or multiple Twitter accounts or create a new account (which is also something you can do from the Twitter screen within Settings, by tapping the Create New Account option).

Although the official Twitter app can be used to create and send Tweets, access your Twitter timeline, and see what the people you're following are tweeting about, you'll now discover that various other core apps, including Photos, Safari, Camera, Contacts, YouTube, and Maps are now fully integrated with Twitter.

> **TIP** For Twitter integration to work with the core apps built in to your iPad (as opposed to just the official Twitter app), you will need to sign in to your Twitter account from within Settings just once.

Figure 4.17 shows the new Twitter option in Photos, which is displayed when you view a photo and tap the Share icon that's displayed to the immediate left of the trash can icon. When the Share menu appears, the last option is to Tweet the photo from directly within the Photos app.

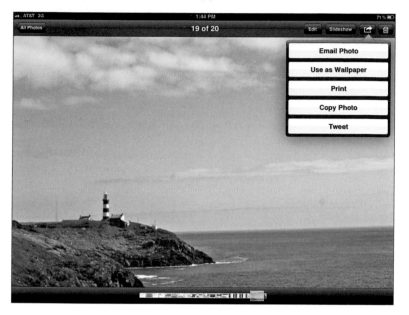

FIGURE 4.17

You can now send tweets from within the Photos app as you're viewing a photo. Tap the Share icon, and then choose the Tweet option.

Tap the Tweet option, and within Photos, a Tweet window appears (shown in Figure 4.18), allowing you to compose an outgoing tweet that will automatically attach the photo. If you tap the Add Location option in the lower-left corner of this window, your exact location will automatically be added to the outgoing tweet as well.

> **TIP** To send a tweet message to your followers to share a website URL from within Safari, tap the Share icon that's displayed to the immediate left of the Address field, and then select the Tweet option from the menu. Similar functionality is also available within a handful of other iPad 2 apps.

FIGURE 4.18

When you choose to send a tweet from within an app, a special tweet window appears allowing you to compose and send the 140-character message and (if applicable) automatically attach a photo, URL, or your exact location.

TAPPING INTO LINKEDIN TO NETWORK WITH BUSINESS PROFESSIONALS

More than 120 million business professionals, working in thousands of different fields and industries, are active participants on the LinkedIn online social networking service (www.linkedin.com).

LinkedIn is a free service that is dedicated exclusively to business professionals, and it can be a valuable tool for communicating with industry colleagues, finding job leads, seeking advice from experts, reaching out to new customers or clients, or exchanging ideas.

To access LinkedIn from your iPad 2, download the free LinkedIn app, called IN. It's available from the App Store. IN is designed for the iPhone but works flawlessly on the iPad 2. You can also utilize the mobile version of the LinkedIn.com website, using Safari, by visiting http://m.linkedin.com.

IN THIS CHAPTER

- An introduction to the Calendar app that comes on your iPad 2
- Using the Notification Center built in to iOS 5
- Additional time-management, project management, To-Do list management, and scheduling tools available from the App Store

5

USING THE CALENDAR APP AND NOTIFICATION CENTER

Appointments, meetings, phone calls, web-based virtual meetings, commuting to and from work, business travel, errands, responding to emails, personal obligations, and vacations are just some of the ways people spend their time.

Those people who are typically the most productive and efficient on the job, and who live with the least amount of day-to-day stress, have often discovered the secrets of effectively managing their time, which enables them to prioritize tasks and their responsibilities, delegate when possible, and keep themselves organized.

Your iPad 2 can be used as a time-management tool for keeping track of your day-to-day schedule. It can also help to keep you well organized and assist with tracking how you utilize your time throughout each and every day, without intruding on your current work habits.

CALENDAR APP BASICS

The Calendar app is preinstalled on your tablet. With multiple viewing options for keeping track of the scheduling information stored within it, Calendar is a highly customizable scheduling tool that enables you to easily sync your scheduling data with your primary computer's scheduling software (such as Microsoft Outlook on a PC or iCal on a Mac). Like many other apps, Calendar works seamlessly with Notification Center and Apple's iCloud service.

Plus, you can share some or all of your schedule information with colleagues and maintain several separate, color-coded calendars of your own to keep personal and work-related responsibilities and projects listed separately while still being able to view them on the same calendar.

For specialized tasks that involve billing customers or clients for your time, handling project management, or employee scheduling, for example, many third-party apps available from the App Store work in conjunction with Calendar to manage these and other time- and scheduling-related tasks.

> **TIP**   The Calendar app is designed to work with Apple's iCloud service, as well as Microsoft Exchange and other software and online-based calendar/scheduling programs (including Google Calendar and Yahoo! Calendar, for example). This file compatibility enables you to easily synchronize your scheduling data between your iPad 2 and other devices.

CONTROLLING THE VIEW

Launch Calendar from your tablet's Home screen, and then choose which viewing perspective you'd like to view your schedule data in. Your five options, selectable by tapping the tabs displayed at the top-center of the screen, include the following:

■ **Day:** This view (shown in Figure 5.1) displays your appointments and scheduled events individually on the right side of the screen, based on the time each item is scheduled for.

■ **Week:** This view uses a grid format (shown in Figure 5.2) to display the days of the week along the top of the screen and time intervals along the left side. With it you have an overview of all appointments and events scheduled within a particular week (Sunday through Saturday).

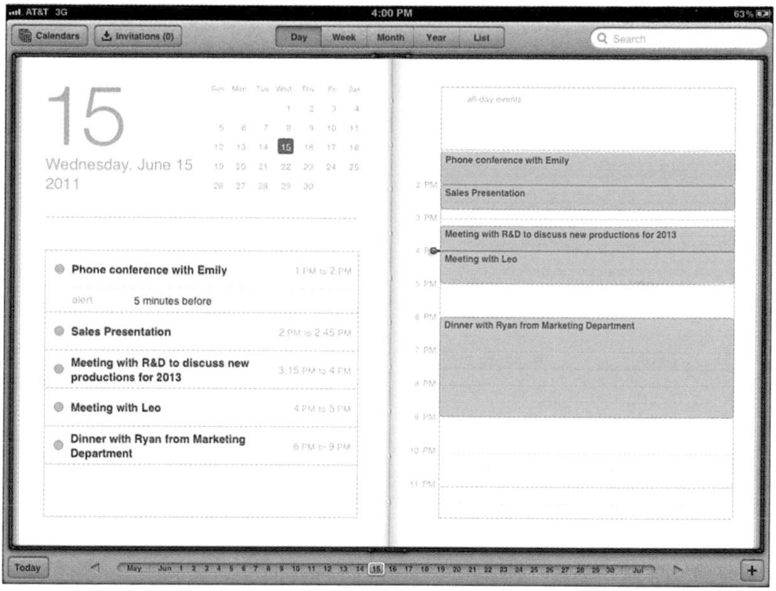

FIGURE 5.1

The Calendar app's Day view.

FIGURE 5.2

The Calendar app's Week view.

■ **Month:** This month-at-a-time view (shown in Figure 5.3) enables you to see a month's worth of appointments and events at a time. You can tap any single day to immediately switch to the Day view to review a detailed summary of appointments or events slated for that day.

FIGURE 5.3

The Calendar app's Month view.

■ **Year:** This view (shown in Figure 5.4) enables you to look at 12 mini-calendars and see an overview of your schedule. For example, you can block out vacation days, travel days, and so on and get a comprehensive view of your overall annual schedule.

■ **List:** See a complete summary listing of all appointments and events stored within the Calendar app (shown in Figure 5.5). You can tap an individual listing to see its complete details. When you're using this view, a listing of all upcoming appointments is displayed on the left, and the current day's appointments and related notes are displayed on the right side of the screen.

Regardless of which view you select, at any time you can view the current day's schedule by tapping the Today button located in the lower-left corner of the screen. On the calendar itself, the current date is always highlighted in blue.

FIGURE 5.4

The Calendar app's Year view.

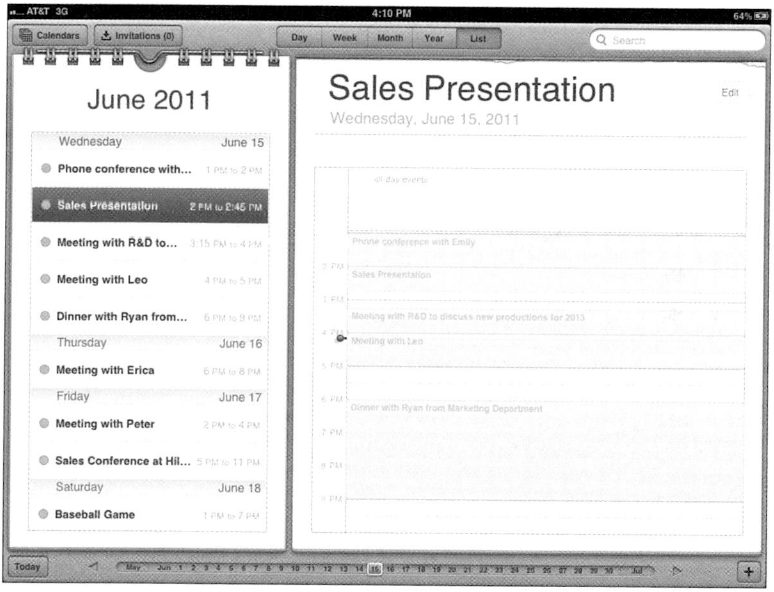

FIGURE 5.5

The Calendar app's List view.

ENTERING A NEW APPOINTMENT

Regardless of which calendar view you're using, to enter a new appointment, tap the plus icon that's displayed in the lower-right corner of the screen. This displays an Add Event window (shown in Figure 5.6). When using the Calendar app, appointments, meetings, and other items you enter are referred to as *events*.

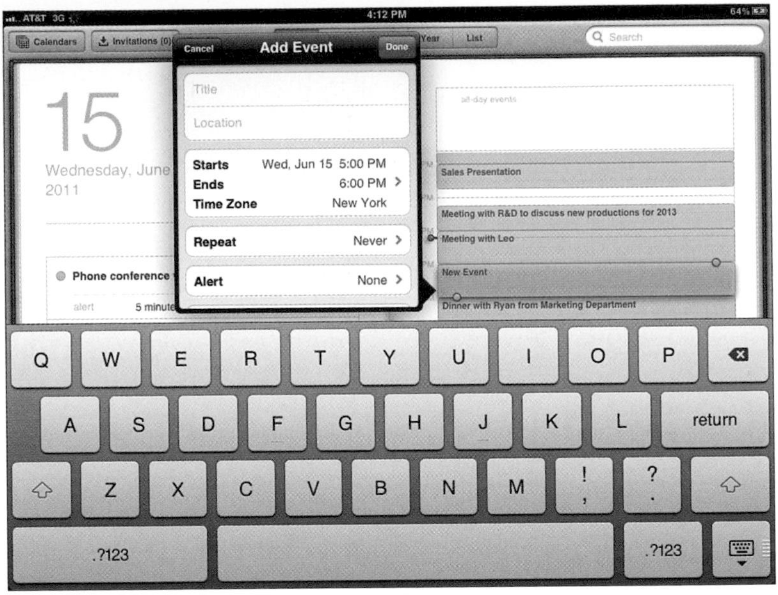

FIGURE 5.6

From the Add Event window, you can add a new appointment to the Calendar app and associate an audible alarm with that event.

The first field in the Add Event window is labeled Title. Using the iPad's virtual keyboard, enter a heading for the appointment or event, such as "Lunch with Bob," "Sales Meeting," or "Call Sally."

Next, if there's a location associated with the meeting or appointment, tap the Location field located below the Title Field, and then use the virtual keyboard to enter the address or location of the appointment. Entering information into the Location field is optional. You can be as detailed as you want when entering information into this field.

To set the time and date for the new appointment to begin and end, tap the Starts and Ends field. A new Start & End window (see Figure 5.7) displays, temporarily replacing the Add Event window.

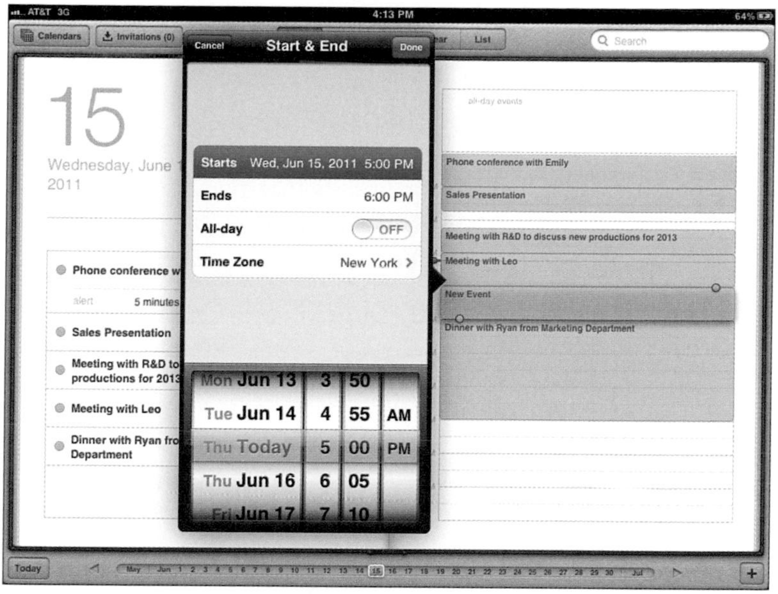

FIGURE 5.7

From the Start & End window, select the start and end time and date for each new appointment you manually enter into the Calendar app.

When viewing the Start & End window, tap the Starts option so that it becomes highlighted in blue, and then use the scrolling Date, Hour, Minute, and AM/PM dials to select the exact Start Time for your appointment.

After entering the Start Time, tap on the Ends option, and again use the scrolling Date, Hour, Minute, and AM/PM dials to select the exact End Time for your appointment. Or, if the appointment lasts the entire day, tap the All-Day virtual switch, moving it from the off to on position.

You can also adjust the Time Zone option if the meeting will be taking place in a different time zone than the one you're currently in. So, if you're based in Los Angeles but the meeting or appointment will take place at 2:00 p.m. (EST) because it will be held in New York, you can enter the correct time for the location of the meeting and the iPad will adjust accordingly when you travel.

After you enter the Start Time and End Time for the appointment, you must tap the blue-and-white Done button to save this information and return to the Add Event window.

If the appointment you're entering repeats every day, every week, every two weeks, every month, or every year, tap the Repeat option and choose the appropriate option. The default for this option is Never, meaning it is a nonrepeating, one-time only appointment.

To set an audible alarm for the appointment, tap the Alert option displayed below the Repeat option within the Add Event window. The Event Alert window (see Figure 5.8) temporarily replaces the Add Event window. In the Event Alert window, tap to specify when you want the audible alarm to sound to remind you of the appointment. Your options are None (which is the default), 5 minutes before, 15 minutes before, 30 minutes before, one hour before, two hours before, one day before, two days before, or On Date of Event. When you tap your selection, a check mark that corresponds with that selection displays on the left side of the window.

FIGURE 5.8

From the Event Alert window, you can set one or two audible alarms to sound to remind you of that obligation.

Tap the blue-and-white Done button that's displayed in the upper-right corner of the Event Alert window to save the information and return to the Add Event screen.

Upon adding an alert, a Second Alert option now displays in the Add Event window. If you want to add a secondary alarm to this appointment, tap the Second Alert option and when the Event Alert window reappears, tap when you want the second alarm to sound. Again, don't forget to tap the Done button.

When you return to the Add Event window, if you're maintaining several separate calendars within the Calendar app, you can choose which calendar you want to list the appointment or event by tapping on the Calendar option and then selecting the appropriate calendar.

As you scroll down within the Calendar window, you will see an optional URL and Notes field. Using the virtual keyboard, you can manually enter a website URL that corresponds to the event or meeting. Or, tap the Notes field and manually type notes pertaining to the appointment (or paste data from other apps within this field).

It is essential that you tap the blue-and-white Done button to save the new appointment information and have it displayed within your calendar. The alternative is to tap the Cancel icon (displayed in the upper-left corner of the Add Event, Start & End, Repeat, or Event Alert window), which is used to exit out of that window without saving any new information.

> **TIP** The Calendar app works with several other iPad 2 apps, including Contacts and Notification Center. For example, within Contacts, you can enter someone's birthday within his record, and that information can automatically be displayed within the Calendar app.
>
> To display birthday listings, for example, from within Calendar, tap the Calendars button, which is displayed in the upper-left corner of the screen, and then tap the Birthdays option to add a check mark to that selection. All recurring birthdays stored within your Contacts app now appear within Calendar.

The alternative to manually entering appointment information into the Calendar app is to enter your scheduling information within a scheduling program on your primary computer, such as Microsoft Outlook (PC), iCal (Mac), or Microsoft Entourage (Mac), and then sync this data with your iPad 2 using the iTunes sync process or a wireless Sync process available through Apple's iCloud service. You can also sync scheduling data with other online or network-based scheduling applications. Later in this chapter, I discuss the various ways to sync your scheduling data.

VIEWING INDIVIDUAL APPOINTMENT DETAILS

From the Day, Week, Month, or List view within the Calendar app, tap any individual event (appointment, meeting, and so on) to view all the details related to that item. When you tap a single event, a new window opens. In the upper-right corner of the window is an Edit icon. Tap it to modify any aspect of the event listing, such as the title, location, start time, end time, alert, or notes.

To delete an event entry entirely, tap the red-and-white Delete Event icon that's displayed at the very bottom of the Edit window. Or, when you're done making changes to an Event entry, tap on the blue-and-white Done button that's displayed in the upper-right corner of the window.

SUBSCRIBING TO CALENDARS

From within Calendar, it is possible to subscribe to read-only Google, Yahoo!, or iCal calendars saved in the .ics format. To subscribe to a calendar, which enables you to read calendar entries created on other devices or services but not edit or create new events within those calendars, follow these steps:

1. From the iPad 2's Home screen, access the Settings app.

2. From the left side of the Settings screen, select the Mail, Contacts, Calendars option.

3. Under the Accounts heading on the right side of the Settings screen, tap the Add Account option.

4. From the bottom of the list of account types, tap the Other option.

5. When the Other screen appears on the right side of the display, tap the Add Subscribed Calendar option.

6. Within the Subscription window that appears, enter the address for the calendar you want to subscribe to within the field labeled Server. Enter this information using the following format: myserver.com/cal.ics.

7. Tap the Next icon that's located in the upper-right corner of the screen to validate the subscription, and then tap the Save icon. Your tablet must be connected to the Internet to do this.

If you use iCal on a Mac, for example, you can publish (and share) a Calendar via a web server, such as iCloud, and make it available to be subscribed to on your iPad 2. From iCal on your Mac, select the calendar you want to publish from the listing on the left side of the iCal screen (on your Mac). After it's highlighted, click the Calendar pull-down menu and select the Publish option. Add check marks next to your desired options, and then click the Publish icon. The URL for the calendar displays. Enter this URL into the Calendar app on your iPad using the steps outlined earlier in this section.

The Apple website also publishes dozens of read-only calendars that you can subscribe to on your iPad. These read-only calendars list major holidays, game schedules for your favorite sports teams, moon phases, new song releases on iTunes, new DVD releases, and more. For a listing of these calendars, visit www.apple.com/downloads/macosx/calendars.

TIP   If your primary work schedule is handled on a computer or network that is compatible with the industry-standard CalDAV or .ics file format, you can easily sync this data with the Calendar app on your iPad 2. To subscribe to a CalDAV or .ics calendar, launch the Settings app on your iPad, and then choose the Mail, Contacts, Calendars option. Tap the Add Account option, and then choose Other from the bottom of the list.

When the Other screen appears, select the Add CalDAV Account option. A CalDAV window displays, and you are prompted to enter the Server address (cal.example. com), your Username, Password, and a description for the calendar. This is information you can obtain from your company's network system administrator or IT department.

After entering all the requested information in the CalDAV window on your iPad, tap the Next button to verify the account. Tap the Save button when this process is completed. The appointments and events included in the calendar you just subscribed to now appear in their own color-coded calendar when you launch the Calendar app on your iPad 2.

FINDING AN APPOINTMENT

In addition to viewing the Day, Week, Month, or List view within Calendar to find individual appointments, you can use the Search field in the upper-right corner of the Calendar app. Tap the Search field and then use the virtual keyboard to enter any keyword or phrase associated with the appointment you're looking for.

Or, from the iPad 2's Home screen, swipe your finger from left to right to access the tablet's main Spotlight Search screen. In the Search field that appears, enter a keyword, search phrase, or date associated with an appointment. When a list of relevant items is displayed, tap the appointment you want to view. This launches the Calendar app and displays that specific appointment.

VIEWING CALENDARS

One of the great features of the Calendar app is that you can view and manage multiple, color-coded calendars at once on the same screen, or you can easily switch between calendars.

To decide which calendar information you want to view, tap the Calendars icon When the Show Calendars window appears, select which calendar or calendars you want to view on your iPad's screen. You can view one or more calendars at a time, or you can select to view data from all of your calendars on one screen simultaneously. Each calendar is color-coded, so you can tell entries apart when looking at multiple calendars on the screen at once.

INVITING PEOPLE TO MEETINGS OR EVENTS

The Calendar app is compatible with Microsoft Exchange. Thus, if you have the appropriate feature turned on and your company uses a CalDAV supported scheduling app on its network, you can invite other people on that network to your events and respond to other people's event invites.

To respond to a meeting, an appointment, or an event invitation, your iPad must have access to the Internet. When you receive an invitation, the event is displayed in your calendar with a dotted line surrounding it. Tap it to see options enabling you to see who the invitation is from and who is attending the event. You can also set your iPad to alert you of the meeting and add comments of your own that pertain to the meeting invite.

As the invitee, you can then accept or decline the invitation or tap the Maybe option. The person who invited you to the meeting or event receives your response.

CUSTOMIZING THE CALENDAR APP

As you begin using the Calendar app, you'll discover there are many ways to customize it beyond choosing between the Day, Week, Month, or List calendar view or subscribing to read-only calendars. For example, from within the Calendar app, you can set audible alerts to remind you of appointments, meetings, and events. To customize the audio alert you hear, launch the Settings app and select the General option from the left side of the screen. Tap the Sounds option displayed on the right side of the screen.

Make sure the Calendar Alerts option, displayed in the Sounds screen that appears, is turned on. If this option is turned off, a text-based message displays on the iPad's screen as an event reminder instead of an audible alarm sounding.

If you have the ability to receive meeting or event invites from others, from the Settings app, tap the Mail, Contacts, Calendars option. Then scroll down to the Calendars heading and make sure the New Invitations Alerts option is turned on (see Figure 5.9). This enables you to hear an audible alarm when you receive a new invitation.

Also from this screen, under the Calendars heading on the right side of the display, you can determine how far back in your schedule you want to sync appointment data between your primary computer and iPad 2. Your options include Events 2 Weeks Back, Events 1 Month Back, Events 3 Months Back, Events 6 Months Back, or All Events.

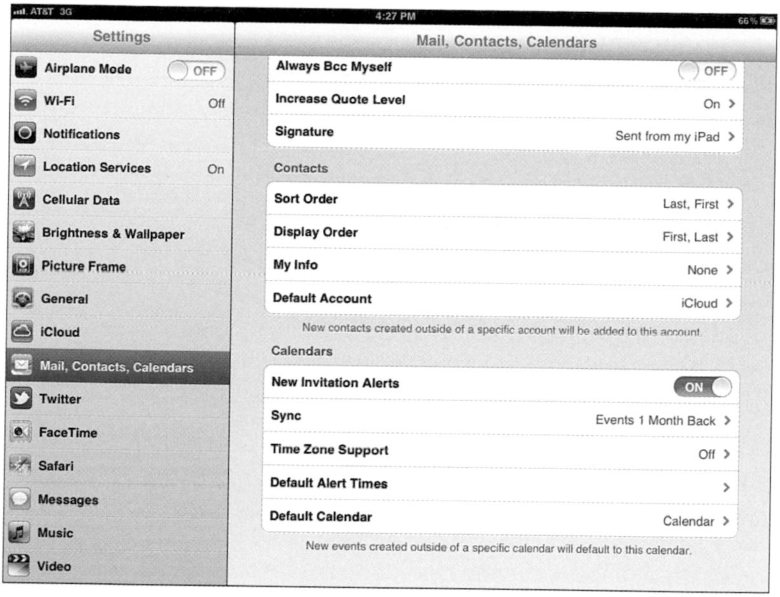

FIGURE 5.9

From the Settings app, you can customize certain settings that relate to the Calendar app.

When the Time Zone Support option is turned on and you've selected the major city that you're in or near, all alarms are activated based on that city's time zone. However, when you travel, turn off this option. With Time Zone Support turned off, the iPad 2 determines the current date and time based on the location and time zone you're in (when it's connected to the Internet) and adjusts all your alarms to go off at the appropriate time for that time zone.

To access the Time Zone Support feature, launch the Settings app and select the Mail, Contacts, Calendars option. On the right side of the screen, scroll down to the options listed under Calendars, and then tap the Time Zone Support option. When the Time Zone Support screen appears, you see a virtual switch for turning this feature on or off. When it's turned on, below the switch is a Time Zone option. Tap it, and then choose your home city (or a city within the time zone you're in).

NOTE When turned on, Time Zone Support displays event times within your Calendar and activates alarms based on the time zone selected. So, if New York City (Eastern Time Zone) is selected, for example, and you have an appointment set for 2:00 p.m. with an accompanying alarm, you see that appointment listed at 2:00 p.m. and hear the alarm at 2:00 p.m. Eastern Time, regardless of where, or in what time zone, you're currently located.

However, if you travel to Los Angeles (Pacific Coast Time), for example, and Time Zone Support is turned on, you hear the alarm go off at 11:00 a.m., not at 2:00 p.m. By turning off this feature when you travel, however, the alarm sounds at 2:00 p.m. in whichever time zone you're in.

SYNCING SCHEDULING DATA WITH YOUR PRIMARY COMPUTER OR SMARTPHONE

Depending on whether you want to sync your Calendar app with a standalone PC or Mac, or wirelessly access scheduling data on a network, the process for setting up the connection and syncing scheduling data is slightly different.

SYNCING WITH A PC OR MAC USING iTUNES SYNC

The process for syncing data between the Calendar app and your primary computer using the iTunes sync process involves connecting the two devices using the white USB cable that came with your iPad 2. You also need the free iTunes software to be running on your primary computer.

For more information about the iTunes sync process, and how to use it to exchange different types of data between your tablet and computer and maintain a complete backup of your iPad 2, be sure to read Chapter 8, "Syncing the iPad Using iTunes or iCloud."

SYNCING CALENDAR DATA WIRELESSLY USING iCLOUD

It's also possible to sync your Calendar data with other devices using a wireless method and Apple's iCloud online service. After you have created an iCloud account, to set up wireless and automatic Calendar syncing, launch the Settings app and select the iCloud option that's displayed on the left side of the screen. On the right side of the screen, when the iCloud screen appears, make sure the Calendars option is turned on.

SYNCING CALENDAR DATA WIRELESSLY WITH SCHEDULING SOFTWARE ON A MICROSOFT EXCHANGE–COMPATIBLE NETWORK

To set up the Calendar app to sync data with Microsoft Exchange–compatible scheduling software used in a corporate environment, launch the Settings app on your tablet and choose the Mail, Contacts, Calendars option.

Tap the Add Account option, and then select Microsoft Exchange from the menu displayed on the right side of the screen. Enter your account information when prompted. This information is typically supplied by your company's system administrator or IT department.

As you're setting up the Microsoft Exchange connection with your iPad, be sure to add a check mark next to the Calendar option so you can sync this data.

TIP   Many company networks and virtual private networks (VPNs) utilize scheduling software that is CalDAV-compatible. To synchronize your scheduling information between your tablet and a CalDAV-compatible calendar/scheduling software package on a corporate network, contact your company's IT department or system administrator to obtain the necessary account settings and passwords to make this connection.

On your iPad 2, you set up this connection from the Settings app. If your company's system administrator or IT department is not able to help you sync your tablet with the company's network, make an appointment with an Apple Genius at any Apple Store or call AppleCare's toll-free phone number (800-APL-CARE) and have a technical support person walk you through the setup process.

SYNCING CALENDAR DATA WIRELESSLY WITH GOOGLE CALENDAR OR YAHOO! CALENDAR

If you maintain your scheduling information using an online-based scheduling application, such as Google Calendar or Yahoo! Calendar, you can use your iPad 2 (when it's connected to the Internet) to wirelessly sync data.

To set this up, launch the Settings app on your iPad 2, select the Mail, Contacts, Calendars option, and then tap the Add Account option.

Choose the Google, Yahoo!, or AOL option based on where you maintain an online-based calendar. When prompted, enter your name and the existing email address and password used for that service and a brief description for the account.

Finally, tap the services you want to link with your iPad, such as Calendars, Contacts, and so on. The available options vary based on the service you use.

KEEPING INFORMED WITH THE NOTIFICATION CENTER

One of the new iOS 5 features that's integrated with a handful of iPad 2 apps is the Notification Center. Whenever an alarm from the Calendar app goes off, you can be alerted by the Notification Center. Likewise, you will be alerted if you receive a new incoming email, a missed call in FaceTime, a new message via iMessage, or other types of notifications within other apps.

The Notification Center is fully customizable. By default, whenever a new alert or alarm goes off, if something happens in an app that requires your attention, Notification Center will display a message within a window that appears at the very top of the display. Or, to access the Notification Center anytime, you can swipe your finger from the top of the iPad in a downward direction.

The Notification Center is always running in the background and works regardless of what apps are currently being used. To customize the Notification Center and determine what alerts, alarms, and messages are displayed, as well as what audible alerts and alarms you hear, launch the Settings app and select the Notifications option on the left side of the screen.

When the Notifications window appears on the right side of the screen, you see all Notification Center–compatible apps listed under the In Notification Center heading. Keep in mind that as you add new apps to your iPad, many of these too will be Notification Center–compatible.

Tap one app listing at a time that's displayed under the In Notification Center heading, starting with Calendar. When you do this, the Notification Center customization options for that app display on the right side of the Settings screen (as shown in Figure 5.10).

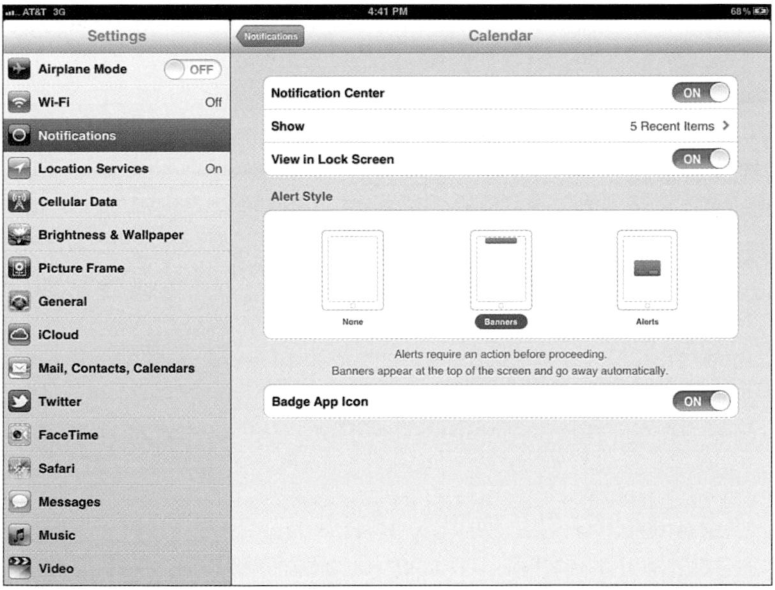

FIGURE 5.10

The Notification Center customization screen for the Calendar app, which can be found within Settings.

From the first option, you can determine whether Notification Center will pay attention to alerts and alarms created using the Calendar app. To use this app with Notification Center, turn this virtual switch to the on position.

Next, determine how many items (individual alerts, alarms, and so on) will display for that app at any given time within Notification Center. Your options include 1, 5, or 10 recent items.

By turning on the View in Lock Screen option, you can determine whether the alerts and alarms associated with Calendar appear on the iPad's Lock Screen when the tablet is in Sleep Mode. You can also adjust the Alert Style and decide whether the visible alert window will display as a banner at the top of the screen or as an alert in the middle of the screen. A banner display appears and then automatically disappears after a few seconds. However, an alert remains on the screen until you tap the appropriate icon in the alert window to make it disappear.

Depending on the app, you can also turn on or off Badge App Icons, which display on the Home Screen as part of that app's icon.

> **NOTE** An app's icon may display a badge on the Home Screen when something has happened in that app. For more information about badges, see Chapter 2, "Customizing iPad Settings."

The great thing about Notification Center is that it serves as a central window where all of your alerts can be displayed in one convenient and easy-to-access location.

When you're viewing the Notification Center window (shown in Figure 5.11), you can tap any item, alert, or alarm listed in it, and the appropriate app automatically launches. For example, if you tap an alert for an upcoming appointment within Calendar, when you tap that listing within Notification Center, the Calendar app launches, and details for that specific appointment appear on the screen. Likewise, if you tap an incoming new email message alert, the Mail app opens and the new email message is displayed.

The Notification Center can also be used to display the current weather or even a stock ticker, depending on what apps you use it with. When a new incoming alert or alarm is set off, the Notification Center window automatically appears at the top of the screen. You can stop whatever you're doing and address that alert or alarm, or you can continue doing whatever you were doing on your iPad uninterrupted, and then address that alert or alarm at your convenience.

FIGURE 5.11

The Notification Center window alerts you about alarms, alerts, incoming messages, missed FaceTime calls, missed iMessages, and other time-sensitive information.

> **TIP**   While your iPad 2 is in Sleep Mode, the Notification Center continues to function. From Settings, you can optionally set the Notification Center to display new alerts, alarms, and related content on your tablet's Lock Screen. Thus, when you wake up your iPad 2, you will immediately see all new alerts, alarms, and messages. From this Lock Screen window, you can swipe any of the Notification Center listings to unlock the iPad and access the appropriate app and content.

After it's set up and customized based on the apps you most rely on, the Notification Center is a powerful tool for helping you stay up to date on all your responsibilities and obligations. As you'd expect, the Notification Center also works with the Reminders app (for maintaining interactive to-do lists), Twitter, Messages, Mail, and FaceTime, so you can better stay connected with your friends, family, co-workers, customers, and clients.

MANAGING TIME AND MORE WITH THIRD-PARTY APPS

The Calendar app is a well-designed and extremely useful general-purpose time-management and scheduling app for your iPad 2. However, if your needs are more specialized, you probably want to use one of the many third-party apps designed to work with the Calendar app to give it added features and functionality.

There's also an ever-growing collection of stand alone iPad-specific apps designed to handle scheduling and time management, as well as time tracking for customer or client billing, project management, and to-do lists.

These apps are available from the App Store. To easily find them, use the Search field in the App Store and enter keywords or phrases such as Time Management, Scheduling, Client Billing, Project Management, or To-Do List Management, depending on your specific needs.

BILL4TIME

The free Bill4Time app for the iPad is designed to work with the Bill4Time online-based service (www.bill4time.com), which has a monthly fee associated with it. Both the app and online service are designed for business professionals, such as lawyers, accountants, and consultants, who need to keep careful track of their time throughout the day and then bill their clients accordingly.

The Bill4Time app offers time tracking, expense tracking, time billing, and invoicing, which can be handled from any computer that's connected to the Internet, or from your iPad 2. This time billing system also offers a project management module, as well as QuickBooks and iCal (for the Mac) integration.

You'll discover that the Bill4Time system, when used in conjunction with your iPad 2, is very customizable and easy to set up. After an initial 30-day free trial, the monthly fee for this service is either $19.99 USD or $39.99 USD per month.

CHOOSING THE RIGHT SCHEDULING APP

With a little research, you'll discover many different scheduling, time-management, project-management, and other related apps, each of which offers a different collection of features and functions, as well as its own user interface.

To help you select the app that's best suited to your unique needs and work habits, first carefully determine those needs. The following are some additional considerations:

- Does the iPad app you select for scheduling, time management, project management, and so on need to be compatible with a software package you're currently using on your PC, Mac, or a company network? Or does the data need to be compatible with an online-based application used within your company or organization?

- Does the iPad app enable you to sync or back up data with your primary computer using a wireless or direct connection method (via a cable)?

- Does the iPad app work seamlessly with other apps already installed on your iPad, such as the Contacts or Maps?

- What current time-management or scheduling challenges or problems will implementing an app help you solve?

- Do the app's features, functions, and user interface fit nicely with your existing work habits?

- Can you easily share data between the app and your employer, co-workers, and clients as needed?

Simply by choosing the right app for the time-management or scheduling tasks you need to handle, you're more apt to be able to use your iPad 2 as a tool to help you become more productive and better organized. Thus, the right app can help you better utilize your time as well as track how you spend your time throughout your workday.

> **CAUTION**   After you opt to begin using an iPad app to help you manage your time or schedule, first test the app carefully to make sure it's properly synchronizing data between your tablet and your primary scheduling tool or software package.
>
> Next, get into the habit of entering all new appointment or scheduling information into the app. Otherwise, you can wind up carrying around an incomplete or inaccurate schedule on your iPad 2, which can be extremely counterproductive.

IN THIS CHAPTER

- An introduction to the Contacts app and how to use it
- Sync your iPad 2's contacts database with your primary contacts management application (whether it's software-based, on a network, or cloud-based)

6

WORKING WITH THE CONTACTS APP

The art of networking is all about meeting new people, staying in contact with them, making referrals and connections for others, and tapping the knowledge, experience, or expertise of the people you know to help you achieve your own career or work-related goals.

If you become good at networking, regardless of which field or industry you work in, over time you establish a contact list comprised of hundreds, or even thousands, of individuals.

In addition to the contacts you establish and maintain within your network, your personal contacts database might also include people you work with, customers, clients, family members, people from your community who you interact with (doctors, hair stylist, barber, dry cleaners, and so on), and friends.

The easiest way to keep your contacts database organized is to utilize some type of contact management application on your primary computer. On a Mac, you might use the popular

Address Book software or Microsoft Entourage. Or, on a PC, Microsoft Outlook is a popular tool. There are also many web-, network-, and online (cloud)-based contact management applications available that are used by businesses of all sizes.

THE CONTACTS APP IS HIGHLY CUSTOMIZABLE

Now that you've become an iPad 2 user, chances are, that same contacts database that you rely on at your office can be synced with your tablet and made available to you using the Contacts app.

As you're about to discover, Contacts is a powerful and customizable contact management database program that works with several other apps that also came on your iPad, including Mail, Calendar, Safari, FaceTime, and Maps.

Of course, Contacts can also be used as a standalone app on your iPad 2, enabling you to enter new contact entries as you meet new people and need to keep track of details about them.

The information you maintain within your Contacts database is highly customizable, which means you can keep track of only the information you want or need. For example, within each contact entry, you can store a vast amount of information about a person, including the following:

- First and last name
- Name prefix (Mr., Mrs., Dr., and so on)
- Name suffix (Jr., Sr., Ph.D., Esq., and so on)
- Job title
- Company
- Multiple phone numbers (work, home, cell, and so on)
- Multiple email addresses
- Multiple mailing addresses (work, home, and so on)
- Multiple webpage addresses
- Facebook, Twitter, Skype, Instant Message, or other online social networking site usernames

You can also customize your contacts database to include additional information, such as each contact's photo, the person's nickname, associated spouse's and assistant's names, birthdays, Instant Messenger usernames, as well as detailed notes about the contact.

Using the Contacts app, your entire contacts database is instantly searchable using data from any field within the database, so even if you have a database containing thousands of entries, you can find the person or company you're looking for in a matter of seconds. And, with the iOS 5 version of Contacts, you can now link contacts together.

> **NOTE** For each entry within Contacts, you can enter as much or as little detail about each person as you want. However, the more information you include, the better. Several other apps on your iPad automatically tap into your Contacts database to obtain relevant information as it's needed.

THE CONTACTS APP WORKS SEAMLESSLY WITH OTHER APPS

After your contacts database has been populated with entries, you discover the Contacts app works with other apps on your iPad 2, such as Mail:

■ When you compose a new email message from within Mail, in the To field you can begin typing someone's full name or email address. If that person's contact information is already stored within Contacts, the relevant email address automatically displays within the email's To field.

■ Or, if you're planning a trip to visit a contact, from the Maps app, you can pull up someone's address from your Contacts database and obtain driving directions to the person's home or work location.

■ Likewise, if you include each person's birthday in your Contacts database, that information can automatically be displayed within the Calendar app to remind you in advance to send a card.

■ As you're creating each contact entry, you can include a photo of that person by either activating the Camera app from within the Contacts app to snap a photo or using a photo that's stored in the Photos app and link it with a contact.

■ From within FaceTime, you can create a Favorites list of people you video-conference with often. You can compile this list from entries in your Contacts database, but you can access it from within FaceTime.

■ From within the Messages app, you can access your Contacts database when filling out the To field as you compose new text messages to be sent via iMessage. As soon as you tap the To field, an All Contacts window appears allowing you to select contacts from your Contacts database (or you can manually enter the recipient's info).

■ Also, if you're active on Facebook, for example, you have the option of adding each contact's Facebook profile page URL within the contact entry. When you do this, the app automatically downloads each entry's Facebook profile picture and inserts it into your Contacts database. (The easiest way to do this is to download and install the free, official Facebook app for the iPhone, which also works on the iPad 2.)

GETTING STARTED USING THE CONTACTS APP

The Contacts app is preinstalled on your iPad 2, and you can access it from the Home screen. When you first launch this app, its contents are empty. However, you can create and build your contacts database in two ways. The first way is to sync the Contacts app with your primary contact management application on your computer, network, or on an online (cloud-based) service, such as iCloud. You can also manually enter contact information directly into the app.

Ultimately, as you begin using this app and come to rely on it, you can enter new contact information or edit entries on either your tablet or within your primary contact management application, and keep all the information synchronized, regardless of where the entry was created or modified.

From the iPad 2's Home screen, tap the Contacts app to launch it. On the left side of the screen are alphabetic tabs. Near the top of the screen, you see the All Contacts heading, and below it is a Search field (as shown in Figure 6.1).

After you have entries within your contacts database, they are all listed alphabetically on the left side of the screen below the Search field. If you tap the Search field, you can quickly find a particular entry by entering any keyword associated with an entry, such as a first or last name, city, state, job title, or company name. Any content within your Contacts database is searchable from this Search field.

You can also tap a letter tab on the left side of the screen to see all entries "filed" under that letter by either a contact's last name, first name, or company name, depending on how you set up the Contacts app from within the Settings app's Mail, Contacts, Calendars option.

To see the complete listing for a particular entry, tap its listing on the left side of the screen. That entry's complete contents then display on the right side of the screen (as shown in the sample entry in Figure 6.2).

FIGURE 6.1

This is the main Contacts screen when the contacts database is empty.

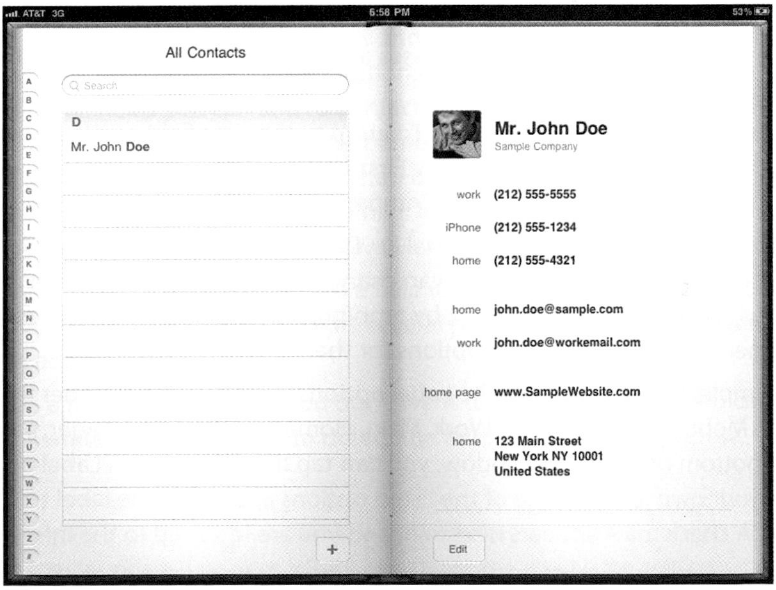

FIGURE 6.2

When you select a contact entry from the left side of the screen, all information pertaining to that particular contact displays on the right side of the screen.

ADDING A PHOTO TO A CONTACT ENTRY

To the immediate left of the First Name field is a square box that says Add Photo. When you tap this field, a submenu with two options—Take Photo and Choose Photo—are displayed. If you tap Take Photo, the iPad 2's Camera app launches from within the Contacts app so that you can snap a photo to be linked to the contact entry you're creating.

If you tap on the Choose Photo option, the Photos app on your iPad 2 launches so that you to choose any digital image that's currently stored on your tablet. When you tap the photo of your choice, a Choose a Photo window displays on the Contacts screen, enabling you to move and scale the image with your finger.

After cropping or adjusting the photo selected, tap the Use icon that's displayed in the upper-right corner of the Choose Photo window to link the photo with that contact's entry.

If you also use an iPhone or FaceTime on your iPad, from the Ringtone option in the Info window, you can select the ringtone you hear each time the contact calls you. Your iPad has 25 preinstalled ringtones (Marimba is the default); however, from iTunes, you can download thousands of additional ringtones, many of which are clips from popular songs.

Each time you add a new mailing address to a contact's entry from within the Info screen, the Address field expands to include a Street, City, State, ZIP, and Country field (as shown in Figure 6.4).

FIGURE 6.4

Using the virtual keyboard, you can add multiple addresses, one at a time, for each contact in your Contacts database. This enables you to include a home address and a work address, for example.

In the Notes field, you can enter as much information pertaining to that contact as you want. Or, you can paste content from another app into this field using the iOS's Select, Copy, and Paste commands and the multitasking capabilities of your iPad 2 to quickly switch between apps.

After you have filled in all of the fields for a particular entry, tap the Done button, which is displayed in the upper-right corner of the Info window. Your new entry displays within your contacts database (see Figure 6.5).

FIGURE 6.5

After entering all the fields as you create a new contact entry, tap the Done button to save the entry and include it in your Contacts database.

EDITING OR DELETING AN ENTRY

As you're looking at the main Contacts screen, you can edit an entry by selecting it from the left side of the screen. Tap its listing, which causes the complete entry to be displayed on the right side of the screen. Now, tap the Edit button displayed near the bottom of the screen to edit the selected entry.

When the Info window appears, tap any field to modify it using the virtual keyboard. You can delete any fields by tapping the red-and-white minus icon.

You can also add new fields within an entry by tapping any of the green-and-white plus icons and then choosing the type of field you want to add.

When you're done editing a contact entry, again tap the Done button.

You can delete an entire entry from your Contacts database. As you're editing a contact entry and looking at the Info window for that entry, scroll down to the bottom of it and tap the Delete Contact button.

TIP Whenever you're viewing a contact entry, tapping a listed email address causes the iPad 2's Mail app to launch, which enables you to compose an email message to that recipient. The To field of the outgoing email is filled in with the email address you tapped from within Contacts. Likewise, from within any entry, tap a website URL that's listed and the iPad 2 launches the Safari web browser with the appropriate web page automatically loaded.

This technique also works with the Twitter field (if you have the Twitter app installed). If you tap a street address, it automatically launches the Maps app, which displays that address (at which point you can tap the Directions icon that's displayed near the upper-left corner of the screen to obtain directions to that contact's location).

When you're in edit mode, modifying content within a contact's entry, if you scroll down to the very bottom of the window, below the red-and-white Delete contact icon, you'll notice a small icon with a silhouette of a head with a plus sign next to it. Tap this icon to Link this contact with one or more other contacts in your database. For example, if you have five employees with the same company listed in your Contacts database, you can use this command to link them. Or, if you have multiple separate contacts for different people within a family, you can link those contacts for easy reference.

NOTE The Contacts app in the iPad 2 doesn't offer a printing method. If you want to print some or all of your contact info, you'll need to find and install an app to add that capability. One app that iPad users highly recommend is PrintCentral for iPad ($8.99 USD), which you can get at the iTunes App Store.

SHARING CONTACT ENTRIES

From the main Contacts screen, tap a contact from the left side of the screen that you want to share details about. When the contact's entry is displayed on the right side of the screen, scroll down to the bottom of the entry until you see the Share Contact button displayed (see Figure 6.6). Tap it.

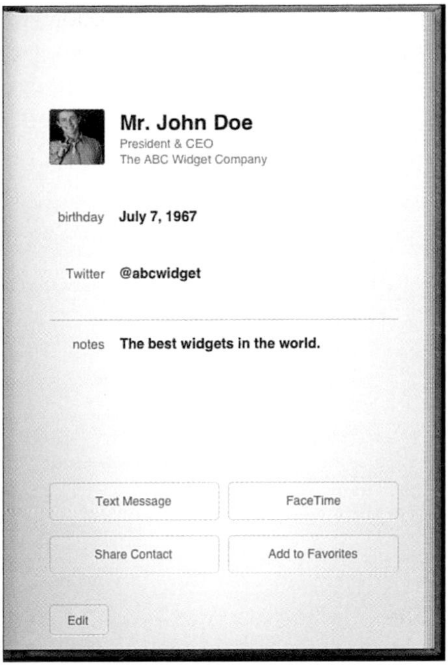

FIGURE 6.6

From within Contacts you can share someone's contact entry with other people by tapping the Share Contact button displayed at the bottom of each contact entry.

An outgoing email message form displays on your iPad's screen. Fill in the To field with the person or people you want to share the contact info with. The default subject of the email is Contact; however, you can tap this field and modify it using the virtual keyboard.

The contact entry you selected (stored in .vcf format) is already embedded within the email message. When you've filled in all the necessary fields in the outgoing email form and added additional text to the body of the message, tap the blue-and-white Send icon that's located in the upper-right corner of the Contact window to send the email message to the intended recipient(s). After doing this, you are returned to the Contacts app.

Within a minute or two, the recipient should receive your email. When she clicks on the email's attachment (the contact entry you sent), she can automatically import that data into her contact management application as a new entry, such as within Address Book on her Mac or Contacts on her iPad 2.

Figure 6.7 shows an incoming email message (using Mail on an iPad 2) with a contact entry attached. After tapping the email's attachment, the contact entry that was emailed is displayed in a window. At the bottom of this window, as the recipient of the contact's information, tap the Create New Contact or Add to Existing Contact option to incorporate this information into your Contacts database.

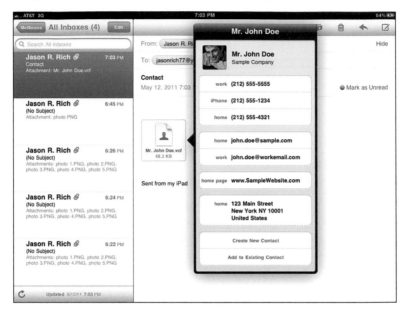

FIGURE 6.7

As the recipient of an email on your iPad 2 that contains someone's contact entry, tap the email's attachment, view the entry, and then tap the Create New Contact option to add that contact entry to your iPad's Contacts database.

ADDITIONAL WAYS TO MAKE CONTACT FROM WITHIN CONTACTS

When viewing any single contact, in addition to the Share Contact button, you'll notice three other command buttons: Text Message, FaceTime, and Add to Favorites. Tap the Text Message icon to send that person a text message via iMessage, or tap the FaceTime app to initiate a FaceTime videoconference with that person.

If you tap the Add to Favorites button, that contact will appear within your Favorites list that's displayed within FaceTime as well as several other apps.

SYNCING CONTACT DATA WITH OTHER CONTACT MANAGEMENT SOFTWARE

If you maintain your primary contacts database using Address Book on your Mac, for example, you can sync the Contacts app via an iTunes sync or you can sync the contacts wirelessly using iCloud.

You can synchronize the contacts database on your iPad 2 with Microsoft Outlook on a PC, Microsoft Entourage on a Mac, any Microsoft Exchange-compatible contact management software that is running on your company's network, or a variety other online (cloud)-based contact management tools. To synchronize contacts data wirelessly, you must do some setup using the Settings app on your iPad 2.

SYNCING WITH MICROSOFT EXCHANGE–COMPATIBLE APPLICATIONS

From the iPad 2's Home screen, tap Settings and then choose the Mail, Contacts, Calendars option. Tap the Add Account option displayed under the Accounts heading on the right side of the screen. Choose to set up a Microsoft Exchange account. When prompted, enter your email address, domain, username, password, and an account description. This is information that should be supplied by your network administrator or IT department. Next, turn on the contacts option and save your new settings.

Contacts is compatible with any contact management software that uses the industry-standard CardDAV and LDAP format. Thus, if you have a MobileMe or Microsoft Exchange account and activate the contacts sync feature, you can wirelessly keep your primary contacts database perfectly synchronized with your Contacts database as long as your iPad has access to the Web.

SYNCING WITH CARDDAV- OR LDAP-COMPATIBLE APPLICATIONS

To set up the wireless sync process between a CardDAV-compatible application and Contacts, access the Settings app on your iPad and select the Mail, Contacts, Calendars option. From under the Add Account heading, tap the Other option. Next, choose either the Add LDAP account or Add CardDAV account option, depending on the application you are syncing with.

You are prompted for a server address, a username, a password, and an account description. Obtain this information from your network administrator or company's IT department.

HOW DOES SYNCING YOUR CONTACTS INFO HELP YOU?

After the iPad 2 is set up to sync your Contacts app with another contact management application (a process that needs to be done just once), whenever you make a change, deletion, or addition to your contacts database (from your iPad, your primary computer, or your smartphone that's also synced with the database), those modifications are automatically reflected on all of the devices that you access your contacts database from.

> **CAUTION** It is important that you initially set up the Contacts sync process correctly, or you could accidentally delete or modify important data. Be sure to make a reliable backup of your contacts database before initiating a first-time sync.

If you have questions about how to configure your iPad 2 to sync correctly with your primary contact management application, make an appointment with an Apple Genius at any Apple Store or call AppleCare's toll-free phone number at (800) APL-CARE, and have a technical support specialist talk you through the setup and initial data sync process.

THIRD-PARTY CONTACT MANAGEMENT APPS

Depending on the contact management application you use on your primary computer, the developer of that software might offer an iPad app that enables you to easily sync and manage your primary contacts database on your tablet without using the Contacts app. The third-party app might offer specialized functionality or data fields that aren't readily compatible with the Contacts app.

Contact the software publisher for the primary contact management application you or your company currently use to determine whether an iPad app (or iPhone app) is currently available.

If you visit the App Store, you can also find a handful of standalone contact management apps that you can use with, or instead of, Contacts.

IN THIS CHAPTER

■ Access the App Store from your iPad 2

■ Access the App Store from iTunes on your primary computer

■ Discover why some apps are free and some are not

■ Find and download the best apps for you

7

FINDING AND INSTALLING APPS FROM THE APP STORE

Yes, the iPad 2 is a sleek piece of hardware with lots of capabilities, but it ultimately comes down to its iOS operating system and apps that make the tablet capable of doing so much. From the App Store, you can find, download, and install apps for your iPad 2 that enable it to perform a much broader assortment of tasks.

However, with more than 100,000 iPad-specific apps currently available, plus more than 350,000 iPhone apps that work on the iPad, the task of finding the right app(s) to meet your needs can become a daunting task.

This chapter introduces you to the App Store, plus helps you find the best apps to meet your particular wants and needs. For every task that for which there is an optional app, there are probably at least a handful of apps, from different developers, that offer very similar functionality. From this chapter, you learn some easy tricks for choosing only the best apps to download and install on your tablet.

FIGURE 7.1

The main App Store app screen. Find, purchase, download, and install apps directly from your iPad 2.

If you already know the name of the app you want to find. Tap the Search field, which is located in the upper-right corner of the screen.

Using the virtual keyboard, enter the name of the app. Tap the Search key on the virtual keyboard to begin the search. You can also perform a search based on a keyword or phrase, such as word processing, to-do lists, time management, or photo editing. The search results can be filtered even more by category, customer rating, and so on.

Within a few seconds, matching results are displayed on the App Store screen. When you access the App Store from your iPad (using the App Store app), iPad-specific apps are always listed first. If you scroll down on the search results screen, iPhone apps (which also work on your iPad) are then displayed.

TIP   Within each App listing is a price icon. In the upper-left corner of the price icon, a plus sign indicates that the app you're looking at is designed for both iPad and iPhone.

In general, when choosing apps for your iPad 2, look for iPad-specific apps first and then look for apps that are designed for both iPad and iPhone. Apps that are iPhone-specific run fine on an iPad 2, but the app's graphics and user interface are formatted for the iPhone's smaller screen.

At the bottom of the main App Store screen are six buttons: Featured, Genius, Top Charts, Categories, Purchased, and Updates. If you don't know the exact name of an app you're looking for, these buttons help you browse the App Store and discover iPad apps that might be of interest to you.

REVIEWING FEATURED APPS

Tap the Featured button that is displayed near the bottom of the App Store screen to see a listing of what Apple considers "Featured" apps. These are divided into two categories, including New and Noteworthy and Staff Favorites.

Near the top of this screen is a large graphic banner that constantly changes. This banner graphic promotes what Apple considers the App of the Week, as well as other noteworthy apps the company wants to promote. To the right of this large banner graphic are three smaller banner ads that promote additional noteworthy apps.

Under the New and Noteworthy section of the Featured screen, you see six app listings. On the right and left side of the New and Noteworthy section are white arrows that point left and right. Tap either arrow to scroll between the four New and Noteworthy sections. You can also tap the See All command that's displayed next to the New and Noteworthy heading.

When you tap on the See All command (see Figure 7.2), the entire screen is replaced by app listings.

FIGURE 7.2

See all the apps that Apple deems as New and Noteworthy as you browse the App Store.

SORTING LISTINGS BY DATE AND POPULARITY

As you're looking at the Featured page of the App Store, you see three tabs displayed at the top-center of the screen: New, What's Hot, and Release Date. These tabs are a more refined sort of the Featured apps (refer to Figure 7.1).

Instead of showcasing New and Noteworthy apps when the New icon is selected, when you tap on the What's Hot icon, a different collection of Apple-recommended apps is displayed under the What's Hot heading. Toward the bottom of the screen are a selection of featured apps that fall into a specific category or area of interest. Shown in Figure 7.3 is a collection of Apple-recommend apps relating to planning a vacation.

FIGURE 7.3

See "what's hot" in terms of iPad 2 apps. By scrolling to the bottom of the What's Hot screen, you'll see a selection of featured apps that relate to a specific and ever-changing topic, which in this case are apps for planning a vacation.

At the very bottom of this screen is a subsection labeled Quick Links. It offers six options for finding apps relating to a particular area of interest. Options include iPad Apps Starter Kit, Games Starter Kit, Hall of Fame, Previous Apps of the Week, Previous Games of the Week, and Game Center. Tap any of these options to see a collection of apps you might be interested in.

For example, if you tap on iPad Apps Starter Kit (see Figure 7.4), you see a collection of apps that Apple recommends for beginning iPad 2 users.

FIGURE 7.4

From the Quick Links section of the App Store, you can access apps that Apple includes within the iPad Apps Starter Kit listing of recommended apps for new iPad 2 users.

If you tap the Release Date tab at the top of the screen (after tapping on the Featured button at the bottom of the screen), what you see displayed are the most recently released apps available from the App Store, starting with the newest and working backward by date.

GENIUS: ANALYSIS AND SUGGESTIONS

The App Store keeps track of all apps you purchase. When you tap the Genius button at the bottom of the App Store screen, the App Store analyzes your past app purchases and offers suggestions for other apps you might be interested in.

TOP CHARTS: POPULAR APPS

When you tap the Top Charts button, on the left side of the screen are the Top Paid iPad Apps listed in order based on their popularity. This is a general listing of all currently popular apps, so it constantly changes.

On the right side of the Top Charts screen (see Figure 7.5) is a listing of the Top Free iPad Apps. Under each heading are 10 app listings. At the bottom of these two charts is a Show More icon. Tap this to see the next 10 apps listed in the chart. You can also scroll down even more to see a listing of the Top Grossing iPad Apps.

FIGURE 7.5

This Top Charts screen shows the most popular paid and free apps in general; they're not broken down or listed by category.

By default, when you tap the Top Charts icon, the Top Charts lists that are displayed are comprised of apps from all categories. However, if you're primarily interested in apps that fall within a specific category, tap the Categories icon that's displayed in the upper-left corner of this screen. A listing of 20 different app categories are displayed (see Figure 7.6). Choose a category by tapping it.

CATEGORIES: TOP APPS BY TOPIC

Although tapping on the Top Charts button reveals a listing of the top-selling apps within a specific category, you can tap on the Categories button at the bottom of the App Store screen to access all of the apps that fall into any one of the App Store's 20 main categories.

Upon tapping the Categories icon, a listing of all 20 app categories displays (see Figure 7.7). The app icon shown for each category is the current number-one most popular paid app within that category.

FIGURE 7.6

You can view Top Charts listed that showcase apps in each of 20 separate categories, such as Business, Finance, News, or Reference.

FIGURE 7.7

Choose which of the 20 app categories you want to browse through from this Categories selection screen.

Tap the category that most interests you, and you can browse through listings of all apps that fall into that category. Keep in mind that there might be thousands of apps within any given category, so you could wind up spending hours looking at app listings as you discover the vast selection of apps available.

After choosing an app category, you can use the right- or left-pointing arrows on either side of the screen to scroll through app listings, which are displayed 12 to a page. By default, the apps are displayed in order based on release date (with the most recently released apps displayed first). However, you can change the sort order by tapping the Sort By button that's displayed in the upper-right corner of the screen. Your options include Name (for an alphabetical listing), Most Popular (starting with the best-selling apps), or Release Date.

As you're looking at the app listings, you can learn more about a particular app by tapping its graphic icon or title. Or, you can purchase, download, and install the app by tapping its price button. (For free apps, when you tap the Free button, the app automatically downloads and installs after you enter your Apple ID password.)

MANAGING YOUR APP STORE ACCOUNT OR iTUNES GIFT CARDS

When you scroll down to the very bottom of the Featured, Genius, Top Charts, or Categories sections of the App Store, you see three buttons labeled Account [Your Apple ID Username], Redeem, and Support.

Tap the Account button to manage your Apple ID account and update your credit card information, for example. Tap on Redeem icon to redeem a prepaid iTunes Gift Card. If you experience problems using the App Store, or have questions, tap the Support icon.

> **TIP** Just above the Account, Redeem, and Support buttons, which can be found at the bottom of many screens within the App Store, you'll see a Show iPhone Apps button. By default, when you shop for apps on your iPad 2 using the App Store app, only iPad-specific apps or hybrid iPad/iPhone apps are displayed. However, when you tap the Show iPhone Apps button, relevant iPhone-specific apps (that will run fine on your iPad) will also be displayed.

MANAGING YOUR PURCHASED APPS

Over time, you'll most likely purchase many apps for your iPad, which the App Store will keep track of. However, at any given time, you might not want all of those apps stored on your iPad.

When you tap the Purchased command icon that's displayed at the bottom of the App Store screen, a complete listing of all apps you've purchased to date displays. This listing includes apps not currently stored on your iPad. These apps can be moved to iCloud for easy (wireless) access from any of your iOS devices, or they can be reinstalled (for free) onto your iPad.

> **TIP** If you also own and use an iPhone 3Gs, iPhone 4 (or a later version of the iPhone), or an iPod touch, anytime you purchase an iPad/iPhone hybrid app, you can install it on any or all of your iOS devices without having to purchase the same app multiple times. The Purchased icon also enables you to find the apps you've purchased and wirelessly install them on your various iOS devices.

UNDERSTANDING THE APP LISTINGS

Each app listing contains the app's name, what category the app falls into (such as Business, Reference, News, Lifestyle, Games, and so on), the app's original release date, the average star-rating the app has received from your fellow iPad users, and a graphic icon that features the app's logo.

Figure 7.8 shows a sample app listing. Also located within each app listing is the app's price button. If the app is free, the word FREE is on the price button. If the app listing is for a paid app, the price of the app is displayed.

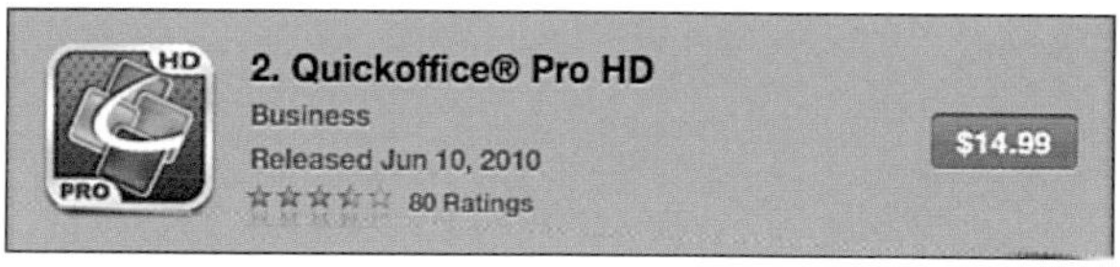

2. Quickoffice® Pro HD
Business
Released Jun 10, 2010
☆☆☆☆☆ 80 Ratings
$14.99

FIGURE 7.8

A sample app listing contains important information about the app, including its price.

> **CAUTION** Some free apps are, in fact, free. However, they might ultimately require you to pay for a content subscription or make in-app purchases to fully utilize the app. How app pricing works is explained later in this chapter.

To purchase an app (or download and install a free app), tap its price icon. The price button changes from gray-and-white to green-and-white. If it's a free app, this new button is labeled Install App. If it's a paid app, the green-and-white button says Buy App. Tap the button to confirm your purchase decision.

An Apple ID Password window displays on the screen. Your Apple ID username is already displayed, but you need to enter your Apple ID password. Type your Apple ID password and then tap the OK button. The app automatically downloads and installs itself on your iPad 2; this process can take between 15 seconds and several minutes. When the app is installed, the app icon for the new app appears on your tablet's Home screen.

Keep in mind that it is necessary to enter your Apple ID Password whenever you attempt to download and install any app, even if it's a free app.

LEARNING ABOUT AN APP BEFORE PURCHASE

Before committing to a purchase, as you're looking at an app's listing from within the App Store, you can tap on its title or graphic icon. When you do this, the App Store screen is replaced with a detailed description of the app.

An app description screen (like the one shown in Figure 7.9) displays the app's title and logo near the top of the screen, along with a detailed description of the app under the Description heading.

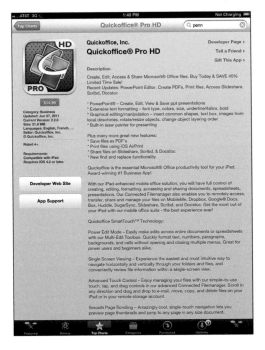

FIGURE 7.9

From an app's description screen, you can learn all about a specific app. This information can help you decide whether it's of interest to you or relevant to your needs.

Below the Description is information about what new features have been added to the app in the most recent version. As you scroll down on this screen, you see one or more actual screen shots from the app. Use your finger to flick from right to left over the screen shots to scroll through multiple images, if applicable.

Displayed under the app's screen shots are the Customer Ratings for that app. You can sort these ratings by tapping the Current Version or All Versions tabs displayed on the right side of the screen.

The Customer Ratings are based on a five-star system. Anyone who purchases or downloads an app has the option to rate it. A top-rating is five stars. From the Ratings Summary chart (shown in Figure 7.10), you can see how many people have rated an app; discover the app's average rating; and then see a breakdown of how many one-star, two-star, three-star, four-star, and five-star ratings the app has received.

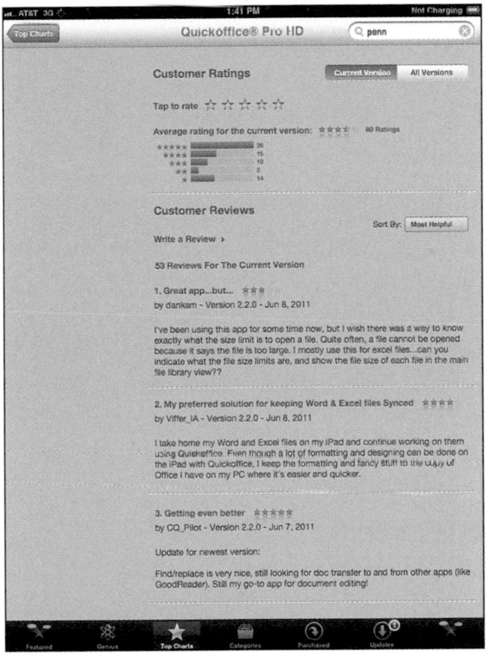

FIGURE 7.10

Every app description contains an average rating and a rating summary chart. Use it to quickly see what other iPad users think about the app you're currently looking at.

Obviously, an app with a large number of five-star ratings is probably excellent, and an app that consistently earns three-stars or less is probably not that great or is loaded with bugs.

As you review an app's description, keep scrolling down to read full reviews that your fellow iPad users have written about that app. These reviews often describe the best features of the app and/or its worst problems.

At the bottom of the app description page is a section labeled Customers Also Bought. These are listings for other apps, usually similar in functionality to the app you're looking at, which other customers have also purchased and downloaded.

The app's price button is displayed below the app's logo on the left side of the description page. Specific information pertaining to that app, including its category, the date it was last updated, the current version of the app, the file size of the app, what language the app is in, and the seller or publisher of the app is also displayed in this area.

Scroll down a little farther to see a summary of what age group the app is suitable for and additional notes related to the app's content, including whether the app requires in-app purchases or a paid subscription to fully utilize it.

The system requirements for the app are also displayed along the left margin of every app description page (when you're using the App Store app). This helps you identify if it's an iPad-specific app, for example, and what iOS operating system version it works with.

> **TIP**   Additional information about the app can also be obtained by visiting the App Developer website or the App Support website, both of which are operated by the app developer. Buttons that launch Safari and take you directly to one of these websites are displayed along the left side of the app description page, as well as in the upper-right corner of an app description page.

After reviewing the app's description page, if you want to be reminded of the app's existence (without downloading it), or you want to tell a friend about the app, tap the Tell a Friend icon that's displayed in the upper-right corner of the app description page to make an email form display.

Within the body of the email are details about the app. Using the iPad's virtual keyboard, fill in the To field to send the app-related information to yourself or someone else via email. Tap the Send button in the upper-right corner of this email form (see Figure 7.11) to send the message.

> **TIP**   Using the Gift This App option in the upper-right corner of an app's description page, you can purchase an app and send it to another iPad or iPhone user electronically.

To exit an app's description page and continue browsing the App Store, tap the left-pointing arrow that's labeled App Store. It's displayed in the upper-left corner of the screen.

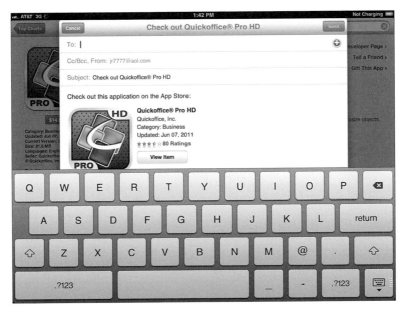

FIGURE 7.11
Share information about an app featured in the App Store with someone else via email or email details about an app to yourself so you can read more about it at a later time.

VISITING THE APP STORE FROM iTUNES ON YOUR COMPUTER

The second method of finding, purchasing, downloading, installing, and updating apps is to use the latest version of iTunes running on your primary computer. With iTunes running, click the iTunes Store option displayed on the left side of the screen under the Store heading. Your computer must be connected to the Internet to access the iTunes Store.

When the main iTunes Store launches within iTunes, click the App Store tab at the top of the screen (see Figure 7.12). You see a similar screen to the Featured page of the App Store when you access it from your iPad 2 using the App Store app.

The functionality of the App Store when accessed through iTunes is the same as when you use the App Store app on your tablet. However, the layout of the screens is slightly different.

FIGURE 7.12
Click the App Store option at the top of the iTunes screen to access the App Store from within iTunes on your primary computer.

> **NOTE** In addition to shopping for apps via the App Store through iTunes, you can use iTunes to purchase and download music, podcasts, audiobooks, and educational content from iTunesU. You can also purchase or rent TV episodes or movies from within iTunes and later transfer that content to your iPad using the iTunes sync process.
>
> To find, purchase, and download content other than apps directly from your iPad, use the iTunes app that comes on your tablet. However, when purchasing TV episodes or movies, for example, a Wi-Fi connection is required because you're downloading large files. However, you can purchase and download music from iTunes on your iPad 2 using a 3G Internet connection.

HOW APP PRICING WORKS

Originally, when the App Store opened, there were two types of apps: free apps and paid apps. The free apps were often demo versions of paid apps (with limited functionality) or fully functional apps that displayed ads within the app. Paid apps were typically priced between $.99 and $9.99 (although some are priced higher).

As the App Store has evolved, additional payment options and fee structures for apps have been introduced, giving app developers new ways to generate revenue and giving iPad users different methods of paying for apps and content.

Here's a summary of the different types of apps from a pricing standpoint:

FREE APPS

Free apps cost nothing to download and install on your tablet. Some programmers and developers release free apps out of pure kindness and to share their creations with the iPad-using public. These are fully functional apps.

There are also free apps that serve as demo versions of paid apps. These are scaled-down versions of apps, or they have some type of limitation in terms of how long they can be used for (usually 30 days). In some cases, basic features or functions of the app are locked in the free version but are later made available if you upgrade to the paid or premium version of the app.

A third category of free apps are fully functional apps that display ads as part of their content. In exchange for using the app, you have to view ads, which offer the option to click on offers from within the app to learn more about the product or service being advertised.

A fourth category of free apps serve as a shell for premium (paid) content that must be loaded into the app to make it fully functional. For example, many newspaper and magazine publishers now offer free apps related to their specific publications but require users to pay for the actual content of the newspaper or magazine, which later gets downloaded into the app.

The final type of free app is fully functional, but it enables the user to make in-app purchases to add features or functionality to the app or to unlock premium content. The core app, without the extra content, is free.

PAID APPS

After you purchase an app, you own it and can use it as often as you like without incurring additional fees. You simply pay a fee for the app upfront, which is typically between $.99 and $9.99. All future upgrades or new versions of the app are free of charge. In some cases, paid apps also offer in-app purchase options to access premium content.

SUBSCRIPTION-BASED APPS

Apps based on subscriptions, such as monthly magazines, are typically free, but you pay a recurring subscription fee for content, which is automatically into the app. Many digital editions of newspapers, such as *The New York Times* and *The Wall Street Journal,* utilize a subscription app model, as do hundreds of different magazines.

The main content of the digital and printed versions of a publication are usually identical. However, you can view the digital edition on your iPad 2 and take advantage of added interactive elements built into the app. If you're already a subscriber to the printed version of a newspaper or magazine, some publishers offer the digital edition for free, and others charge an extra fee to subscribe to the digital edition as well. Another option is to subscribe to just the digital edition of a publication.

With some magazines, you can download the free app for a specific publication, and from within the app purchase one issue at a time, such as the current issue or a single past issue. There is no long-term subscription commitment, but you must purchase and download individual issues of the publication. You can also purchase an ongoing subscription, and new issues of that publication are automatically downloaded to your iPad as they become available.

The Daily, which is a digital newspaper published by News Corp., is created and published exclusively for use on the iPad. The app and a two-week trial subscription to *The Daily* are free. After that you need to pay for an ongoing subscription to have the daily publication automatically sent wirelessly to your tablet.

Like iBookstore, the Newsstand app is used to find, subscribe to, download, and read digital editions of newspapers and magazines in one centralized location. You learn more about the Newsstand app in Chapter 14.

> **NOTE** You can purchase digital editions of magazines and newspapers from the App Store or Newsstand apps. These publications require their own proprietary app to access and read the publication's content. You can discover digital editions of many popular business-oriented publications, as well as industry-specific magazines, available from the App Store and Newsstand. However, you purchase, download, and read eBooks using the iBooks app.

IN-APP PURCHASES

An in-app purchase is a special type of app that may be free, or it might be a paid app. The important thing to note is that, as you're actually using the app, you can purchase additional content or add new features and functionality to the app by making in-app purchases. The ability to make in-app purchases has become very popular and is being used by app developers in a variety of different ways.

As you read an app's description within the App Store, carefully read the text included within the left margin of the app description screen to see if in-app purchases are required.

> **CAUTION** The price you pay for an app does not translate directly to the quality or usefulness of that app. There are some free or very inexpensive apps that are extremely useful and packed with features and that can really enhance

your experience using your iPad 2. However, there are costly apps (priced at $4.99 or more) that are poorly designed and filled with bugs or that don't live up to expectations or to the description of the app offered by the app's developer or publisher.

The price of each app is set by the developer or programmer that created or is selling the app. Instead of using the price as a determining factor if you're evaluating several apps that appear to offer similar functionality, be sure to read the app's customer reviews carefully and pay attention to the star-based rating the app has received. The user reviews and ratings are a much better indicator of the app's quality and usefulness than the price of the app.

QUICK TIPS FOR FINDING RELEVANT APPS

As you explore the App Store, it's easy to be overwhelmed by the sheer number of apps that are available for your iPad 2. If you're a new iPad user, spending time browsing the App Store introduces you to the many different types of apps that are available and provides you with ideas about how you can utilize your tablet in your personal or professional life.

However, you can save a lot of time searching for apps if you already know the app's exact title or if you know what type of app you're looking for. In this case, you can enter either the app's exact title or a keyword description of the app within the App Store's Search field to see a list of relevant matches.

So, if you're looking for a word processing app, you can either enter the search phrase "Pages" into the App Store's Search field or enter "word processor" to see a selection of word processing apps.

If you're looking for vertical market apps with specialized functionality that caters to your industry or profession, enter that industry or profession (or keywords associated with it) within the Search field. For example, enter keywords such as medical imaging, radiology, plumbing, telemarketing, or sales.

NOTE Pages is an extremely powerful, yet easy-to-use word processing app that was designed by Apple, specifically for the iPad. It's compatible with Microsoft Word and enables you to create documents on the iPad and then transfer them to your primary computer or access documents created on another device and then view or edit them on your tablet. Pages is a must-have business app for your iPad 2 and is described in greater detail in Chapter 9, "Using Pages, Numbers, Keynote, and Other Must-Have Business Apps."

As you're evaluating an app before downloading it, use these tips to help you determine if it's worth installing on your tablet:

■ Figure out what type of features or functionality you want to add to your iPad 2.

■ Using the Search field, find apps designed to handle the tasks you have in mind. Chances are, you can easily find a handful of apps created by different developers that are designed to perform the same basic functionality. You can then pick which is the best based on the description, screen shots, and list of features each app offers.

  Compare the various apps by reading their descriptions and viewing the screen shots. Figure out which app works best for you based on your unique needs.

■ Check the customer reviews and ratings for the app. This is a useful tool to quickly determine if the app actually works as described. Keep in mind that an app's description within the App Store is written by the app's developer and is designed to sell apps. The customer reviews and star-based ratings are created by fellow iPad users who have tried out the app firsthand.

  If an app has only a few ratings or reviews and they're mixed, you might need to try out the app for yourself to determine if it will be useful to you. However, if an app has many reviews that are overwhelmingly negative (three stars or less), that's a strong indication that the app does not perform as described or that it's loaded with bugs.

CAUTION A few less scrupulous app developers opt to post positive reviews of their own apps, or they get friends and family members to do this for them. If an app has only a handful of reviews or ratings and they're all overwhelmingly positive, you might need to download and try out the app for yourself to see whether it is indeed useful.

■ If an app offers a free (trial) version, download and test out that version of the app first before you purchase the premium version. You can always delete any app that you try out but don't wind up liking or needing.

■ Ideally, you want to install apps on your iPad that were designed specifically for the iPad, so if you have a choice, opt for the iPad-specific app first.

KEEPING YOUR APPS UP TO DATE

Periodically app developers release new versions of their apps. To make sure you have the most current version of all apps installed on your iPad 2, while visiting the App Store using the App Store app on your tablet, tap the Updates button displayed at the bottom of the screen.

A red-and-white circle in the upper-right corner of the Updates button (as shown within Figure 7.13) indicates that one or more of your apps has an update available. The number in the red circle tells you how many app updates are available. You can download updates directly from your iPad 2 if it's connected to the Internet.

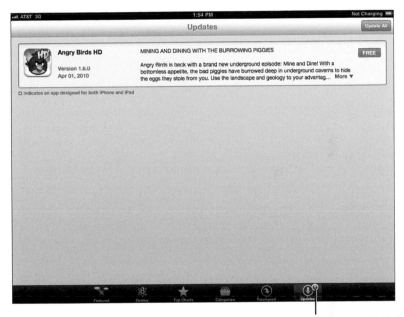

This number indicates how many installed
apps have updates ready for download.

FIGURE 7.13

Keep your apps up to date with the latest versions. In this example, only the Angry Birds app installed on this iPad 2 has an update available.

Tap the Updates icon to display a list of apps with updates available and then tap the Update All button or an individual app icon that's displayed on the Updates screen to automatically download the new version of the app and install it. Doing this replaces the older version of the app.

Using the App Store app to check for updates helps you determine whether there are updated versions for apps currently installed on your iPad 2. However, if you check for app updates using iTunes on your primary computer, it checks for updates for all of the apps you have ever downloaded for your tablet (including backups of apps stored on your primary computer that aren't currently installed on your iPad).

To check for app updates from within iTunes on your primary computer, click the Apps option displayed under the Library heading on the left side of the iTunes screen. The app listings for every app you've downloaded for your iPad (and iPhone, if applicable) display—even apps not the currently installed on your tablet are included.

In the lower-right corner of the iTunes screen, when you have the Apps option selected, is an option that says how many app updates are currently available. Click this option. You can then click individual apps you want to update, or click the Download All Free Updates option that's displayed in the upper-right corner of the My App Updates screen.

After the app updates have been downloaded to your primary computer, perform an iTunes sync with your iPad 2 to transfer the updated versions of the apps currently installed on your tablet.

TIP   To ensure you have the latest versions of your most commonly used apps installed on your iPad 2, check for app updates once every week or two. Each time Apple releases an update to the iOS operating system, it's common for app developers to also release an updated version of their apps.

IN THIS CHAPTER

- How and when to use the iTunes sync process
- How and when to use iCloud to sync and share files
- Learn about the types of data you can transfer between your computer and tablet with iTunes sync versus iCloud, and how to do it

8

SYNCING TO YOUR COMPUTER VIA iTUNES OR iCLOUD

Your iPad 2 is a powerful standalone mobile-computing device, and when operating with iOS 5 with iCloud, it no longer needs to be connected to your primary computer via a USB cable to transfer documents, sync data, or back up files.

However, you still have the option to use the iTunes sync process, which requires you to occasionally connect your iPad 2 to your primary computer using the white USB cable that came with the tablet. When the two devices are connected via the iTunes software and a USB cable, you can transfer files and apps between your primary computer and your tablet, and back up your tablet by using your primary computer's hard drive to store your iPad's archived backup files.

You can also use your primary computer to shop for and download apps, music, movies, TV show episodes, audio books, eBooks, and other content to your primary computer,

copied to your primary computer and stored in a backup file. Thus, as long as you maintain a current backup of your iPad 2 using the iTunes sync process, you can always restore the contents of your tablet from that backup and not worry about losing important information if the iPad experiences a problem.

UNDERSTANDING THE iTUNES SUMMARY SCREEN

After a connection is made between your iPad 2 and primary computer using the iTunes sync process, when the iPad 2 is selected and highlighted on the left side of the iTunes screen what you see in the main area of the iTunes screen on your computer is the Summary screen.

The Summary screen is comprised of three sections: iPad, Version, and Options. Near the top of the Summary screen is the iPad section. Within this box (see Figure 8.1), your iPad 2's device name (which you created when you first set up the tablet), its memory capacity, what version number of the iOS operating system is installed on the tablet, and its serial number are displayed.

FIGURE 8.1

The section of the Summary screen within iTunes that is labeled iPad.

Within the Version section of the iTunes Summary screen is an option to check for updates related to the iOS operating system running on your tablet. Click the Check for Update button to determine if an updated version of the operating system is available. As you can see from the message displayed to the right of the Check for Update button, the iTunes software automatically checks for iOS updates periodically and informs you when the next check will take place.

If an iOS update is available, follow the onscreen prompts to download the new version of the operating system from Apple and then install it on your iPad 2. This process is almost totally automated, but it takes as long as 15 minutes. It's important that your iPad's battery has enough power remaining to handle the process and that you leave your tablet connected to your computer during the entire iOS upgrade process.

Should you have a problem with your iPad 2 that requires you to restore its entire contents from a saved backup, use the Restore option that's displayed within the

Version section of the Summary screen. This option also enables you to restore your iPad to its factory settings, which undoes any settings you've adjusted yourself.

The Options section of the Summary screen includes a handful of other customizable settings. To turn on any of these options, use the mouse to add a check mark within the checkbox that corresponds to the desired option.

The first option displayed in the Options section (see Figure 8.2) enables you to set iTunes to automatically launch as soon as you connect the iPad 2 with your computer using the USB cable. Some of the other options enable you to set preferences related to the type of content you download from the iTunes Store.

For example, when you download TV show episodes or movies, you can select the default resolution option to be Standard or High Definition. A TV show or movie you watch on your iPad 2's screen in high definition looks more vibrant and detailed, but it costs you slightly more to purchase or rent high-resolution content, plus these files take up more storage space on your tablet.

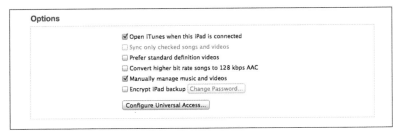

FIGURE 8.2

When the Open iTunes When This iPad Is Connected option is turned on, the iTunes software automatically launches and the sync process begins as soon as you connect your iPad to your primary computer.

TIP If you're using your iPad 2 for work and are storing data you need to keep private, be sure to add a check mark next to the Encrypt iPad Backup option and then select a password for this feature.

When you activate the iTunes sync process, a backup of your iPad 2 is created and stored on your primary computer. Activating the Encrypt iPad Backup option encrypts the data within this backup file, making it much more difficult for an unauthorized person to access this backup data that is stored on your primary computer.

On the iPad 2 itself, you also want to activate the Passcode option from the Settings app. This protects the data stored on your tablet and keeps unauthorized people from using your iPad 2 because it is passcode protected.

ADJUSTING SYNC OPTIONS WITH THE iTUNES INFO SCREEN

Click on the Info icon displayed near the top of the iTunes screen to access a selection of options that relate to the syncing of data between your primary computer and the Contacts, Calendar, Mail, Safari, and Notes apps on your iPad 2.

The Info screen enables you to customize the sync options related to your address book contacts (see Figure 8.3). If you want to sync the contents of the Contacts app on your iPad 2 with the contents of your primary contact management application, add a check mark next to this option's heading and then select the appropriate options within this section.

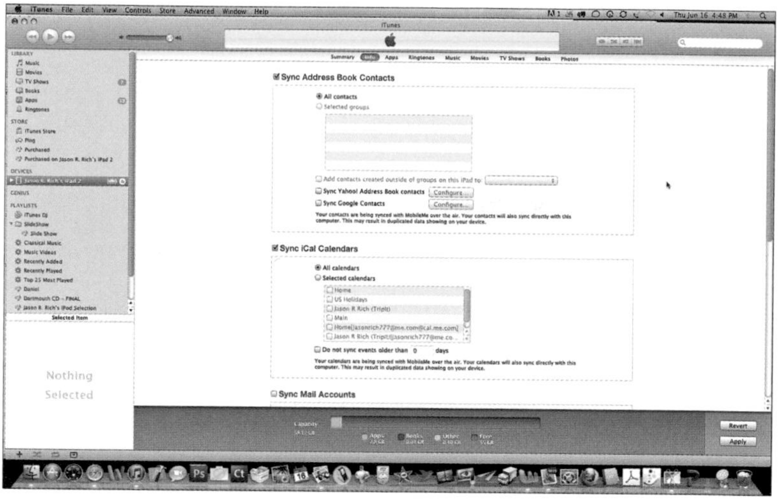

FIGURE 8.3

From within iTunes, you can set up the process for syncing your contacts database between your primary contact management application and the Contacts app on your iPad 2.

For example, you can choose to sync all your contacts or just specific groups of contacts. If you use the online-based Yahoo! Contacts or Google Contacts apps, you can adjust the settings under these options to sync your contact information with the Contacts app on your iPad 2. Click the Configure icon next to Sync Yahoo! Address Book Contacts or Sync Google Contacts to do this.

Below the Sync Address Book Contacts section within the Info screen is the Sync iCal Calendars section. To sync your scheduling data between the Calendar app on your iPad 2 and your primary scheduling app, use the mouse to add a check mark next to this option's heading and then choose which options listed within this section are appropriate to your needs.

Moving down the Info screen, add a check mark to the Sync Mail Accounts option and then select which of your email accounts you want to sync between your primary computer and your iPad 2. This feature is used to sync account information, not the actual email messages within each account.

From the Other section, you can add a check mark next to the Sync Safari Bookmarks option if you want your saved bookmarks to be consistent on Safari on your iPad 2 with Safari on your Mac (or another compatible web browser) or with Microsoft Internet Explorer (or another compatible browser) on your PC.

You can also sync notes created using the Notes app that comes on your tablet if you add a check mark next to the Sync Notes option.

The options within the Advanced section of the Info screen enable you to decide if specific types of content should be synced between your primary computer and tablet or if the iTunes sync process should replace (not merge) specific types of content on your iPad 2 with the data from your primary computer (see Figure 8.4). After you make any changes to the iTunes sync options, they will not take effect until your next sync between the two devices.

FIGURE 8.4

The Advanced section of the Info screen gives you the option to replace iPad 2 content, not sync it with your primary computer.

CAUTION If you add a check mark to the Contacts, Calendars, Mail Accounts, Bookmarks, or Notes option within this Advanced section, the content currently stored on your tablet is overwritten (deleted) and replaced by the content currently stored on your primary computer.

Typically, when you initiate an iTunes sync, data between the two devices is synced or merged. Data from one device does not overwrite the other. Adding check marks to the options within the Advanced section of the Info screen could result in the accidental loss of important data if these features are not used properly.

After you've made changes to the options offered from the Info screen of iTunes, be sure to click the Apply or Sync button, one of which is displayed in the lower-right corner of the screen. Your changes go into effect immediately.

SYNCING YOUR APPS WITH THE iTUNES APP SCREEN

The iTunes App Screen is used to manage all the apps you've downloaded from the App Store. It enables you to determine which apps should be installed on your iPad 2. To use the features within this section of iTunes, first add a check mark next to the Sync Apps heading.

On the left side of the iTunes App Screen (see Figure 8.5) is a complete list of all apps you've downloaded and that are stored (or backed up) on your primary computer.

FIGURE 8.5

You can manage the apps on your iPad 2 from this iTunes screen.

On the right side of the iTunes App Screen is a copy of your iPad 2's Home screen, which displays all of the apps currently installed on your tablet. From the left side of the screen, use the mouse to move apps around on your Home Screen to change their location.

From the right side of the screen, add check marks to the apps stored on your primary computer that you want to transfer and install on your iPad 2. You can also remove check marks that correspond to listed apps to uninstall them from your tablet, but still keep copies of the apps stored on your primary computer.

At the bottom of the app listing, on the left side of the screen, is the Automatically Sync New Apps option. When this option is turned on, anytime you download a new app for your iPad from within the App Store using iTunes, that new app is automatically transferred to and installed on your tablet when a sync is next initiated.

If you make any changes to the options displayed within the App screen, be sure to click the Apply button to save those changes. Or, to undo the changes you've made, click the Revert button. You can find both the Apply and Revert buttons in the lower-right corner of the iTunes screen.

TRANSFERRING APP-SPECIFIC DATA OR FILES BETWEEN YOUR COMPUTER AND iPAD 2

Some apps enable you to use the iTunes sync process to transfer app-specific data between an iPad app and specific software on your primary computer, such as Microsoft Word, Microsoft Excel, Microsoft PowerPoint, and many others.

If you install an app that allows for app-related files to be transferred using the iTunes sync process, those apps are displayed within the File Sharing section, which appears at the bottom of the App screen (see Figure 8.6).

FIGURE 8.6

From the File Sharing section of the App screen within iTunes, you can transfer files between spe-cific apps that can be accessed with software running on your computer.

The Pages word processor for the iPad is one example of an app that enables you to transfer documents between the Pages for Mac software or Microsoft Word (PC or Mac version).

To transfer an app-specific file, from the File Sharing section, click the app name listed on the left side of the screen, under the Apps heading. If you click on Pages, for example, on the left side of the screen, a Pages Documents section within iTunes displays. Click the Add button in the lower-right corner of the screen to choose documents stored on your computer's hard drive to be transferred to your iPad 2 during the next sync (see Figure 8.7).

FIGURE 8.7

Select documents or app-specific files stored on your computer that you want to transfer to your iPad 2.

Repeat this process for each document you want to transfer and then, if applicable, click another app listed under the Apps heading within the File Sharing section and select compatible files stored on your computer. For example, you can transfer Excel spreadsheet files to your iPad 2 and access them using the Numbers app.

SYNCING YOUR MUSIC WITH THE iTUNES MUSIC SCREEN

If you use iTunes on your primary computer to manage your digital music library, and you want to transfer some or all of your music so you can enjoy it on your iPad 2 using the iPod app that comes on the tablet, click the Music option near the top of the iTunes screen and then place a check mark next to the Sync Music heading.

Within the Sync Music section are several customizable options that enable you to determine which music files should be synced with your iPad 2. For example, you can sync your entire music library or pick and choose specific songs, playlists, music within a specific genre, or music from a particular artist. You can also select entire albums to be synced between the two devices, not just individual songs.

After you've made your selections, click the Apply icon that's displayed in the lower-right corner of the screen. In the upper-right corner of this screen, the number of songs that will be synced with your iPad are displayed.

From the iTunes Music screen, you can also opt to sync music videos and voice memos.

TIP If you don't plan on transferring any music between your computer and iPad 2, you can simply leave the Sync Music heading unchecked. The same is true for many of the other section headings within iTunes, such as Sync Movies, Sync TV Shows, or Sync Photos.

SYNCING YOUR MOVIES WITH THE iTUNES MOVIES SCREEN

If you have purchased and downloaded movies from iTunes and want to transfer those movie files to your iPad 2 to view them using the Videos app, click the Movies option displayed near the top of the iTunes screen and then place a check mark in the checkbox displayed next to the Sync Movies heading. You can choose which movies you want to transfer to your iPad 2 (or vice versa).

However, if you have used iTunes to rent movies, you need to click on the Movies option and use the Rented Movies section to choose which movies you want to transfer from your primary computer to your iPad 2 (or vice versa) by clicking the Move icon that's associated with each rented movie (see Figure 8.8). On the left side of the screen are the rented movies currently stored on your primary computer. The box on the right side of the Rented Movies screen represents your tablet and the rented movie content stored (or to be stored) on it.

Unlike movies you have purchased, rented movies can only be stored on one system (your primary computer or your iPad 2) at any given time.

Keep in mind that movie files, including those you shoot and edit on your iPad 2, are large and require a lot of storage space. That's why it's good to store movies on your computer and move them to your iPad when you want to view them on the tablet.

NOTE Using the iBooks app to find, purchase and download eBooks from the iBookstore is covered in Chapter 17, "Using iBooks." You can purchase eBooks from many best-selling business and self-help books from a wide range of publishers and authors.

As with any type of content, if you know you won't be using your iPad 2 as an eBook reader (using iBooks) or you won't be listening to audiobooks, you can leave the Sync Books and Sync Audiobooks headings within iTunes unchecked.

SYNCING YOUR DIGITAL IMAGES WITH THE iTUNES PHOTOS SCREEN

If you use a Mac, you might be happy to know that the iPhoto software that comes on your computer is designed to work seamlessly with the Photos app on your iPad 2. Thus, you can quickly and easily transfer digital images between the two devices using the iTunes sync process. You can also transfer digital images between your PC and the iPad 2 using the iTunes sync process.

To sync digital images (pictures) between the two devices, click the Photos option displayed near the top-center of the iTunes screen and then add a check mark to the Sync Photos From heading (see Figure 8.10).

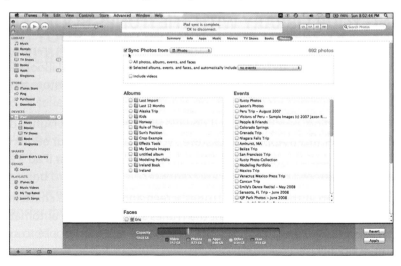

FIGURE 8.10

Using the iTunes sync process, you can pick digital images to transfer between your iPad 2 and primary computer.

You can then choose to sync photos from a particular application on your primary computer, such as iPhoto, or choose a specific directory on your computer's hard drive (such as Pictures) that contain images that you want to copy over to your iPad 2.

From this screen, you can also sync videos you've shot that are stored on your primary computer or videos that you shot using the Camera app of your iPad 2. As you scroll down the Photos screen within iTunes, you can pick and choose which images you want to sync.

For example, if you use a Mac you can choose specific Albums or Events from iPhoto or choose specific people based on iPhoto's Faces face-recognition feature. The photos you transfer from your primary computer are then accessible from the Photos app on your iPad or from other apps that can access images stored on your tablet (such as Contacts).

Based on your selections, the number of photos to be synced between your primary computer and tablet are displayed in the upper-right corner of the screen. Keep in mind that this is a syncing process, so your images remain intact at their current location, but you can also duplicate, transfer, and save them on the other device.

After you make your selections from the Photos screen, be sure to click the Apply or Sync button in the lower-right corner of the screen to save your changes.

ADDITIONAL iTUNES COMMANDS AND FEATURES

When your iPad 2 is linked with your primary computer via the iTunes sync process, you can see a graphic depiction of your tablet's memory at the bottom of the iTunes screen. This display (see Figure 8.11) shows how much of the iPad 2's storage space is currently being utilized and what type of data is taking up the space.

FIGURE 8.11
At the bottom of the iTunes screen is a graphic depiction of how the storage space within your tablet is being utilized.

After you adjust the settings to personalize the iTunes sync process, those settings remain intact and are immediately utilized the next time you initiate the sync process. At any time, however, you can adjust the settings to change what data, files, apps, and content are transferred or synced between your primary computer and tablet.

During the actual sync process, a rotating circle is displayed in the upper-left corner of the iPad's screen (to the immediate right of the 3G and Wi-Fi signal indicators). At the same time, the progress of the sync is displayed at the very top of the iTunes screen on your primary computer. This is shown within Figure 8.12.

FIGURE 8.12

During a sync, you can see the progress of the sync process in a window displayed at the very top of the iTunes screen.

CAUTION When a sync is in process, don't disconnect your tablet from the computer and don't try to use your tablet. Disconnecting the tablet prematurely could result in lost or corrupted data. On the iTunes screen, wait to see the Okay To Disconnect message. When the sync process is completed, your iPad 2 displays the Lock screen or Home screen.

Maintaining a backup of your iPad's contents and data is a smart strategy to use on an ongoing basis. Get into the habit of performing a sync at least once every few days, or more often if you make significant changes to data stored on your iPad 2, or need additional apps or content transferred between your tablet from your primary computer.

Depending on your primary computer, the USB connection between the two devices may be adequate to charge your iPad 2's battery. If this is the case, the battery icon displayed in the upper-right corner of your tablet's screen shows a lightning bolt within it to indicate that the device is charging.

However, if you see the Not Charging message next to the battery icon, your computer's USB port does not provide enough power to the iPad 2 to recharge its battery. This does not impact its ability to transfer data between the two devices, however.

Some Macs and PCs (more than two or three years old) have USB 2.0 ports that don't supply enough power to recharge your iPad 2's battery. If this is the case, you need to connect the two devices to perform an iTunes sync, but you ultimately need to plug your iPad 2 into an electrical outlet (using the USB cable and the power adapter supplied with your tablet) to charge its battery.

WORKING WITH iCLOUD

Launched with OS X Lion for the Mac and iOS 5 for the iPad, Apple's new iCloud serves a handful of functions, including the ability to transfer files between computers and your various iOS devices.

iCloud is a remote file-sharing service that stores your music, photos, apps, calendar data, contacts, documents, and other types of files and then makes them available (wirelessly) via the Internet to your various computers and devices.

The majority of services offered by iCloud are free. When you set up your free iCloud account, you're given a unique email address and 5GB of online storage space. Additional online storage space can be purchased if you need it.

You can equate iCloud to a hard drive storage solution in cyberspace that gives you access to all the data and files you transfer to it. However, iCloud does much more than just store data and files. It can automatically sync your iPad with your primary computer and/or other iOS devices (such as your iPhone or iPod touch). It can even manage and store all your iTunes purchases so they're available on all your computers and devices.

For example, you can purchase a song on iTunes using your computer, store that song on your computer's hard drive and on the iCloud service, and then wirelessly access that song purchase (for no additional charge) on your iPad via the Internet.

> **NOTE** If you upgrade your iCloud account to include the iTunes Match feature (for an additional fee of $24.99 USD per year), your entire music collection, including content not purchased on iTunes, can be shared wirelessly between your Mac, Apple TV, and all your iOS devices. This includes music you've ripped from your own CD collection.

iCloud also offers a Photo Stream service that enables you to store up to 1,000 digital photos on the iCloud servers, and this service can keep your individual photos or digital photo albums synced between all your devices. So if you take a photo on your iPad 2, it can automatically be sent to iCloud and synced with the photos stored on your primary computer, your Apple TV, and your iPhone, for example.

When using the Photo Stream service through iCloud, a complete master photo library is maintained on your PC or Mac; however, up to 1,000 images remain instantly accessible to all your devices via iCloud.

One of the most convenient features of iCloud is that you can easily transfer documents, data and work-related files between your primary computer and iPad 2 wirelessly. So you can take a Microsoft Word, Excel, or PowerPoint file created on your PC or Mac, for example, send it to iCloud, and make it instantly accessible to your iPad that's connected to the Web.

Not only does this feature make it easy to transfer files and documents between your own devices, it also makes collaboration with other people easier because the latest edited version of your file or document will automatically be synced with iCloud. On your iPad, files stored on iCloud can be retrieved or directly sent by a variety of business-related apps (see Chapter 10, "Finding Other Business Apps").

Many other business-related apps that are compatible with online file sharing services, such as DropBox or WebDAV, are now compatible with iCloud (or soon will be).

> **NOTE** With the launch of iOS 5, new versions of Pages, Numbers, and Keynote were released that have document/file import and export options that work seamlessly with iCloud.

Your iPad can also use iCloud to back up and access your collection of apps and eBooks. All your app purchases, whether they're currently stored on your iPad or not, can automatically be stored in iCloud and accessible to you at any time (assuming your iPad is connected to the Web). iCloud also keeps a backup of all your eBook purchases from the iBookstore.

Another use for iCloud is to sync all your Contacts, Calendar, and iCloud email account messages between all your devices. Thus, as soon as you update a contact in your iPad's Contacts database, for example, that change is reflected on both your primary computer and your iPhone. Likewise, the free iCloud email account also automatically remains synchronized between all your devices.

Finally, instead of backing up your iPad by connecting it to your primary computer via a USB cable and using the iTunes sync process, you can create and maintain a daily backup of your tablet wirelessly using iCloud. To make the backup process quick, only information that has changed on your iPad is sent to the iCloud service and incorporated into your backup archive.

After a backup has been stored on iCloud, you can perform a wireless restore if something goes wrong with your tablet causing data to be deleted. When set up to do so, iCloud automatically backs up a host of information from your iPad:

- Music, app, and eBook purchases
- Photos and videos shot using your tablet
- Your iPad 2 personalized settings
- Apps and related data

- Home Screen data and settings
- Text messages sent and received via iMessage
- Downloaded ringtones

Some third-party apps also utilize iCloud for data backup purposes.

When you initially set up your iPad 2 after purchase (or upgrade to iOS 5), you are prompted to set up a free iCloud account. You can then customize that account from within the Settings app. To do this, launch Settings from your iPad's Home Screen.

On the left side of the screen, tap the iCloud option. When the iCloud screen appears on the right side of the screen (shown in Figure 8.13), you see a variety of iCloud-related options you can customize, starting with the email account that's associated with your iCloud account. All new iCloud accounts will have an email address that starts with your unique username and ends with @me.com, so your email address will look like [username]@me.com.

FIGURE 8.13

You can decide which iCloud features you'll utilize from your iPad, plus customize how your various apps will tap into this service from within Settings.

However, if you opt to port over your older MobileMe email account, that account might end with @.mac. After you assign an email address to your iCloud account, you can then decide which of your iPad's apps will automatically (and wirelessly) sync with the iCloud service.

Right from the start, your options include Mail, Contacts, Calendars, Reminders, Bookmarks, Notes, and Photos. However, after you begin adding apps to your iPad, such as Pages, Numbers, Keynote, or some other third-party apps, you should be able to adjust their iCloud-related settings from this screen or by tapping the specific app listing on the left side of the Settings screen.

Toward the bottom of the iCloud screen within Settings you can also set up the Find My iPad service and manage your online storage and backup. To manage your iPad 2 wireless backups, tap the Storage & Backup option to access the Storage & Backup screen within Settings (shown in Figure 8.14).

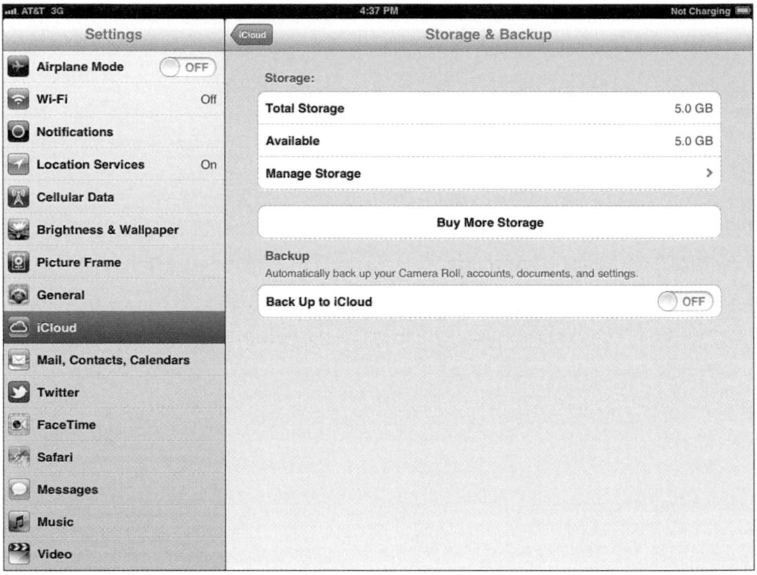

FIGURE 8.14

From the Storage & Backup screen, you can see how much of your free 5GB of online storage space you're utilizing, purchase more online storage space, or turn on (or off) the automatic wireless backup feature.

The Back Up to iCloud feature is a wireless backup option that replaces the need to back up your iPad using the iTunes sync process described earlier in this chapter.

As you begin using your iPad with iCloud, you'll discover the convenience that the various features and functions offered by this online-based file sharing service offers, not just for backup purposes, but for sharing and automatically (and wirelessly) syncing important work-related documents and files between computers and your iOS devices.

Keep in mind that, to access the iCloud service from your iPad, the tablet must have access to a Wi-Fi or 3G internet connection. If you know you're about to board an airplane that doesn't offer Wi-Fi, or you're leaving a 3G wireless data coverage area, access and store whatever files you'll need on your tablet before the Internet connection is shut down or lost.

CAUTION Apple's iCloud service has replaced its older and now obsolete MobileMe online service, which officially goes offline forever in June 2012. If you utilized MobileMe to store files or digital photos, be sure to download them to your computer or iPad before they're permanently deleted.

OTHER OPTIONS FOR SYNCING DATA WIRELESSLY

You can sync some data and files on your iPad 2 with your primary computer (or network) wirelessly, whenever your tablet is connected to the Internet. This applies to the Contacts and Calendar apps as well as data from a bunch of other apps.

You can do the wireless transfer process through iCloud or through Microsoft Exchange. Some other third-party apps allow for wireless file transfers using online-based cloud services, such as Dropbox or WebDAV. If you plan to use iCloud with your iPad 2, these other services may prove to be obsolete, but they are an alternative to wireless file sharing.

TIP The free Dropbox app enables your iPad to wirelessly link to the Dropbox cloud-based online service, which can be used for sharing all kinds of files between your tablet and other devices, including your primary computer. Dropbox works with a growing number of iPad 2 apps, including Photos, Pages, Numbers, Keynote, and many others.

You can create a Dropbox account, which includes 2GB of online storage for free. Or you can pay for a premium account that offers up to 100GB of online storage space. All data stored on the Dropbox service is encrypted and secure. Dropbox also makes it easy to share files with others, so you can collaborate on projects using your iPad 2 from wherever you happen to be.

To learn more about the Dropbox cloud service and the Dropbox app, visit www.DropBox.com or download the app directly from the App Store. Similar (free) Dropbox software is also available for the PC and Mac, making it easy to share files wirelessly between your primary computer, your iPad 2, and your iPhone.

There are also a handful of third-party apps available from the App Store, such as GoToMyPC and Splashtop Remote Desktop, that enable you to access files on your PC or Mac remotely via the Internet directly from your iPad 2.

The process for transferring data wirelessly between specific apps and your primary computer varies based on the app. However, wireless transfer can be a fast and easy way to share files and data with other devices when you're on the go with your iPad 2, and have access to the Internet.

IN THIS CHAPTER

- An introduction to Pages
- Get acquainted with FileMaker Go, Bento, and Things (database management)

USING PAGES, NUMBERS, KEYNOTE, AND OTHER MUST-HAVE BUSINESS APPS

If you plan to use your iPad 2 for work-related purposes or to help you be more productive while on the go, there are a handful of apps that can help dramatically enhance your tablet's capabilities, enabling it to perform more like a netbook or notebook computer.

> **TIP** If you have the iCloud feature turned on with Pages, Numbers and/or Keynote, any time you alter a document or file using one of these apps (on any of your iOS devices or computers), an updated version will automatically be saved online in your iCloud account and be almost instantly updated on all your other devices or computers that are linked to the iCloud account (and connected to the Internet). This feature happens in the background, without you manually having to import or export the documents or files. Thus, no matter which system or device you're working on, you'll always be accessing the latest version of your Pages, Numbers, or Keynote document or file.

With a battery life that averages 10 hours, the iPad 2 is lighter, sleeker, and easier to carry around than a notebook or netbook computer, and with the addition of certain apps, your tablet can be just as useful. You may ultimately discover that the iPad 2 can replace your need to carry around a laptop computer.

This chapter focuses on a handful of must-have business-related apps that add word processing, spreadsheet management, digital slideshow presentation, and database management capabilities to your tablet.

The optional iPad-specific apps featured here also offer file compatibility with Microsoft Office (Word, Excel, and PowerPoint) or other popular software applications (such as FileMaker Pro, Bento, and Things). Thus, you can transfer files created using these software packages to use on your tablet or create files on your tablet that work with these software applications on your primary computer. In addition, most of the apps described in this chapter are compatible with iCloud for easy document importing and exporting to and from your tablet.

> **TIP** As you begin using your iPad 2 for work-related tasks that involve a lot of data entry, such as word processing, managing spreadsheets, or database management, you might find it more convenient to use an optional external keyboard with your tablet, as opposed to the onscreen virtual keyboard.

In addition, many of these apps enable you to create PDF files that are easy to share. On your iPad 2, reading, viewing, or printing PDF files transferred from your computer, for example, can be done with the optional (free) iBooks app, or with a third-party PDF reader app, such as PDF ($3.99 USD), PDF Reader – iPad Edition ($.99 USD), or PDF Reader Pro Edition for iPad ($9.99 USD), all of which are available from the App Store.

WORD PROCESSING WITH THE PAGES APP

When visiting the App Store, if you perform a search using the search phrase "word processing," you can find a handful of third-party apps that offer word-processing or text-editing capabilities. However, if you're looking for a full-featured, well-designed, and extremely robust app for word processing, that's also fully compatible with Microsoft Word, the app you're looking for is Apple's own Pages ($9.99 USD).

Pages is part of a trio of business-related apps for the iPad that were created by Apple as part of its iWork suite (which includes Pages, Numbers, and Keynote). Each app is sold separately. In addition to being compatible with Microsoft Office files, these apps are also fully compatible with the Pages, Numbers, and Keynote software available for the Mac.

Pages offers much of the same functionality as Microsoft Word when it comes to formatting documents, as well as incorporating photos, graphics, various fonts, and even charts or graphics created using another app (such as Numbers) into your documents.

Aside from enabling you to create documents from scratch on your iPad 2, you can easily import Word or Pages documents from your primary computer or another user. The Pages app makes it easy to transfer these documents using the iTunes sync process or a wireless transfer process via iCloud or email. Plus, if you have a wireless printer compatible with the AirPrint feature, you can print documents directly from your tablet.

From the opening Pages screen (shown in Figure 9.1), you can manage your document files. This includes renaming or deleting documents currently stored on your tablet; importing documents from another device; or exporting documents via Email, iCloud, iTunes sync, or an online-based cloud service.

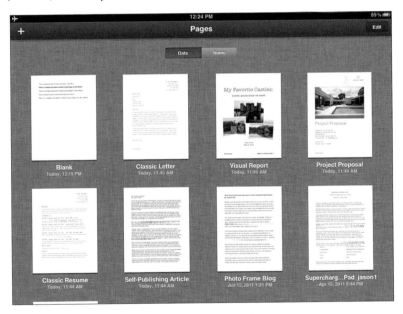

FIGURE 9.1

From the opening Pages screen, you can manage the documents stored on your tablet.

From the Pages opening screen, to rename a document file, tap its current filename, which is displayed below its image thumbnail. The iPad's virtual keyboard displays. Type the new filename within the blank field displayed directly above the keyboard (shown in Figure 9.2), and then tap the blue-and-white Done button to save your changes. This same method for renaming files also works in Numbers and Keynote.

FIGURE 9.2

Once a document has been created, you can rename it by tapping its current filename when looking at the document's thumbnail on the opening Pages screen.

To delete a Pages document that's saved on your iPad, from the Pages opening screen, tap the Edit button that's displayed near the upper-right corner of the screen, or hold your finger on any document thumbnail for several seconds. When the document thumbnails begin to shake, tap the document thumbnails you want to delete. As you select each of them, a yellow frame appears around each thumbnail. To delete the selected documents, tap the trash can icon that's displayed near the upper-left corner of the screen. From the opening screen, you can also create a copy of a document with a single tap of the Copy Document icon, which is located to the immediate left of the trash can icon.

You can view the Pages opening screen and your document thumbnails based on the date they were created (in reverse chronological order) or alphabetically by filename by tapping the Date or Name tab, respectively. To create a new document from scratch, tap the plus sign–shaped icon displayed in the upper-left corner of the Pages opening screen. A menu window displays in the upper-left corner of the screen that gives you the option to Create Document or copy (import) a document from iTunes (via sync), iDisk, or WebDAV. Tap the Create Document option.

The next step in creating a new document is to select a template from the Choose a Template screen (shown in Figure 9.3). There are 16 different templates to choose from, ranging from a blank document to a business letter, résumé, project proposal, report, or flyer. Tap the template thumbnail to select the template of your choice.

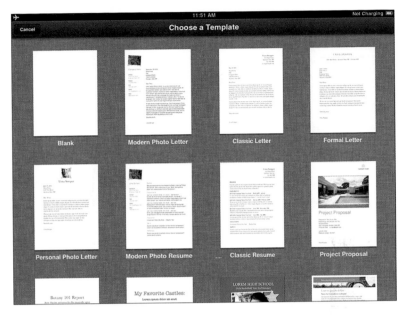

FIGURE 9.3

From the Choose a Template screen, select a document template to help with formatting or create and format a document from scratch by selecting the Blank template.

When the main Pages screen appears, you have a wide range of word processing features and functions at your disposal. You can now position your iPad 2 in either landscape or portrait mode as you type. If you're using the virtual keyboard for typing, however, landscape mode offers a larger-size onscreen keyboard layout (but there's less area to actually view the document you're creating).

Figure 9.4 shows Pages in landscape mode, and Figure 9.5 shows the same document being edited with Pages in portrait mode.

Located along the top of the Pages screen as you're creating or editing documents are a handful of command buttons, many of which reveal additional menus. In the upper-left corner of the screen is the Documents button. Tap it to return to the Pages opening screen.

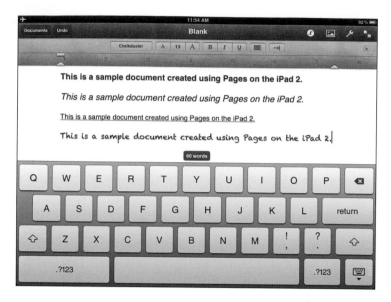

FIGURE 9.4

Here, a document is being created with the iPad held in landscape mode. The onscreen keyboard is larger, making it easier to type.

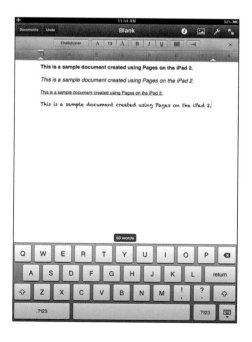

FIGURE 9.5

When you hold the iPad in portrait mode, you can see more of the document you're creating or editing, but the onscreen keyboard is smaller.

Directly to the right of the Documents icon is the Undo button. Tap it to undo or delete the last action done using the Pages app. Numbers and Keynote also have an Undo button in approximately the same onscreen location. Displayed at the top-center of the Pages screen is the document's current title.

CAUTION Any time you transfer documents created using a Microsoft Office application (Word, Excel, or PowerPoint) to your iPad, you could run into compatibility issues if your tablet does not possess the same fonts as those used in the document or file created on another computer.

During the import process, you are notified if any font conflicts arise. A substitute font is automatically used, but this could alter your document or file's formatting, requiring you to make adjustments on your iPad. Common fonts, such as Arial, Times New Roman, or Helvetica, transfer with no problem.

FORMATTING TEXT

Located in the upper-right corner of the Pages screen are four command buttons that are used for formatting and sharing your documents. Tapping the circular icon with an "i" within it reveals a window that offers a handful of formatting options. At the top of this window are three command tabs (shown in Figure 9.6), labeled Style, List, and Layout. When you tap each of these tabs, different formatting options become available:

- **Style:** Use these options to control the font size (by selecting a heading style), or scroll to the bottom of this window and tap the Text Options command, which reveals a submenu (see Figure 9.7) for selecting the font size, font color, and the actual font that is used in your document.

- **List:** Here you can create bulleted or numbered lists in your document. You can also tap the left- or right-pointing arrows that appear in this window to reposition the text on the page.

- **Layout:** These settings modify your document's paragraph alignment, create columns, or adjust the line spacing of the text.

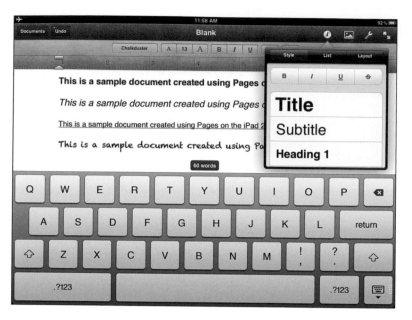

FIGURE 9.6

From this menu window, you can tap on one of three tabs (Style, List, and Layout), each of which reveals different document formatting options.

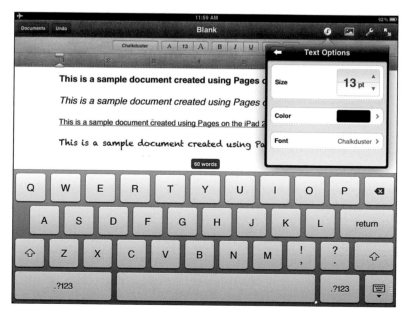

FIGURE 9.7

To access this Text Options window, tap the Style tab and scroll down to the Text Options command.

INSERTING GRAPHICS

Tap the picture frame–shaped icon that's displayed near the top-right corner of the Pages screen to access a handful of commands that enable you to import photos, create tables, import charts, or add graphic shapes to a document.

The window that appears after tapping the picture frame icon has four tabs at the top of it, labeled Media, Tables, Charts, and Shapes. Tap the Media tab (shown in Figure 9.8) to import a photo that's currently stored on your iPad 2, and then place the photo into your document. After the photo is imported, you can use your finger to position and resize it on the screen within the document.

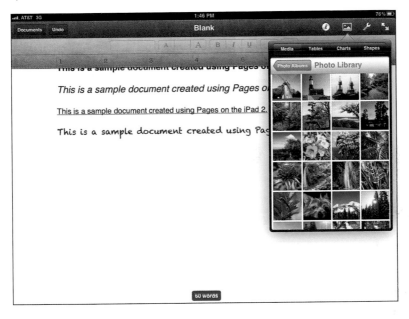

FIGURE 9.8

You can import any photo that's currently stored on your iPad into your Pages document, place it anywhere, and resize it as needed.

From the Tables tab, you can create tables to be embedded into your document. Or, if you've created a chart or graph using another app, such as Numbers, you can import and place it in your Pages document. By tapping the Charts tab, you also have the option to create several different types of charts (using different pre-formatted color schemes) from scratch using the tools built in to Pages.

Tap the Shapes tab to import and incorporate graphic shapes, such as lines, circles, arrows, and triangles, into your document. As you're looking at this window, you can swipe your finger from right to left to scroll through the available options.

The font selection icon enables you to quickly select a font. Tap it to reveal a pull-down menu of available fonts (shown in Figure 9.11). To the right of the font selection icon are three font size selection icons. Tap the small "A" button to reduce the font's type size by one point per tap. Tap the number button displayed between the two "A" icons to access a pull-down menu that enables you to choose a pre-defined font size (such as 10-, 12-, 14-, 18-, 24-, or 36-point type), or tap the large "A" button to increase the font size by one point.

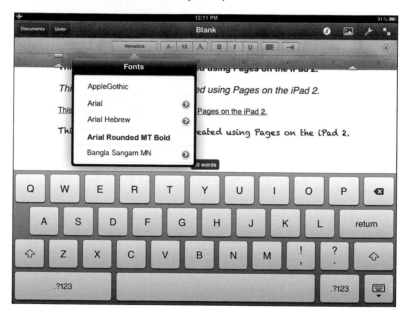

FIGURE 9.11

Tap the font selection icon to reveal a pull-down menu of available fonts.

When you change the font or font size or the type style, everything you type from that point on reflects your new selections. Alternatively, you can first select existing text so that it's highlighted, and then make adjustments; the highlighted or selected text is modified. To select text, double-tap a word and then drag the blue dots that appear so that all the desired text is highlighted.

Also, as you're typing you can tap the **B**, *I*, or U icons to instantly switch between normal text and bold, italic, or underlined text (or mix and match these formatting options). By tapping one of the options located to the right of the U icon, you can choose the paragraph formatting or justification you want to use in your document. Your options include left-aligned, centered, right-aligned, or right/left justified.

The icon located next to the paragraph formatting icon (shown in Figure 9.12) reveals a window that enables you to add a Tab, Line Break, Column Break, or Page Break to your document.

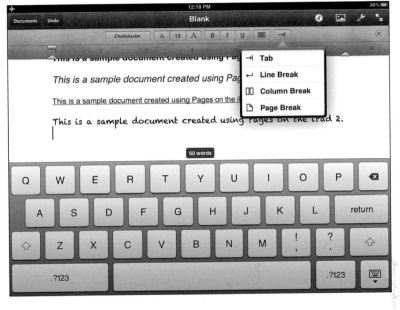

FIGURE 9.12
Tap the icon located next to the left/right justification icon to add a Tab, Line Break, Column Break, or Page Break to your document.

The onscreen ruler is used for formatting text and controlling your right and left margins. Using your finger, you can move the margin controls (small, upward facing arrow icons displayed on the ruler) to the left or right to modify your right or left document margin.

EXPORTING A DOCUMENT

You can exit out of Pages at anytime, and whatever document you're creating, editing, or reading is automatically saved. However, when you tap the wrench icon and choose the Share and Print option, before you export or email a document, you have the option to save or send it in one of three formats, including Pages, PDF, and Word (shown in Figure 9.13). These same options are also offered in Numbers and Keynote. Exporting to a Word document makes your document fully compatible with Microsoft Word on your primary computer. Exporting to a PDF file means the document can be opened using any PDF file reader on any device. Pages-formatted documents can be opened with any version of Pages on a Mac, an iPad, or an iPhone.

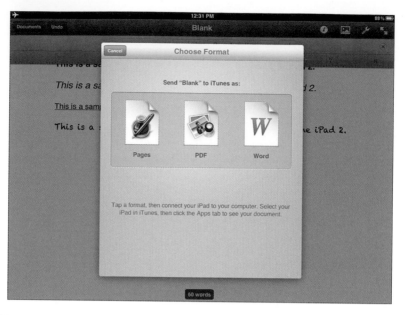

FIGURE 9.13

Before sending or exporting a document, choose its format. Your options include Pages, PDF, or Word.

As new features and functions are added to the iOS operating system, Apple periodically releases updated versions of Pages, which adds new word-processing features and capabilities to this app. With each new version that's been released thus far, this app has come closer to rivaling what's offered in a full-featured word processor, such as Microsoft Word.

> **TIP** iOS 5's Select, Copy, Cut, and Paste commands work well in this app and enable you to easily move blocks of text or graphics around and paste content imported from other apps into your document.

MANAGING SPREADSHEETS WITH THE NUMBERS APP

Creating, viewing, managing, and sharing complex spreadsheets has never been easier than when you use Numbers on an iPad. Using this $9.99 USD app, you can create tables, charts, and graphics from spreadsheet data; perform complex calculations; and keep data up to date within spreadsheets while you're on the go.

Everything is done from the app's slick interface that's user-friendly but loaded with features.

If you're already familiar with how to use Microsoft Excel or Numbers for the Mac, you should have no trouble learning to use and getting the most out of Numbers on the iPad. In terms of its interface, this app is similar in design to Pages and Keynote, plus it enables you to easily select, copy, and paste content between these apps.

Data entry is also simple with Numbers. Your tablet's virtual keyboard modifies itself automatically based on the type of data being entered. Built in to the app is a calculation engine with more than 250 different functions and formulas, as well as 16 spreadsheet templates that are easily customizable.

You can import spreadsheet data from Excel (PC or Mac) or Numbers for the Mac, or you can export it for use with these software applications. You also can create a PDF document of your spreadsheet data.

> **TIP** You can wirelessly transfer and share Numbers spreadsheets, as well as documents created using Pages or presentations created using Keynote, to other devices using Apple's iCloud service or another compatible file-sharing (cloud-based) service. You can also send Numbers files from an iPad via email or transfer them to a computer using the iTunes sync process.

When you launch the Numbers app from your iPad 2's Home screen, you see the app's opening screen (shown in Figure 9.14), which looks and acts similar to the Pages opening screen. From here, you can manage existing spreadsheet files, create a new spreadsheet from scratch, rename files, or delete files using the same methods described earlier in this chapter for Pages.

To create a new spreadsheet, tap the plus sign icon displayed near the upper-left corner of the Numbers opening screen, and then tap the Create Spreadsheet option. From the menu window that appears, you also have the option of importing a spreadsheet file from iTunes, iCloud, or a few other online-based file-sharing services.

When you opt to create a new spreadsheet, the Choose a Template screen displays, enabling you to choose between 16 time-saving templates. For example, there's a checklist, loan comparison, budget, mortgage calculator, expense report, employee schedule, and team organization template to choose from, or you can create a spreadsheet from scratch by tapping the Blank template option.

When you make a template selection, the main Numbers screen displays. Just like when using Pages, there are command buttons along the top of the page. Figure 9.15 shows a sample spreadsheet that's utilizing the Budget template.

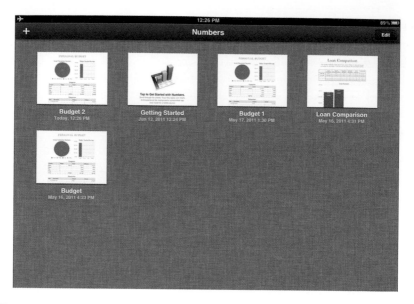

FIGURE 9.14

The opening screen of the Numbers app enables you to easily manage your spreadsheet files. This includes importing or exporting files, renaming files, or deleting files from your iPad.

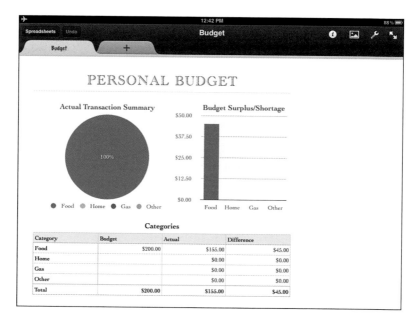

FIGURE 9.15

The main Numbers app screen with the Budget template loaded.

The menu options offered under the four command buttons at the upper-right corner of the screen change depending on what type of data you're looking at, creating, or editing. For example, if you tap the circular icon with an "i" in it and you're currently editing a table, the menu window that displays offers commands and options related to modifying that table. However, if you're working within a table, that same "i" command icon reveals a totally different set of menu options (shown in Figure 9.16) that relate to modifying cells in the table.

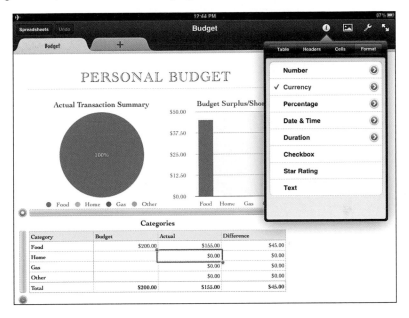

FIGURE 9.16

When you're working within tables to modify cells, tap the "i" icon to access an entirely different set of menu options.

When you tap the picture frame button, the menu options offered are for adding media (photos), tables, charts, and shapes into the spreadsheet. Tap the command tab at the top of the window (see Figure 9.17) to determine what type of content you want to add, and then use your finger to position and size the content within the main Numbers screen.

Use the Spreadsheets icon, found near the upper-left corner of the screen, to return to the Numbers opening screen. Use the four command buttons displayed near the upper-right corner of the screen to edit and manage the spreadsheets.

The commands found under the wrench icon (shown in Figure 9.18) enable you to share and print your spreadsheets wirelessly from your iPad 2, find content within a spreadsheet file, adjust some of the app's settings (such as turning on or off the spelling checker, the Center Guides, and the Edge Guides), or access the online-based help and tutorial content offered by Apple.

Use the icon that looks like two arrows moving away from each other to enter the Numbers full-screen mode.

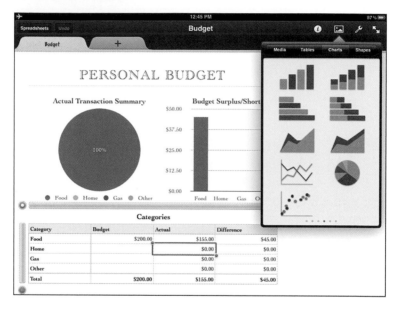

FIGURE 9.17

Using the command options displayed after tapping the picture frame button, you can insert media, tables, charts, or shapes into your spreadsheet, and then adjust the position and size by dragging your finger on the screen.

How you manage a spreadsheet for "number crunching" by programming formulas and so on is all similar to using Excel on a PC or Mac. However, entering data is much easier on the iPad 2 because the virtual keyboard automatically adjusts itself based on the type of data you're entering. For example, if you're entering dollar amounts, those numbers will be formatted as $###.##, while numeric dates can be formatted as ##/##/##.

The Numbers app is extremely versatile in terms of how it can be used. The savvier you are at using spreadsheets in general, the better you'll be at getting the most use out of this powerful app.

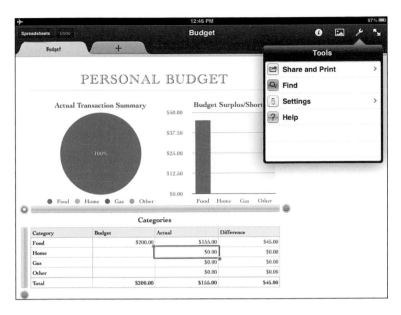

FIGURE 9.18

Several command options, such as the ability to print spreadsheets, are offered when you tap the wrench button that's displayed near the upper-right corner of the screen.

USING KEYNOTE TO CREATE DIGITAL SLIDESHOW PRESENTATIONS

If your work responsibilities involve giving presentations, teaching, or conducting meetings, for example, chances are that you regularly utilize PowerPoint or Keynote on your primary computer to create, view, and give digital slideshow presentations. With the addition of the Keynote app ($9.99 USD) on your iPad, you can import your PowerPoint presentations to your tablet and then edit or present them. You also can create eye-catching and professional-quality presentations directly on your iPad 2 and then show off those presentations on your tablet's screen to a small group.

Using an optional Apple VGA Adapter cable ($29.00 USD), it's possible to connect your tablet to an LCD projector to make a presentation in front of a large crowd. With the optional iPad Digital AV Adapter cable ($39.00 USD), you can connect your tablet to any size high-definition television or monitor (that has an HDMI In port) to show off your presentation.

> **TIP** When giving a presentation, your iPad must be connected to a monitor, television set, or LCD projector via a cable. The length of this cable determines how much mobility you have as the speaker or presenter. However, with the optional Keynote Remote app ($.99 USD), available from the App Store, you can wirelessly control your iPad using an iPhone or another iOS device, which gives you greater mobility as you're presenting or speaking.

Keynote on your iPad offers much of the same functionality as PowerPoint on your primary computer. You can create digital slides, add graphics and text to those slides, insert animations and slide transitions, and group the slides together into a cohesive presentation.

From the opening Keynote screen, you can also import PowerPoint presentations into your iPad 2 to view, edit, or present them. By tapping the wrench icon when using Keynote, you can select Share and Print to easily export presentations you create on your tablet and use them with PowerPoint (on a PC or Mac) or Keynote (on a Mac).

If you opt to create a presentation from scratch on your iPad, from the opening screen, tap the plus button (displayed near the top-left corner of the screen) and choose the Create Presentation option. Then, choose one of 16 theme templates offered from the Choose a Theme screen. You can then personalize the template and add text, photos, graphics, charts, graphs (created using Numbers, for example), and animations to the slides, plus add a wide range of eye-catching slide transitions.

The interface and layout of the Keynote app is similar to Pages and Numbers. From the Keynote opening screen (see Figure 9.19), you can manage your presentation files, import a presentation, create a new presentation, copy a presentation, or delete a presentation. From this screen, you can also rename a presentation.

Scroll through the presentation thumbnails to choose which one you want to work with. Tap a presentation thumbnail to open the file and begin editing and viewing it, or use one of the command icons to export (share), rename, or delete the file.

> **TIP** The process for renaming a file is identical to how you rename a document in the Pages app or how you rename a spreadsheet file in the Numbers app.

As you're creating or editing a presentation, from the main slide creation page, you can then create or edit one slide at a time using the command options available by tapping any of the five command icons that are displayed near the top-right corner of the screen.

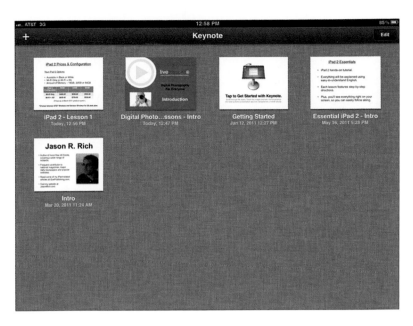

FIGURE 9.19

Use the opening screen of Keynote to manage your presentation files. This includes importing presentations, renaming presentations. or deleting presentations.

CAUTION In general, PowerPoint presentations imported and viewed using Keynote on your iPad look the same; however, you might encounter minor compatibility issues with fonts, animations, slide formatting, and/or slide transitions. When you import a new PowerPoint presentation, be sure to preview it yourself on your iPad 2 before presenting or sharing it with others. You might need to make minor adjustments to compensate for compatibility and inconsistent formatting issues.

To create a new slide in a presentation, tap the plus-sign button near the bottom-left corner of the screen. Thumbnails on each slide in your presentation display along the left margin of the screen. Tap any slide thumbnail to view that slide in the main slide viewing area of Keynote and edit that slide (see Figure 9.20).

At the top-center of the screen, the presentation's title is displayed. To edit each slide or actually give a presentation, use the command buttons found near the upper-right corner of the screen.

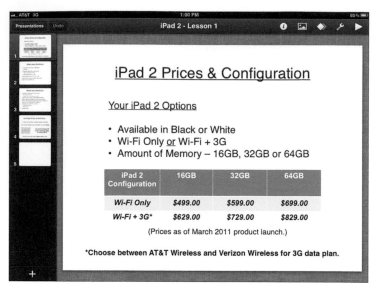

FIGURE 9.20

From the slide editing screen of Keynote, you can view thumbnails of slides in your presentation, plus edit one slide at a time in the main slide viewing area of the screen.

The circular command icon with an "i" in it is used to add special effects (such as frames, borders, shadows, and reflections) to graphics or photos that are selected and highlighted in the main slide viewing area. For example, you can change a photo's opacity.

However, if you're working with text within a slide, the circular command icon with an "i" is used to access menu options for editing and manipulating the text and creating bulleted or numbered lists, for example.

The picture frame button is used to import and include media (photos), tables, charts, and shapes into your slide presentation, whereas the diamond command button is used to add animations in each slide and slide transitions between slides.

The wrench button offers a handful of commands, including the ability to print slides wirelessly to a printer; manage Presenter Notes; and share or export your presentation via email, iCloud, or another compatible service. As you export a Keynote presentation, you can choose between the Keynote, PDF, or PowerPoint file format.

When you're ready to give your presentation or preview it for yourself, tap the right-pointing, arrow-shaped Play icon. Your slides are viewable in full-screen mode on your tablet. Alternatively, if the iPad is connected to a monitor or projector, a totally different presenter's view of each slide is displayed.

As you're viewing a slideshow on your tablet, use finger swipes to move between slides, one at a time. Swiping your finger from right to left advances the slides forward; swiping your finger from left to right moves backward in the presentation.

You'll be pleasantly surprised how easy it is to use Keynote but how complex you can make your slide presentations if you invest the time to add special effects, animations, and details.

MANAGING DATABASES WITH FILEMAKER GO, BENTO, AND THINGS

When it comes to database management, companies of all sizes and in all industries rely on FileMaker Pro. This is one of the most widely used and versatile database management software applications available for PCs, Macs, and networks. The uses of customized databases created and managed using FileMaker Pro are as diverse as the millions of companies that rely on this software.

Using the FileMaker Go for iPad app ($39.95 USD), you can easily access, view, manage, and share databases created using FileMaker Pro and work with database content from virtually anywhere.

The FileMaker Pro software comes with more than 30 "starter" solutions for creating custom databases. However, you can easily build your own database from the ground up and then access it using FileMaker Go on your tablet. Creating and managing databases using this software and app requires no programming skill whatsoever. However, depending on the complexity of your database, creating it from scratch requires a learning curve and time investment.

Instead of having a custom iPad app developed for your business, in many situations it's much easier, faster, and less expensive to develop a custom FileMaker Pro database to be used with the FileMaker Go app. As you're developing a database with mobile access via your tablet in mind, you can incorporate features such as the ability to display charts and graphics, print information wirelessly from your tablet, and capture onsite signatures using the iPad 2's touch screen.

> **TIP** To access a list of 50 ways companies in a variety of industries are using FileMaker Pro combined with FileMaker Go on the iPad, visit www.filemaker.com/products/filemaker-go/tasks.html.

If your database needs are not as complex as what FileMaker Pro is designed to handle, the same development team behind FileMaker Pro has created a more consumer-oriented database management tool, called Bento, that has both Mac ($29.00 USD) and iPad ($4.99 USD) versions available.

Bento is a more simplistic, yet still powerful, database management application that enables you to easily create custom databases and then sync data between the Mac and iPad versions of the program. You can use it to organize contacts, track projects, plan events, manage things, print labels or charts, and much more.

Although you can manage contacts using the Contacts app and coordinate your schedule using the Calendar app on your iPad, Bento for iPad offers highly customized solutions for handling these tasks using a single app.

You can also use Bento for iPad as a standalone program. It comes with more than 25 database templates to help you get started using it quickly and efficiently.

To learn more about the many different uses of Bento for iPad (whether or not you plan to use it with Bento for Mac), visit www.filemaker.com/products/bento/ipad.html.

Yet another database management tool that's more simplistic than FileMaker Pro but still offers the capability to create rather complex and highly personalized databases is called Things. It's a software package from CulturedCode (www.culturedcode.com) that is available both for the Mac ($49.95 USD) and iPad ($19.99 USD).

The two versions of Things are fully compatible, so you can easily exchange data between a Mac and an iPad. Or, you can use the iPad version as a standalone database app.

Being able to create a customized database and utilize it on both your primary computer (or network) and on your tablet—while keeping the data fully synced—offers an incredible opportunity for companies of all sizes to streamline a wide range of tasks and make available highly specialized information from almost anywhere. For example, using a database application, you can check on inventory in your warehouse while sitting in your customer's office or manage a detailed project while traveling.

OTHER APPS FOR MANAGING MICROSOFT OFFICE FILES

The Pages, Numbers, and Keynote apps described earlier in this chapter enable you to create, edit, view, store, and share Microsoft Office or Apple iWork documents and files with other computers, devices, or users.

From the App Store, there are also a handful of other apps that offer the capability to view or, in some cases, create, edit, view, store, and share Microsoft Office-compatible files. Here's a small sampling of these apps. You can find additional apps with similar functionality in the App Store, using the Search field and the search phrase "Microsoft Office," for example.

> **TIP** Need help deciding which of these third-party apps can best meet your
> specific needs when it comes to accessing, viewing, editing, and sharing Microsoft
> Office files using your iPad 2? Read each app's description carefully when visiting
> the App Store; pay attention to the user ratings and reviews; and, if applicable,
> download the free trial version of the app to test it out for yourself. Each of these
> apps, however, provides relatively straightforward solutions for accessing Word,
> Excel, and PowerPoint files and documents with your iPad.

MAIL

If you receive a Microsoft Office document as an email attachment, you can open
and view it (but not edit it) using the free Mail app that comes installed on your
iPad. After you download a document by tapping the attachment thumbnail
within the email message, you can open it in Quick Look mode within Mail.

While viewing an attachment in Quick Look mode, tap the Share icon that's displayed near the upper-right corner of the screen. If it's a Word or Pages document
and you have Pages installed on your iPad, select the Open in Pages option to
transfer this document into the Pages app to be able to view, edit, and share it.

You also can wirelessly print the document from the Quick Look mode within Mail
by tapping the Share icon followed by the Print option. Tap the blue-and-white
Done icon, displayed near the upper-left corner of the screen, to exit out of Quick
Look mode.

Or, if the email attachment is a Word, Excel, or PowerPoint file, you can bypass
Quick Look altogether (if you have Pages, Numbers, or Keynote installed on your
iPad) and select the Open in Pages, Open in Numbers, or Open in Keynote option
that's displayed when you hold your finger on the email attachment's thumbnail
for a second or two within Mail (as shown in Figure 9.21).

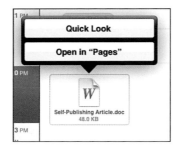

FIGURE 9.21

*In Mail, you can download an attachment and then open a Microsoft Office file in Pages,
Number, or Keynote, depending on the file type (you must have the appropriate app installed
on your iPad). Otherwise, you can view the document in Mail's Quick Look mode.*

DESKTOP CONNECT

When you want or need to access important files or data on your primary computer but you're away from your desk, you can use your iPad to remotely access your computer via the Internet. This can be done using a variety of different third-party apps, including Desktop Connect ($14.99 USD).

This is a fast, full-featured desktop viewer that enables you to remotely access your PC or Mac and run software on your computer. This app enables you to access any and all Microsoft Office files, for example, without worrying about compatibility issues or porting content between your tablet and computer.

To be able to access files and software on your primary computer remotely, your iPad must have access to the Internet via a 3G or a higher-speed Wi-Fi connection. Other apps that offer similar functionality include GoToMyPC and Splashtop.

> **CAUTION** Some remote desktop applications for the iPad are free but charge a monthly fee to be able to access your primary computer from your tablet via the Internet. Others are paid apps but charge no ongoing monthly fee. All offer fully secure connections between your computer and tablet.

DOCUMENTS TO GO PREMIUM – OFFICE SUITE

The Documents To Go Premium – Office Suite ($16.99 USD) is designed to be used with an included free program that runs on your primary computer. When they're used together, you can easily access, view, and create Microsoft Word, Excel, and PowerPoint files from your iPad, and you can view Adobe PDF files. You also can use this app suite for transferring and managing Apple iWork files with corresponding iPad apps, as well as accessing Google Docs files.

To easily transfer Office documents between a computer and iPad (or vice versa), you can use email, you can use a cable-based synchronization process that is similar to iTunes sync, or you can take advantage of one of several cloud-based online file sharing services, including Dropbox.

Documents To Go Premium – Office Suite enables you to easily access all types of Microsoft Office documents and files. This app even supports Office documents sent to your iPad as an email attachment.

If you rely heavily on Microsoft Office applications and want access to your main Office-related files and documents while you're on the go without having to worry about any compatibility issues, this app offers a comprehensive and straightforward solution.

To learn more about this app, visit the App Store or www.dataviz.com/products/documentstogo/iphone/index.html.

QUICKOFFICE CONNECT MOBILE SUITE FOR iPAD

Another solution for easily accessing Microsoft Office documents and files using your iPad is the QuickOffice Pro HD for iPad ($19.99 USD). Using this app, you can access and sync Office documents in a variety of ways, including through the use of a compatible cloud-based online file-sharing service or via the iTunes sync process.

The app also enables you to easily create and share PDF files created from your Office files or documents and enables you to create, edit, and share Microsoft Word, Excel, and PowerPoint files.

This suite of apps includes QuickWord (for word processing), Quicksheet (for creating, viewing, and editing Excel spreadsheets), and QuickPoint (an advanced PowerPoint presentation editor), all of which allow for the sharing and syncing of files using email or a cloud-based file sharing service.

If you need access to your Microsoft Office documents and files while on the go using your iPad 2, QuickOffice Pro HD for iPad is one viable file sharing solution. To learn more about this app, visit the App Store or www.quickoffice.com/quickoffice_pro_hd_ipad.

PICSEL SMART OFFICE

Picsel Smart Office for iPad ($9.99 USD) offers the same overall functionality as the Documents To Go and QuickOffice apps but uses a really slick user interface that makes full use of the iPad 2's high-definition touch-screen display. Smart Office enables you to access, view, and edit Microsoft Office files and documents on your tablet. It maintains full compatibility with fonts, graphics, and formatting as you transfer files between the computer and iPad.

One unique feature of this app is the "3D stereo visual capability" that enables you to place content on the z-axis to add depth and emphasis to spreadsheets and presentations, for example.

Like its competition, Smart Office also enables you to transfer files and documents between your computer and iPad (plus share files with others) in a variety of ways, including through the use of a compatible cloud-based online file sharing service, such as Dropbox.

To learn more about Picsel Smart Office for iPad, visit the App Store or www.picsel.com/products/smart-office.

TIP The apps featured here have general appeal among business professionals, salespeople, freelancers, and consultants, but this is just a small sampling of the apps available from the App Store that can be found under the Business, Finance, Productivity, Reference, and Social Networking categories. Even if some of the apps described in this chapter are not directly relevant to your needs, they may help you understand the many different ways your tablet can be used for handling tasks you might not have realized were possible.

DROPBOX

With so many new apps being "invented" that allow files and documents from software running on a PC, Mac, or network to be accessed and used with the iPad, the need to easily and wirelessly transfer files and documents between a computer, network, smartphone, and iPad has become increasingly prevalent.

The iTunes sync method for transferring or syncing data between a computer and iPad is certainly viable, however, making that direct cable connection isn't always possible. One solution that's being adopted by a growing number of app developers is the use of an online cloud-based file sharing service, such as iCloud or Dropbox, to wirelessly import and export files from the iPad.

These services enable you to transfer a document or file to a remote service and then pull that file from the server using another device. This makes it easy to share documents, data, and files with others or to wirelessly transfer content between your own devices.

Currently, in addition to iCloud, there are many different cloud-based file-sharing services that iPad users can subscribe to. In fact, many large companies have established their own, secure, online file-sharing solutions. In terms of those that work with the iPad, some are free and others have a monthly or annual usage fee associated based on the amount of online storage space that's utilized.

All of Apple's iWork apps, including Pages, Numbers, and Keynote, have taken advantage of cloud-based services such as iCloud or iWork.com for wireless file and document transfers.

Meanwhile, many third-party app developers have created iPad apps that utilize the popular, easy-to-use, and low-cost Dropbox cloud-based file-sharing service for moving files between the iPad and other computers or devices.

Setting up a Dropbox account is initially free (for up to 2GB of online storage space). However, premium accounts that offer much more online storage space are available for a fee.

Dropbox offers free PC and Mac software for securely transferring files from a computer to the password-protected and encrypted online-based service. A free proprietary app for the iPad (see Figure 10.1) is also available that allows the tablet to send and receive files utilizing the Dropbox service as long as a 3G or Wi-Fi Internet connection is available.

More and more iPad apps are becoming compatible with Dropbox, as well as Apple's own iCloud service. Using this type of service to wirelessly transfer and share files, documents, and data is convenient and simple.

FIGURE 10.1

The Dropbox app for iPad gives your tablet direct access to the popular Dropbox online (cloud-based) file-sharing service.

To get started using the Dropbox app, download it from the App Store and set up a free account the first time you use it. Or you can download the free Dropbox software for your PC or Mac from www.Dropbox.com and set up your account using the software.

> **NOTE** The premium Dropbox service is priced at $9.99 USD per month for up to 50GB of online storage space or $19.99 USD per month for up to 100GB of online storage space. In addition to sharing files between devices or users, Dropbox and other services like it can be used as an online-based remote data and file backup solution.

INVOICE2GO FOR iPAD

For small business operators, consultants, and freelancers, the need to generate and send invoices in a timely and efficient manner in order to be paid is essential. Using the Invoice2Go software on a PC or Mac ($99.00 USD to $149.00 USD per year), in conjunction with the Invoice2Go for iPad app ($14.99 USD), you have the ability to create professional-looking, customized invoices that you can design from scratch or adapt from more than 300 invoice templates offered with the software and app.

A free Invoice2Go Lite for iPad version is available (see Figure 10.2). It includes 20 built-in invoice templates. This is a slightly scaled-down version of the paid app,

FIGURE 10.2

Create and send professional-looking and customized invoices, purchase orders, estimates, and credit memos from your iPad using the Invoice2Go for iPad app.

Finding and generating the perfect invoice to bill a customer or client for your products, services, or time is possible using this app. For invoices sent electronically, you can also add an interactive PayPal button, so you can be paid with a click of the mouse by the recipient. As you're generating the invoice, subtotals, sales tax, and totals are automatically calculated.

> **NOTE**   You can also use the Invoice2Go for iPad app to create and generate personalized purchase orders, estimates, and credit memos that can contain all of your company information, including your logo.

In addition to simply generating the invoices, this app generates sales and business reports in 16 different formats, enabling you to email invoices directly to clients or customers from your iPad and track incoming payments. You can print invoices and reports wirelessly from the iPad, or you can transfer all data and sync it with Invoice2Go on your computer. Data from Invoice2go can also be exported for use in Intuit's QuickBooks accounting and bookkeeping software that's running on your primary computer or network.

Invoice2Go can meet all of your customer and client invoicing needs, yet the software and app (either of which you can use as a standalone product) are extremely user friendly and require no accounting knowledge to fully utilize. For more information, go to www.Invoice2go.com.

OMNIGRAFFLE

The OmniGraffle app for iPad ($49.99 USD) is a powerful diagramming tool that enables you to use your tablet's screen as a canvas for creating detailed charts and diagrams that utilize lines, shapes, objects, and text, all of which are fully customizable in terms of sizing, color, and visual effects.

Use this app to help organize your thoughts, present information in an easy-to-understand format, graphically showcase complex tasks or ideas with flow charts, demonstrate the hierarchy within a team or organization, or graphically explain any type of multistep process.

You use a simple drag-and-drop interface that requires just one finger to format diagrams using a vast library of stencils (predrawn shapes). However, you can also draw diagrams freehand on the tablet's display. The app has a large collection of diagram templates and charts built in, and you can easily customize them to meet your needs.

After you've created diagrams on the iPad, you can print them wirelessly, convert them into PDF files for easy sharing, or export them to the Mac version of OmniGraffle (priced at $99.95 USD for the standard edition or $199.95 USD for the professional edition). The developer of this app, The Omni Group (www.omnigroup.com), also offers a handful of other Mac and iPad apps designed for task management, outlining, and graph drawing and data plotting. Go to www.omnigroup.com/products/omnigraffle for more information.

PENULTIMATE

When it comes to word processing on your iPad, Apple's Pages app is one of the best solutions for on-the-go writing. However, there are many other apps available from the App Store that also offer word processing and text-editing capabilities. One such app is Cocoa Box's Penultimate ($1.99 USD).

What sets this app apart from Pages is that, in addition to using the iPad's virtual keyboard (or an external keyboard) for typing, the Penultimate app (see Figure 10.3) enables you to write text directly onto the iPad's screen, and also create sketches by drawing on the screen using your finger or an optional stylus.

FIGURE 10.3

Using the Penultimate app, you can write or draw on the iPad's screen to create notes or sketches. It's an alternative to typing using the tablet's virtual keyboard.

This app is ideal for people who are more comfortable writing notes and ideas using a traditional pen and paper. As you're writing on your tablet's screen, you can quickly swap digital ink colors or change the look of the virtual paper you're writing or drawing on.

In addition to the three photo-realistic paper styles that come with the app, you can add a collection of other virtual paper styles (using in-app purchases, priced between $.99 USD and $2.99 USD each). For example, you can add music paper, games paper, graph paper, time and task management forms, and various designer papers to the app.

Using this app, you can create separate "notebooks" to differentiate between top-ics, projects, or categories. You can easily rearrange, duplicate, or delete individual note pages. After you've created individual notes or entire "notebooks," you can export them into PDF format and easily share them with others via email. You can also wirelessly print files from this app, or you can use it as a whiteboard during meetings by connecting your iPad to a monitor with the optional Apple Digital AV Cable ($39.00 USD). For more information, go to www.cocoabox.com/penultimate.

> **TIP**   For any app that requires precision drawing or writing on the iPad 2's screen, one optional accessory that can help is the Bamboo Stylus ($29.95 USD) from Wacom (http://wacom.com/en/Products/BambooStylus.aspx). This pen-like device has a soft and narrow tip that's good for precision drawing, writing, or tap-ping on the iPad's screen without fear of scratching it. See Chapter 19, "Must-Have Accessories," for more information about this and other useful iPad 2 accessories.

QUICKBOOKS CONNECT

QuickBooks from Intuit Software (www.intuit.com) is one of the most widely used bookkeeping, accounting, and financial management software packages in the world. Now, it's easy to keep your small business' financial records up-to-date from anywhere, using the QuickBooks Connect app, which is designed to work seam-lessly with QuickBooks Online or QuickBooks for the PC or Mac.

If your business uses the QuickBooks Online accounting and bookkeeping soft-ware, you can freely use the QuickBooks Connect app. However, if you use the PC- or Mac-based software, you must pay a monthly subscription to use QuickBooks Connect on your iPad.

Using QuickBooks Connect, you can easily access financial records from anywhere and generate estimates, invoices, and sales receipts while you're away from the office.

SQUARE: CREDIT CARD PROCESSING

Whether you're a small business, consultant, or freelancer, or even an artisan show-casing your work at a local crafts show, one of the easiest ways to set up a mer-chant account and be able to accept credit card payments within a few minutes is to use the Square app and credit card processing service.

Begin by visiting http://squareup.com to set up a free account. Next, from the App Store, download the free Square app. To use the Square service in order to accept and process credit card transactions, there are no upfront costs, no contracts to sign, no recurring monthly fees, and no hidden charges. You simply pay a flat 2.75% fee per transaction (as long as you swipe the customer's credit card). Without the card swipe, each transaction costs $.15 plus 3.5% of the transaction.

Square even provides a free, and extremely small, credit card swiper that attaches to the iPad through the unit's headphones jack. You can use it to swipe credit cards and process transactions, or you can manually enter credit card information from your customers or clients.

The free Square app accepts an onscreen signature from your customer, processes the transaction, and promptly emails your customer a detailed receipt. The proceeds from the transaction are transferred directly to the checking or savings account you have linked to your Square account.

Within minutes of setting up a Square merchant account, you are able to accept Visa, MasterCard, American Express, Discover, and debit card payments using your iPad.

Before using the app for the first time to process credit card transactions, you can set up onscreen icons that represent each item you're selling. You can include the item name, price, whether sales tax should be charged, and a brief item description. You also can attach a photo of that item.

When you're ready to accept a credit card payment, simply launch the Square app, enter the transaction amount or tap a preprogrammed Item icon (based on what's being purchased), swipe the customer's credit card, and have the customer sign your iPad's screen. Then the app connects to the Internet and securely processes the transaction within seconds.

Being able to accept major credit cards and debit cards, especially while working offsite, offers a huge advantage to small businesses, consultants, freelancers, and entrepreneurs while also offering added convenience to customers.

Square offers an efficient and low-cost way to be able to handle credit card transactions from any location and automatically maintain detailed records of each transaction that you can later export to bookkeeping or inventory management software on a primary computer.

VOICE RECORDER HD

Using the Voice Recorder HD app ($1.99 USD), or one like it, with a tap on the iPad's screen you can record audio using the device's built-in microphone, and then play back your recordings on your iPad. You also can share the recordings with others via email or use the iTunes sync process to transfer recorded files to your primary computer. This app is also compatible with Dropbox (described earlier in this chapter).

Recording meetings, classes, conversations, workshops, phone conversations, or your own dictation is extremely easy. The onscreen controls are straightforward, allowing for one-tap recording and playback. For more information, go to www.efusion.co.jp/app/voice-recorder-hd/en/.

APPS FOR OTHER BUSINESS NEEDS

Aside from apps designed specifically for business professionals, there are thousands of apps that can help you become more efficient in handling a range of tasks associated with your personal life. Using your iPad to stay organized, save money, and better utilize your time, for example, helps you enjoy all that your life has to offer.

The following are additional apps that can be useful in either your personal or professional life.

ACCESSING COMPUTERS REMOTELY

In addition to the apps described thus far, many business professionals have discovered the benefit of being able to access the files and content on their primary computer remotely, via the Internet, using their iPad.

You can do this using a handful of different remote desktop apps, such as Splashtop Remote Desktop for iPad, Jump Desktop, Remoter: Remote Desktop RDP, and GoToMyPC. To find a handful of apps that offer this functionality, visit the App Store. In the Search field enter the keywords "Remote Desktop."

PARTICIPATING IN VIRTUAL MEETINGS

You can also participate in virtual (online) meetings from anywhere using the GoToMeeting, WebEx for iPad, or Skype apps, for example. More information about these apps, and others that are useful for video conferencing, are featured in Chapter 13, "Conducting Videoconferences and Virtual Meetings."

READING PDF FILES

Another type of app that's helpful to many business professionals is a dedicated PDF file reader. These apps enable you to import PDF files and view them on your tablet's screen.

Although the free iBooks app (featured in Chapter 17, "Using iBooks") serves as a PDF file reader, several dozen other apps for accessing and reading PDF files, such as PDF Reader Pro Edition, FastPDF+, and iAnnotate PDF, are available. When visiting the App Store, enter the search phrase "PDF Reader" in the search field to find a selection of these apps.

PDF files are useful because they retain their exact formatting and appearance, even when transferred across multiple viewing platforms. A PDF file looks the same on a PC, Mac, iPad, or smartphone screen regardless of the software used to create it.

SAVING TIME IN YOUR EVERYDAY LIFE

Beyond apps that are strictly for business, you can find a plethora of apps within the App Store that can save you time in your personal life. For example, there's the Walgreen's app, which enables you to manage your prescription medications and order refills from anywhere.

Many of your favorite chain stores also have their own apps, enabling you to shop online or find the store's nearest retail location. If you're a business professional who's constantly on the go, the FedEx Mobile app helps you ship and track packages, but it also helps you find the nearest FedEx location wherever you happen to be. To order office supplies or find the closest Staples location, the free Staples app can prove helpful.

Or, If you're in need of a jolt of caffeine, the MyStarbucks app helps you find the nearest Starbucks location and decide what you want to order. You can use the Starbucks Mobile Card app to actually pay for your in-store purchases.

ONLINE BANKING MADE EASY ON YOUR iPAD

Many major banks, such as Bank of America, Capital One, PNC, Citizens Bank, and TD Bank, now offer specialized apps for handling your online banking from the iPad. You can easily check your balances, transfer money between accounts, pay bills online, and more using these free, bank-specific iPad apps.

STAYING ACTIVE WITH ONLINE SOCIAL NETWORKING SERVICES

If you're active on any of the online social networking sites, such as Facebook, Twitter, MySpace, or LinkedIn, you can find specialized apps that greatly expand the capabilities of these services when you access them using your tablet.

You can use an app such as Pingle to keep multiple online account statuses up to date simultaneously. Meanwhile, in addition to the official Facebook, MySpace, Twitter, and LinkedIn apps, all of which are free and available from the App Store, dozens of other apps offer added features and functionality for using these online social networking services. For example, there's Twitterific, which is ideal for managing multiple Twitter accounts.

The official Twitter app, which can be downloaded for free from within the Settings app (as opposed to the App Store), also enables you to manage multiple Twitter accounts from your iPad 2.

If you use AIM or another instant messaging service to stay in contact with people, many apps are fully compatible with these services, so you can communicate via instant messaging from your iPad. In terms of using AIM, the AIM for iPad app is available.

> **TIP** iOS 5 has been designed to work with Twitter, enabling you to send tweets to your followers from several different core apps, including Photos, Safari, Camera, YouTube, and Maps. To do this, however, you must sign in to Twitter from within the Settings app (select the Twitter option).

TRACKING YOUR CUSTOMER LOYALTY REWARDS

If you're a member of a frequent buyer or customer loyalty program at a handful of different stores that you shop at regularly, including supermarkets, pharmacies, pet stores, and restaurants, there are a handful of apps, such as AwardWallet, that help you manage these memberships without carrying around a stack of membership cards.

FINDING BUSINESSES OR SERVICES YOU NEED

Thanks to the GPS capabilities built in to your iPad, the free AroundMe app can pinpoint your exact location and then help you find whatever type of business or service you're looking for, such as the closest gas station, ATM, supermarket, restaurant, hospital, dry cleaner, or hotel. Apps such as AroundMe work with your tablet's preinstalled Maps app.

Similar to the AroundMe app is the free Yelp app. It too ties in to your tablet's GPS capabilities and can be used to find nearby businesses, services, and restaurants. Speaking of finding nearby restaurants, if you need a recommendation and directions, check out the free Urbanspoon for iPad app. It offers a nationwide database of restaurants and enables you to find selections based on location, food type, or menu prices.

There are also apps to help you obtain the latest weather forecasts and plan your travel (see Chapter 11, "Using Travel-Related Apps"). Using an app such as Moviefone, Fandango, or OneTap Movies, with a few taps on the screen, you can find the closest movie theaters to where you are, determine what movies are playing, view a list of show times, and even preorder tickets.

AMERICAN AIRLINES HD (OR ANY AIRLINE APP)

Many of the major airlines offer their own free apps that you can use to book travel and manage itineraries that relate to that specific airline. The American Airlines HD app (see Figure 11.1) also offers a handful of other features, such as the ability to set a parking reminder (so you always remember where you leave your car at the airport's parking lot), monitor your position on a flight's standby list, manage your AAdvantage frequent flier account, create and access mobile boarding passes for your flights, view terminal maps, and even play a game of Soduku to help pass the time.

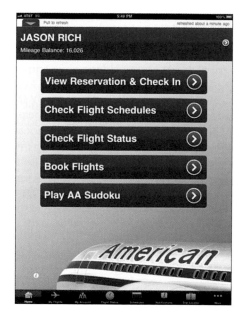

FIGURE 11.1

The American Airlines HD app is one of the more feature-packed and useful iPad-specific apps offered by a major airline.

Using this particular app, you can also wirelessly check in for flights, receive flight status notifications, check flight schedules and the status of flights, and view terminal maps for the airports through which you're traveling.

The American Airlines HD app is one of the most feature-packed of all the various airline-specific apps. And, because American Airline flights offer Wi-Fi access, you can use the app to book travel or change your itinerary while you're aboard a plane.

To find the free app that's offered by your favorite airline, visit the App Store. In the Search field, enter the airline's name.

> **TIP** Some of the "discount airlines," such as JetBlue, Southwest Airlines, and Virgin America, do not participate with the various online services used for finding cheap airfares, such as Kayak.com, Hotwire.com, or Priceline.com. Thus, if you want to find the lowest fares offered by these airlines and manage your travel itinerary, you need to use the iPad apps offered by these airlines or visit their respective websites directly.

AWARDWALLET

Many frequent fliers wind up becoming members of numerous airline frequent flier programs, as well as participating in the rewards programs offered by multiple hotel chains and rental car companies. Keeping track of membership numbers, award balances, and other details pertaining to each account can become a cumbersome task—unless, of course, you use the free AwardWallet app (or upgrade to the AwardWallet Plus app for $4.99 USD). This easy-to-use app keeps track of reward programs from airlines, hotels, rental car companies, and credit cards. The app (see Figure 11.2) is compatible with more than 350 loyalty programs. After you install the app, simply enter each of your membership account numbers and passwords once.

FIGURE 11.2

Use the AwardWallet app to manage a handful of different frequent flier and membership-based customer loyalty programs. For obvious reasons, I've blanked out my personal info from this shot, but it will give you an idea of the kind of data AwardWallet can store and track for you.

The free TripIt app offers all the features and functionality of using the TripIt.com website, but it utilizes a specially created interface for the iPad's touchscreen. Using the basic TripIt service is free; however, you can register for a premium account (for an annual fee of $49) that offers a handful of additional features that are useful to frequent business travelers.

With a TripIt Pro premium account, some of the added benefits include the capability to quickly learn about flight cancellations and be able to find alternative flights fast. You'll also receive a free membership to the Hertz #1 Club Gold, be able to track your frequent flier mile accounts, and be able to share your itineraries with others.

WEATHER CHANNEL MAX FOR iPAD

As you're preparing for your trip and deciding what to pack or determining what to do each day when you arrive at your destination, knowing the local weather forecast is extremely useful. The free Weather Channel Max for iPad app (see Figure 11.5) enables you to pick any city in the world and obtain a detailed current weather report, as well as an extended weather forecast. Plus, you can watch streaming Weather Channel television reports, view animated weather radar maps, and use other features within this colorful app as you monitor the weather in one or more cities.

FIGURE 11.5

This colorful and detailed app enables you to obtain real-time, current weather reports, and long-term forecasts for virtually any location in the world.

Use this app as you're packing to figure out the average daily temperature at your destination so you know in advance whether to pack extra sweaters, jackets, hats, and gloves, for example. There are many weather-related apps available for the iPad; however, the Weather Channel Max for iPad app is created specifically for the iPad and offers forecast information and weather reports from a reliable and well-respected source. Go to www.weather.com/services/ipad.html for more information.

ZAGAT TO GO

If you're looking for a restaurant recommendation, you can take advantage of the Zagat To Go Restaurant Guide app ($9.99 USD) or one of many other apps available that offer fully searchable restaurant listings based on location, food type, price, quality, and a number of other factors.

The Zagat To Go app combines the content from 45 of the publisher's highly respected printed city-specific guides and offers reliable reviews and ratings relating to thousands of restaurants. After you choose a restaurant, your iPad pinpoints your exact location and maps out walking or driving directions to that dining establishment. See http://mobile.zagat.com for more information.

Keep in mind that many of your favorite chain restaurants, such as Starbucks, McDonald's, Pizza Hut, Chipotle, Papa John's, Ruth's Chris Steakhouse, Outback Steakhouse, The Capital Grille, Subway, and Baja Fresh also have their own custom apps that can help you find the closest location to wherever you happen to be.

TIP   Many of the travel app developers have created both an iPad-specific and iPhone edition of their app(s). Although both versions work on your iPad, in most cases, the iPad-specific version makes better use of your tablet's display and offers more functionality. So, when possible, be sure to purchase and download the iPad edition of the app(s) you select.

12

iPAD APPS FOR PRODUCTIVITY, ORGANIZATION, AND BRAINSTORMING

You can use the Calendar app that comes preinstalled on your iPad 2 (featured in Chapter 5, "Using the Calendar App and Notification Center") to keep track of appointments. However, there are a wide range of other to-do list management programs designed exclusively to help you create lists, prioritize each item on your lists, associate individual alerts and alarms with list entries, and track your progress in completing your tasks and goals.

One of the most powerful to-do list management apps available comes preinstalled on your iPad 2 with iOS 5, and it's called Reminders. You learn all about this app and how it works with other apps later in this chapter.

From the App Store, you can find a selection of related apps designed to replace the sticky notes and loose slips of paper you might use for memos, as well as apps that can help you generate new ideas.

Especially when it come to using the iPad 2 for business-related tasks, one of the most appealing aspects of this tablet is the established collection of vertical market applications currently available. These are apps designed to handle very specialized tasks that cater to particular fields, industries, or occupations.

Using vertical market apps, you can go beyond accessing, reading, editing, and sharing documents and spreadsheets, and you can use the tablet for much more than a web-surfing tool. This chapter examines some of those possibilities.

This chapter features a small sampling of iPad-specific apps designed to enhance your productivity, improve your organization, and facilitate the generation of new ideas. As you're about to discover, the various apps available for these purposes adopt vastly different approaches to these tasks, enabling you to choose one that best fits your work habits and unique way of thinking.

> **TIP** Whenever you discover a task that you believe your iPad can be a useful tool for, either in your personal or professional life, make a point to search the App Store to find an app specifically design for that purpose. Yes, "there's an app for that." With so many apps to choose from, chances are there's an app that can serve as the perfect solution for your need.

ORGANIZING YOUR LIFE WITH LIST MANAGER APPS

There are numerous benefits to utilizing a to-do list management app on your iPad to help enhance your productivity and organization, including the following:

- You can store all of your to-do items in one place, so you can have your lists with you anytime and anywhere. After all, you probably keep your iPad with you throughout the workday.

- You can consolidate dozens of separate scrap papers or sticky notes into one well-organized list without worrying about misplacing any important information. At the same time, you get to remove clutter from your desk or workspace.

- Using any of these to-do list management apps, you can easily prioritize your tasks, associate deadlines with them, and set audible alarms or text-based alerts to remind you throughout your day to stay on track.

- As needed, you can easily import to-do items into your calendar and incorporate them into your daily, weekly, or monthly schedule.

USING THE REMINDERS APP

If you've just acquired a new iPad 2 or have recently upgraded to iOS 5, you'll discover the Reminders app that's preinstalled on your tablet. On the surface, this is a straightforward to-do list manager. However, after you start using this innovative but easy-to-use app, you'll discover it offers a plethora of interesting and useful features.

Reminders works seamlessly with Notification Center and iCloud and easily syncs with iCal or Outlook on your primary computer. Plus, you can create as many separate to-do lists as you need to properly manage your personal and professional life or various projects you're responsible for.

To make it easier for you to juggle tasks and keep track of deadlines and ongoing responsibilities, you can give every item on your to-do list a unique alarm, which can be associated with specific times, dates, or both. However, each alert can also be location-based.

Because your iPad 2 has GPS capabilities, it always knows exactly where it is. Thus, you can create a to-do list or item on a list that is associated with an alarm that alerts you when you arrive at or depart from a particular destination, such as your home, office, or a particular store.

For example, you can have your morning to-do list or call list automatically display on your iPad's screen when you arrive at work. Or, if you're maintaining a list of office supplies you need to purchase at Staples, you can have your shopping list that you created using Reminders pop up on the screen when you arrive at your local Staples office supply superstore.

In addition, you can set a reminder alarm to warn you of an upcoming deadline and then have a second alarm alert you when that deadline has arrived.

When you launch Reminders for the first time, on the left side of the screen you see the control center for this app. On the right side of the screen (shown in Figure 12.1) is a simulated sheet of lined paper, with the heading Reminders at the top.

To begin creating a single to-do list under this Reminders heading, tap the top empty line of the simulated sheet of paper or tap the plus sign button that's displayed near the upper-right corner of the screen. The iPad's virtual keyboard displays. Enter the first item to be added to your to-do list, and tap the Return key on the keyboard.

Upon tapping on the Return key, an empty checkbox displays in the margin to the left of the to-do list item you just entered (as shown in Figure 12.2). You can mark the completion of this task later by tapping this checkbox to add a check mark to it. The item then moves to the master Completed list, which is accessible from the left side of the screen under the Completed heading.

When it comes to managing your to-do list and accomplishing tasks listed within it, as you complete each listing, tap the checkbox associated with that item. This causes a check mark to appear within the checkbox, and the to-do list item is moved to the Completed section (displayed on the left side of the screen).

At any time, you can view your list of completed items by tapping the Completed heading on the left side of the screen.

MANAGING MULTIPLE TO-DO LISTS SIMULTANEOUSLY

The Edit button is in the upper-left corner of the Reminders screen. Tap this button to create a new list, delete an existing list, or change the order your lists are displayed on the left side of the screen.

To create a new list, tap the Create New List option. You can create a list to be stored on your iPad or one that is automatically sent to and stored on iCloud. As soon as you tap one of the Create New List options, the iPad's virtual keyboard displays, and you can enter a name or title for the new list (see Figure 12.7).

FIGURE 12.7

In Edit mode, you can create a new list, delete entire lists, or change the order of lists.

Also while in Edit mode, you can delete a list by tapping the red-and-white circular icon with a negative sign displayed in it that is associated with the list you want to delete. Or, to change the order of your lists, place your finger on the icon that looks like three horizontal lines, and drag it upward or downward. To exit Edit mode, tap the Done icon in the upper-left corner of the screen.

When the List button that is displayed near the top-left corner of the screen is selected, the left side of the Reminders screen lists the various list names, enabling you to view any of them with a single tap. However, when you tap the Date button that's displayed to the immediate right of the List button, the left side of the Reminders screen is replaced with month-by-month calendars. You can tap a specific date to view upcoming deadlines or due dates associated with specific to-do list items.

> **TIP** To quickly find items within any of your to-do lists, tap the Search Reminders field displayed in the upper-left portion of the screen, and then use the virtual keyboard to enter any text that is associated with what you're looking for.

After you get into the habit of entering all of your to-do list items, upcoming deadlines, or various other tidbits of information into the Reminders app, you quickly discover it can be used to manage many different types of information in your personal and professional life. Chances are you'll quickly find that Reminders, when used with Notification Center, iCloud, and Calendar, is a wonderfully powerful to-do list management tool that's extremely versatile and customizable to meet your needs and work habits.

OTHER HELPFUL LIST MANAGEMENT APPS

Each of the following to-do list management apps enables you to view your lists using an intuitive but unique graphic interface, so you can color-code lists or individual items, plus view them in a variety of formats on your iPad's screen. In many cases, you can print your lists directly from your tablet or share them with others.

2DO

2Do ($6.99 USD) is a practical to-do list manager. As you create each of your to-do list items, you can assign deadlines and alarms, have them also appear within your calendar, and prioritize them as you go.

You can sync individual items or entire lists with your PC or Mac email them to others, tweet them, password-protect them for privacy, and incorporate them with text, photos, graphics, URLs, and audio clips as attachments. You also can associate individual to-do items with GPS map locations, enabling you to obtain maps, find directions, and utilize other features built in to your iPad's Maps app.

2Do's user interface (see Figure 12.8) is easy to navigate and is customizable, so you can display all of your most important information at once. Simply tap an item to view all content associated with it. Managing multiple lists and projects, each with numerous individual items, is a simple and straightforward process.

FIGURE 12.8

The 2Do app is one of many to-do list management apps created specifically for the iPad.

You sort, search, and prioritize items or entire lists using a simple, onscreen drag-and-drop method, which enables you to navigate to and access information quickly with a few taps of your finger.

This inexpensive app can help you juggle a wide range of responsibilities, tasks, or tidbits of information; stay organized; and more easily plan for upcoming deadlines. It's highly customizable, so the app adjusts to your work habits and needs.

GOODREADER FOR iPAD

Many of the apps featured in this chapter are used to create to-do lists or document your ideas using what starts off as some type of virtual blank canvas. GoodReader for iPad ($4.99 USD) is a brainstorming tool, but it enables you to import almost any type of document (such as a PDF document, a Word or Pages file, or a saved web page) and then use a collection of colorful virtual markers and tools to add handwritten notes, comments, ideas, and feedback that get overlaid on the document you're reviewing and annotating.

> **TIP** As you're reviewing and annotating a document using GoodReader, you can use touch-screen finger motions to scroll up, down, left, or right. You can also zoom in or zoom out on specific areas of a page. You can perform text searches or utilize hyperlinks within a document to easily navigate around the app. In addition, you can encrypt and password-protect documents.

Using this app, you can import digital versions of books, manuals, magazines, reports, or other documents and view them on your tablet's screen. As you're reading, you can easily add drawings, handwritten notes (entered directly onto the iPad's screen with your finger or an optional stylus), incorporate typed text (entered using the virtual keyboard), and other content. You also can highlight text, add virtual sticky notes to the document, or add text underlines or strikeout text.

After you've marked up a document, it's possible to wirelessly share it with others using MobileMe, iDisk, DropBox, or a handful of other cloud-based online file-sharing services.

GoodReader (see Figure 12.9) is a powerful and versatile tool for reviewing and annotating documents, and you can easily share ideas or edits that relate to those documents with others. Thus, it becomes a perfect tool for collaborating and brainstorming. Because GoodReader accepts PDF files, these documents can include full-color graphics and photos as well as traditional text.

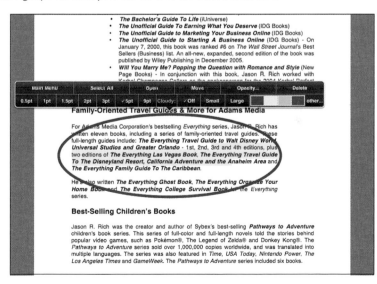

FIGURE 12.9

Using the GoodReader app, you can annotate documents and write down or draw your ideas or comments on the page as you're reading.

GOTASKS

The free GoTasks app is designed for use with a Google App account. It's a basic to-do list manager that utilizes a traditional outline format on the tablet's screen.

After creating each master list, add headings, as well as an unlimited number of subheadings, and then assign separate priorities, deadlines, and alarms to each item. You can also sort items by date, title, or status and color-code them to quickly see which items on your list are due, overdue, or pending.

Because this is an iPad-specific app, you can use various onscreen finger motions to quickly add items or move them around on the screen. You can share items or entire lists with others and wirelessly sync with your Google Apps account.

IDEAWALLETS

The IdeaWallets app ($5.99 USD) is much more than a basic text-based to-do list manager. It's capable of helping a user brainstorm, organize ideas, manage entire projects, or juggle numerous to-do lists simultaneously.

IdeaWallets (shown in Figure 12.10) enables you to create virtual index cards on the iPad's screen. Each card can contain text, photos, graphics, voice memos (sound clips), sketches, or elements created using other apps and imported into IdeaWallets (using the iOS Select, Copy, and Paste commands). You can color-code cards as you create them, and cards can contain information on both their virtual fronts and backs.

You can name and date each virtual card. In addition, cards can include a text-based description, be associated with a project, and tagged with related keywords for easy reference. You can group individual cards so that you can organize them into projects and later reorganize or prioritize them as deadlines or objectives change.

The user interface of IdeaWallets is visually impressive, yet surprisingly simple and intuitive.

FIGURE 12.10

The IdeaWallets app offers yet another solution for managing a vast amount of information that's broken down into notes, individual ideas, or to-do list items.

INDEX CARD

On the surface, Index Card ($2.99 USD) looks like a simplistic app. It transforms your iPad's screen into a corkboard and then enables you to create simulated index cards that you can place on the board. However, the app offers a lot of extra features and functions that make it a powerful to-do list manager, as well as a comprehensive project-management tool.

For example, you can capture ideas, notes, or to-do items on individual virtual index cards (covering both sides of the card with text-based content), color-code the cards themselves, arrange them in any order on your corkboard, and edit the cards at any time.

You can use each card to represent one item or task within a to-do list, which you can then prioritize by moving your cards around on the corkboard display or by assigning different colors to them. This app is also useful for storyboarding a concept.

With the Index Card app (see Figure 12.11), you can easily create multiple virtual corkboards to manage different projects or keep everything on the same board but utilize many index cards. From within the app, you can email individual index cards to others or copy your entire corkboard (including all cards) and send it to your desktop or laptop computer using the iTunes sync process.

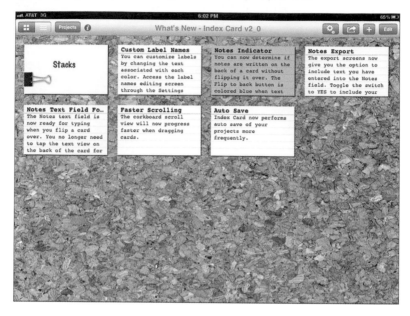

FIGURE 12.11

Index Card is yet another example of an information management app that can help you keep track of and organize notes, to-do items, ideas, and other tidbits of information.

Index Card does more than create and manage to-do lists; it's also ideal for outlining text-based content and organizing projects, brainstorming, and gathering research notes.

INFINOTE

Designed specifically for the iPad, the Infinote app ($2.99 USD) transforms your iPad's screen into a virtual corkboard (or a series of separate onscreen corkboards) onto which you can place an unlimited number of color-coded virtual sticky notes. On each sticky note you can add text (using any font, color, or type size) plus utilize a library of more than 100 graphic symbols. You can color-code individual notes and the corkboard background for easy visual reference.

You can associate each sticky note on your board with a deadline and alert or alarm. One nice feature of this app is that each virtual corkboard is not limited by the size of your iPad's screen. It can scroll infinitely in any direction (up, down, left, or right), so you can have dozens or hundreds of individual sticky notes placed on each board, positioned anywhere, and move them around freely using your finger.

You can keep notes separate or group them together. You also can create separate boards to manage different lists, projects, or assignments. The app is highly customizable, so you're not restricted by how you display or position the sticky notes as you create or organize them on the screen. As a result, you can use the Infinote app (see Figure 12.12) as a visual to-do list or a versatile organizational, project-management, or brainstorming tool.

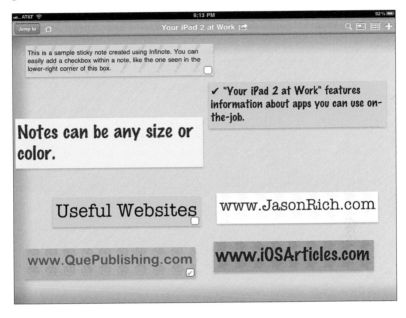

FIGURE 12.12
Infinote serves as a corkboard onto which you can post an unlimited number of color-coded virtual sticky notes, each of which can represent an idea or to-do list item.

You can also export individual notes or your entire board into a PDF file (or a .PNG or .JPG graphic) for easy sharing. If you connect your iPad to an LCD projector, television set, or HD monitor, Infinote can be a useful brainstorming tool for use in a group meeting.

OMNI OUTLINER

If you tend to organize your thoughts using structured outlines, Omni Outliner ($19.99 USD) is a powerful but highly intuitive app that enables you to document your ideas using a traditional outline format. However, you can customize the format in terms of its layout and color scheme. In addition to using text in your outlines, you can associate photos with the outline as you create headings and unlimited subheads.

You can manage an unlimited number of outlines and expand or collapse outlines as you're viewing them on the screen. Each outline can incorporate checkboxes, formatted and numbered lists, or pop-up lists. As part of any heading or subhead, you can attach a separate note or link attachments (such as photos) to it.

In addition to being able to email your outlines to others or share them wirelessly using any of several compatible cloud-based online file-sharing services, you can transfer outlines between the iPad edition of Omni Outliner and the Mac version (sold separately, $39.95 USD for the standard version or $69.95 USD for the professional version).

This is a useful tool for managing to-do lists, formulating ideas, or managing projects in a structured and organized way that's visually familiar.

THINGS

As opposed to calling itself a to-do list manager, Things is an "intuitive task manager," with three distinctly different but fully compatible versions available for the iPhone ($9.99 USD), iPad ($19.99 USD), and Mac ($49.95 USD). Thus, your projects, outlines, to-do lists, and related files can easily be transferred between devices wirelessly or via iTunes sync.

Each version of Things has the same core functionality but is scaled to work well on the device it was designed for, taking into account the size of the screen, for example.

The iPad-specific Things app enables you to manage multiple lists or projects simultaneously, keeping track of each item and the item's associated deadlines. Thus, it becomes easy to take a massive project, divide it into smaller, more achievable goals, set deadlines for each goal, monitor your progress, adjust priorities as you go, and work toward your primary objectives while keeping yourself and your team well organized.

One of the most appealing aspects of Things is that the user interface is simple. Each screen is intuitive and easy to navigate, so you can focus on creating, managing, prioritizing, and tracking your projects and lists, as opposed to figuring out how to work the app itself.

UPAD

Building upon the virtual notepad or bulletin board with sticky note concept, the slick-looking UPad app ($4.99 USD) serves as a memo pad onto which you can "handwrite" notes, memos, and drawings directly onto the iPad's screen. It's designed to look and feel like a traditional notepad (see Figure 12.13). You write or draw on the touch screen using your finger or an optional stylus (such as the Wacom Bamboo Stylus, which is featured in Chapter 19, "Must-Have Accessories").

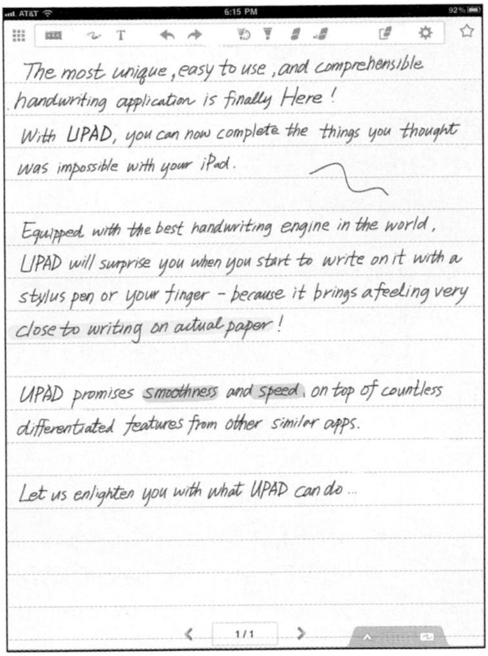

FIGURE 12.13

The UPad app nicely re-creates the look and feel of a traditional notepad and writing utensil, giving you the freedom to handwrite or draw your ideas on the tablet's screen.

When used as a virtual notebook, you can select from many different paper styles and virtual writing utensils. You can add colors and simulate the appearance of writing in pencil, pen, marker, or highlighter. You can make your iPad look like a chalkboard, lined notepad, graph paper, music paper, a storyboard, or colorful stationery onto which you literally write your notes or ideas.

CAUTION When "writing" on your tablet's screen, use your finger or an optional stylus that is designed for this purpose, or you could accidentally scratch the iPad's screen. In other words, don't use a real pen or pencil to "write" when using an app that accepts onscreen handwriting or drawing.

In addition to the handful of paper templates, UPad also has a Weekly Planner and Monthly Planner template built in, so you can manage your schedule in a freestyle and creative way.

Another way to use this app is to import a PDF file containing the contents of a book, magazine, report, photo, drawing, or document and then annotate it by writing or drawing on the screen. Your entries are superimposed onto the PDF document you're viewing.

The versatility of UPad extends to how you can view your photos. This app enables you to view the digital images stored on your tablet so that you can associate comments or annotations to them.

UPad is very much a creativity and brainstorming tool for people who are more comfortable writing, composing, drawing, or documenting their thoughts and ideas in a freehand style on traditional paper, as opposed to typing on a keyboard and using a structured format.

You can export anything you "create" using this app into a PDF file or as a .PNG graphic. You also can email files to others from within the app. Alternatively, you can connect your iPad to an LCD projector, television set, or HD monitor (using an optional cable) to use this app during group brainstorming sessions.

You'll quickly discover that the UPad app is extremely versatile, customizable, and powerful while still being extremely easy to use.

> **TIP** UPad is one of many apps that offers a free, scaled-down version that you can download from the App Store and try firsthand before purchasing it. The free edition of UPad is called UPad Lite.

USING THE iPAD IN VERTICAL MARKETS

According to SearchCIO.com, "A vertical market is a particular industry or group of enterprises in which similar products or services are developed and marketed using similar methods (and to whom goods and services can be sold). Broad examples of vertical markets are: insurance, real estate, banking, heavy manufacturing, retail, transportation, hospitals, and government."

Vertical market apps are designed for use with the iPad and targeted to specific vertical markets. This is slightly different from general business apps, such as word processor or spreadsheet programs, which are considered "horizontal market" apps (meaning they cater to the needs of many industries).

As developers are creating vertical market apps to cater to the unique needs of particular industries, Apple and other third-party app programmers are developing high-level security and encryption technology for the iPad that ensures confidential data cannot be compromised when the tablet is used to remotely access a company's network, for example.

By combining these cutting-edge security measures (described more in Chapter 18, "Protecting Your iPad 2 and Its Data") with the highly specialized, vertical market apps being released for the iPad, your iPad 2 offers a unique set of tools that can easily and inexpensively be implemented by people working in a wide range of different fields.

> **TIP**   The easiest way to find vertical market applications that have already been developed for your industry or occupation is to visit the App Store. Using the Search field, enter your occupation or industry, such as medical, plumber, electrician, lawyer, writer, photographer, musician, investment banker, or dentist.
>
> You can also enter a keyword or search phrase associated with the task you want the vertical market app to handle, such as medical imaging, medical practice management, retail sales tools, retail cash register, car sales, electrical engineering, stock portfolio management, investing, or time billing for lawyers.

When deployed in the field, the iPad can be used to give employees access to important files stored on your corporate network, and it can be used to streamline how employees record and track vital business information by transforming traditional paper-based workflows into more automated processes. All types of paper-based forms, for example, can be replaced with an iPad app.

You can also use vertical market apps to perform highly specialized mathematical calculations or to showcase information in a particular way. For example, there are apps designed for salespeople that allow for an interactive, branded product catalog to be created for a specific product line, which can then be used as an impressive sales tool when making in-person sales calls and presentations. The same app can be used to enter orders, which are immediately sent to the home office for processing.

Depending on your occupation, the possibilities for how the iPad can be used are limitless, and new applications are constantly being developed to further enhance the way Apple's tablet caters to the vertical market needs of today's businesses.

To read articles from a variety of publications about how companies have implemented the use of iPads, visit www.apple.com/ipad/business.

Getting back to the concept of transforming traditional paper-based workflows into more automated processes, one of the easiest and most cost-effective ways to do this, without incurring the cost of having a custom app developed for your business, is to utilize the FileMaker Pro (www.FileMaker.com) database management software for a PC, Mac, or network. You can use this software to create and implement a customized database for accessing documents or completing specialized forms.

Then, using the FileMaker Go app, your custom-designed FileMaker Pro database becomes readily accessible from an iPad using a 3G or Wi-Fi Internet connection. Companies in many industries have discovered ways to utilize this database technology with the FileMaker Go app to streamline paper-based tasks and gain remote but secure access to databases stored on a network.

For small businesses, the ability to perform a wide range of specialized or industry-specific financial management and bookkeeping tasks is possible by combining the popular QuickBooks Online Plus with Payroll service with Intuit Software's iPhone/iPad app. This online-based service and app combo enables small business operators to remotely handle tasks such as creating business reports, tracking sales and expenses, printing checks, tracking payments, accepting credit card payments, managing payroll, creating estimates, creating and managing invoices, entering and managing bills, tracking inventory, handling time tracking, and much more—all for less than $75.00 (USD) per month. Less costly monthly plans, with slightly different functionality, are also available.

> **TIP** Also available for the iPad are digital editions of industry-oriented magazines and publications, which can help you stay on the cutting edge of industry-related trends and news.

TRANSFORMING HOW DOCTORS PRACTICE MEDICINE

When it comes to the truly innovative implementation of the iPad within a specific industry, the medical profession has been affected most. In fact, according to an article published on CNBC.com, "Analysts at Chilmark Research estimate 22 percent of doctors in the U.S. were using iPads by the end of 2010. In February 2011, four out of five doctors surveyed by health marketing company Aptilon said they planned to buy an iPad this year."

GE Healthcare, which provides doctors and hospitals with cutting-edge technology, software, and equipment to meet a wide range of specialized needs, has developed iPad apps to work with some of its software and technology.

For example, GE Healthcare's Centricity Advance is a fully integrated electronic medical record (EMR), medical practice management, and patient portal solution that, according to the company, addresses the challenges facing today's small practices and primary care physicians. This software consolidates medical records online. When doctors use Centricity Advance with an iPad they have unprecedented and speedy access to patient records and information from virtually anywhere there's an Internet connection.

NOTE At the Mobile World Congress held in February 2011, the results of studies were released that indicate that heavy adoption of the iPad will come from the healthcare industry and that sales of tablets to this industry will reach $63 million by 2013.

Jim Corrigan, vice president and general manager of GE Healthcare IT, explained, "GE has some of the best solutions in the world, and we now have the mobile platforms to extend the use of those solutions to help customers leverage them even further. We have made something easy to adopt while still ensuring an extremely powerful tool. The possibilities for rolling out iPad applications to the physician community are truly exciting."

Mike Friguletto, vice president of GE Healthcare's Centricity Advance business added, "By accessing our electronic medical record systems on the iPad, doctors are able to view the most important patient information and enter clinical notes from the patient appointment room, from home, on the road—wherever makes the most sense and is most convenient."

Meanwhile, when it comes to reading ECG images, GE Healthcare reports that the tiniest change in a patient's heartbeat can indicate the presence or absence of a heart condition. With the introduction of the GE Healthcare MUSE Cardiology Information System data now being made available on the iPad via AirStrip Cardiology, cardiologists can now see these small changes in great detail.

This single vertical market iPad app is enabling clinicians to move away from faxed pictures or blurry cell phone images, and it helps detect .5-millimeter differences, which ultimately give physicians the information needed to help speed accurate clinical diagnosis of heart conditions without needing to leave the patient's presence.

This cutting-edge technology combined with the iPad app is now being used at major hospitals around the world to help doctors quickly determine the best treatment paths for their patients and to save lives.

GE Healthcare isn't alone in pioneering highly specialized apps for the iPad targeted to the medical profession. Using Citrix Receiver for iPad, for example, healthcare workers can access their electronic medical record system securely, giving them quick and easy access to patient data, including X-ray images, as well as other radiology imaging results using an iPad that's connected to the Web. This same app and back-end technology (Citrix XenApp, www.citrix.com) can also be adapted for use in a wide range of other industries that require wireless access to a company's secure network.

According to the Citrix website, "Citrix XenApp 6 introduces exciting new enhance-ments for advanced management and scalability, a rich multimedia experience over any network and self-service applications with universal device support from PC to Mac to Smartphone."

To learn more about this technology and how it can be used with Apple's iPhone or iPad, the Citrix website offers a free 28-minute video, which you can watch at www.citrix.com/tv/#videos/1622.

CHANGING THE PRACTICE OF LAW

As the Apple iPad is quickly changing how doctors practice medicine, this same tablet, when used with totally different vertical market software, is also dramati-cally altering how many other professions perform specialized work-related tasks.

Some of the country's largest law firms have implemented the iPad, providing a tablet to each of their lawyers along with a traditional desktop or laptop computer. Lawyers are using the iPad for numerous tasks, including logging client time and billable hours, as well as for reviewing and annotating PDF files (using more gen-eral business-related apps, such as DocsToGo and Goodreader).

For example, storing digital versions of massive case files on an iPad greatly reduces the amount of paperwork lawyers have to lug between their offices and the courtroom when trying cases. Plus, using the iPad makes it easier to quickly locate specific documents or tidbits of information within those documents during a trial.

One vertical market app being used by an increasing number of attorneys is called The Deponent ($9.99 USD). It's designed to assist legal professionals in drafting questions when preparing for a deposition, as well as for organizing exhibits.

The Deponent app contains a database of more than 150 questions that are orga-nized by category; you can also enter customized questions. You can modify the order of the question list and add customized text for specific witnesses. Then you can link questions to exhibits.

Another indication of the adoption of iPads by lawyers is the steadily increasing number of paid subscriptions to the digital (iPad) edition of *The American Lawyer* magazine that have been downloaded to date from the App Store.

TIP   To discover some of the ways lawyers are using the iPad and what apps are being used, read the Court Technology and Trial Presentation blog (http://trial-technology.blogspot.com).

THE iPAD IS MAKING ITS WAY INTO MANY INDUSTRIES

While the iPad is still a relatively new technology, it has already had a tremendous effect on many industries aside from the medical field and legal profession. However, what we've seen to date in terms of innovative uses of the tablet in the workplace is still in its infancy.

As time goes on, companies in thousands of different industries will continue to realize the potential benefits of using the iPad to enhance communication, productivity, and efficiency. For example, companies will find new ways to streamline how various tasks are performed to reduce or eliminate traditional paperwork.

To stay current in whatever field you work in, one added responsibility you now have is keeping tabs on emerging trends and newly released tools available to you and your business. Hundreds of new vertical market apps for the iPad, catering to the needs of many different occupations, industries, and fields, are being released every week.

At the same time, companies are pioneering new ways to utilize the iPad with vertical market apps and other existing technologies, which further enhances the tablet's potential. Chances are, with a small amount of research on your part, you'll discover vertical market apps available right now that cater to your industry or occupation. However, you can bet that in the near future, many more will most likely be introduced.

IN THIS CHAPTER

■ Introduction to the FaceTime app and how to use it

■ How to use the Messages app to send/receive text messages with iMessage

■ Using the Skype app to make and receive calls from your iPad

13

CONDUCTING VIDEOCONFERENCES AND VIRTUAL MEETINGS

One of the most significant improvements between the original iPad and the iPad 2 is the introduction of the front- and rear-facing cameras. With the addition of the cameras and the FaceTime app, real-time videoconferencing between iPad 2, iPhone 4, iPod touch, and Mac users has become possible.

Mac users can download the FaceTime software ($.99 USD) from the online-based Mac App Store. It comes preinstalled on the iPad 2, iPhone 4 (or later models), and iPod touch.

> **NOTE** The FaceTime app works with an iPad 2, but only when a Wi-Fi Internet connection is available. Videoconferencing is not possible using a 3G Internet connection, even if you have an iPad 2 Wi-Fi + 3G model.

FaceTime utilizes the front- or rear-facing camera built in to your iPad 2, along with the tablet's built-in microphone and

speaker, and provides for a true videoconferencing experience that enables you to both see and hear the person you're communicating with.

You can use the FaceTime app to more easily collaborate on projects with co-workers who are located in different locations, stay in touch with friends, or actually see your young kids as you say goodnight to them whenever you're away on a business trip or working late at the office.

NOTE Another way to communicate with fellow iOS 5 device users is via text messaging through Apple's new iMessage service and the Messages app, which now comes preinstalled on the iPad 2. You find out how to use this text messaging app, and read about the pros and cons it offers compared to other text messaging services, later in this chapter.

As an iPad 2 user, the first time you launch the FaceTime app, you need to set up a free Apple ID account or enter your existing Apple ID username and password.

You are asked to enter an email address to be associated with your FaceTime account. This serves as your unique FaceTime identifier (which acts just like a phone number), so others can initiate connections with you when you both have FaceTime running on your devices. Likewise, if you want to call another FaceTime user with this app, you must know the other person's email address (the one associated with FaceTime) or iPhone phone number.

After you complete this set-up process (it takes less than a minute), as long as you have FaceTime running on your tablet and it's connected to the Internet through a Wi-Fi connection (and you remain within the Wi-Fi hotspot's radius), you are able to initiate or receive calls and participate in videoconferences.

TIP Users of FaceTime on an iPad 2, iPod touch, or Mac utilize an Apple ID as their identifier when making connections using this app or software. However, if you're making contact with an iPhone 4 user via FaceTime, you should use the iPhone's mobile phone number.

USING FACETIME FOR VIDEOCONFERENCING

To launch the FaceTime app, first look near the upper-left corner of your iPad's Home Screen and make sure the tablet is connected to the Web using a Wi-Fi connection (as shown in Figure 13.1). The Wi-Fi signal strength icon is displayed to the right of your wireless data provider's 3G signal bars if you're using an iPad 2 Wi-Fi + 3G model. (The Wi-Fi signal icon is displayed in the extreme upper-right corner of the screen if you're using an iPad 2 Wi-Fi Only model.)

FIGURE 13.1

For FaceTime to work, you must be connected to the Internet using a Wi-Fi connection. Check to make sure a Wi-Fi signal is available by looking at the upper-left corner of your iPad 2's screen.

If no Wi-Fi connection is present, you don't see signal bars. If you're in Airplane mode, you see a tiny airplane-shaped icon in the upper-left corner of the screen.

To turn on Wi-Fi and establish an Internet connection, launch the Settings app, and tap the Wi-Fi option. Then, on the right side of the screen, select the Wi-Fi network you want to join. Available networks are displayed under the Choose a Network heading.

While in Settings, on the left side of the screen, tap the FaceTime option to turn on the FaceTime app and allow your email address to be shared with people you call. You can also set up one or more email addresses at which you can be reached via FaceTime.

After your iPad 2 is connected to a Wi-Fi network, launch the FaceTime app by tapping its app icon from the Home screen. If no Wi-Fi connection is present, the app doesn't launch and you see an error message that states, "FaceTime Unavailable. Turn on Wi-Fi to use FaceTime."

As soon as the FaceTime app is launched, the iPad's front-facing camera turns on, and you should see yourself on your iPad's screen. On the right side of the screen is a window requesting that you sign in with your Apple ID username and password. Use the virtual keyboard to enter this information, and then tap the Sign In button. Alternatively, you can tap the Create New Account option to set up a free Apple ID account from within the FaceTime app.

You're now ready to initiate or receive FaceTime calls and participate in a video-conference via the Web. Displayed near the lower-right corner of this app screen are three command buttons: Favorites, Recents, and Contacts (see Figure 13.2).

FIGURE 13.2

After FaceTime is running on your iPad, you see three command buttons near the lower-right corner of the screen.

CREATING A FACETIME FAVORITES LIST

A Favorites list within FaceTime is a list you can customize to include the people with whom you plan to FaceTime videoconference the most. In essence, this Favorites option serves as a one-touch speed dial list.

To add a contact, tap the plus sign in the upper-right corner of the Favorites window, and then select people from your established contacts database.

In the Contacts entry for each person, if the person is an iPhone 4 (or later) user, be sure to associate the mobile phone number with the iPhone label as opposed to the mobile phone label. Doing so helps the FaceTime app easily identify and connect with the person.

> **NOTE** See Chapter 6, "Working with the Contacts App," for more on working with Contacts entries in your database.

USING FACETIME'S AUTOMATIC RECENTS LIST

When you tap the Recents icon while using FaceTime, you see a list of people with whom you've already communicated using FaceTime. Tap any of the contacts in this list to videoconference again with the person. Obviously, the first time you launch this app, your Recents list is empty.

If this is the first time you're using the FaceTime app, this window is empty except for the All and Missed tabs displayed at the top of the window.

After you begin using the app, the All tab displays all FaceTime videoconferences you've participated in, as well as any incoming missed calls. Tap the Missed tab to see a list of only the incoming FaceTime calls you didn't answer.

CHOOSING PREFERRED FACETIME CONTACTS

The Contacts icon that's displayed near the lower-right corner of the FaceTime screen enables you to select any person listed in your Contacts database to call using this app.

Remember that FaceTime only works with other iPad 2, iPhone 4 (or later), iPod touch, or Mac users. iPad 2, iPhone 4 (or later), and iPod touch users must also have access to a Wi-Fi Internet connection; Mac users must have a high-speed Internet connection for the FaceTime software to work. Also, when calling another iPad 2, iPod touch, or Mac FaceTime user, the FaceTime app or software must be running on that person's device so that he can accept a call. As long as the person's iPhone 4 (or later) is turned on and connected to the Internet (via Wi-Fi), he can automatically accept incoming FaceTime calls.

To initiate a call with someone who also has FaceTime installed and operating on her computer or device, select that person from your Contacts list and tap on her email address or iPhone phone number that she uses to register with FaceTime. If a connection can be made, a FaceTime icon automatically appears next to her name within the FaceTime app (see Figure 13.3).

FIGURE 13.3

Next to a FaceTime contact's name, a FaceTime icon appears if the contact has FaceTime running and is available to videoconference.

When you initiate a call, at the bottom center of the screen, the FaceTime With message and the person's name are displayed. Next to this label is the End button, which you can tap at any time to terminate the connection.

PARTICIPATING IN A FACETIME CALL

If the person you're calling with the FaceTime app answers, your own image that was displayed in full-screen mode on the tablet's screen shrinks and is now displayed in the upper-left corner of the screen. The rest of the iPad 2's screen displays the person you're connected with using FaceTime.

> **NOTE** If you initiate a FaceTime call but the person you're calling does not answer, after a minute or so, you see the "FaceTime Unavailable. [Insert Name] is not available for FaceTime." message.

Notice that near the bottom of the screen are three command buttons: Mute, End Call, and Switch Camera. Use them for the following purposes:

- Tap the Mute button to retain the video connection but mute the iPad 2's built-in microphone, so the person you're communicating with is able to see you but not hear you.

- Tap the End Call button to terminate the FaceTime connection and promptly end the call.

- Tap the Switch Camera button to alternate between the two cameras built in to your iPad 2. The front-facing camera is facing toward you, whereas the camera on the back of the iPad shows off whatever it's pointing at.

The FaceTime app is pretty simple to use, and it is a powerful tool for video-conferencing. The best thing about using FaceTime is that it's free, and you can communicate with anyone in the world that also uses the FaceTime app or software. In other words, you never have to pay long-distance phone charges, international calling fees, or cell phone roaming charges when using FaceTime. Nor do you have to worry about using up your cell phone minutes or your monthly 3G wireless data usage allocation from your wireless data provider. Perhaps the biggest benefit to using FaceTime is that you can actually see *and* hear the person you're communicating with.

TEXT MESSAGING WITH iMESSAGE

If you use a cell phone or smartphone, such as the iPhone 4 or a BlackBerry, you're probably familiar with the concept of text messaging. Through your cell phone service provider, you can use your phone to send a private text message to a recipient's phone. This text message can include a photo, short video clip, or another data attachment. Within a second or two after sending your text message, the recipient receives the message and can reply to it, which enables you to conduct a text-based conversation.

The primary drawback to text messaging via your cell phone is that your cell phone service provider typically charges extra for this feature or allows only a predetermined number of text messages to be sent or received as part of your service plan per month.

With the release of iOS 5, Apple has introduced its iMessage service, which allows any iOS device that's connected to the Web via a Wi-Fi or 3G connection to send and receive text messages using the Messages app that now comes preinstalled on the iPad 2.

iMessage has some pros and cons. On the plus side, this is a totally free service. You can send and receive as many text messages as you want. On the negative side, this service currently works only with other iOS 5 devices. Eventually, software or apps might be developed for PCs and Macs, or other types of wireless devices, so they too can communicate using the iMessage service. For the time being, though, iMessage only supports iPad, iPad 2, iPhone 3Gs, iPhone 4, and iPod touch users.

Within a text message composed and sent via your iPad 2, you can include basic text or attach a photo, short video clip, map location, or information from your Contacts database.

Like any text messaging app, Messages for use with iMessage enables you to participate in multiple text message "conversations" simultaneously, but each one is kept separate. As you participate in a text-based dialogue, the text messages you send are displayed in a different color than the messages you receive from the recipient, so tracking the progression of a dialogue is easy.

Before you start using the Messages app, launch Settings and tap the Messages option that's displayed on the left side of the screen. On the right side of the screen, turn on the iMessage virtual switch. Now you can customize the settings.

To initiate an iMessage conversation or receive text messages, you must set up an email address that is associated with your iMessage account. This email address serves as your unique identifier (like a phone number). You can use your Apple ID or any other existing email address. The email address you plan to use must be added to the Receive At option within the Messages screen of the Settings app.

When you launch the Messages app, you can compose a new outgoing text message or respond to an incoming message using the iPad's virtual keyboard. To create and send a new text message, fill in the To field in the New Message window (see Figure 13.4).

FIGURE 13.4

To create a new text message, begin by filling in the To field of the New Message window.

In the To field, you can manually enter the email address that the recipient has associated with iMessage. Alternatively, you can select this information from your Contacts database by typing the recipient's name in the To field and then selecting the appropriate email address from the Contacts listing.

To manually search your Contacts database, tap the blue-and-white plus sign that's located to the right of the To field.

After filling in the To field, tap the empty Subject window, which is just above the virtual keyboard (refer to Figure 13.4). Using the keyboard, type your text-based message.

To attach a digital photo or short movie clip to the outgoing text message, tap the camera icon to the left of the Subject window and select the Take Photo or Video option or the Choose Existing option.

If you select Take Photo or Video, the iPad's Camera app launches. If you select the Choose Existing option, the Photos app launches and you can choose a digital photo or video clip that's stored on your iPad.

After composing your message, tap the blue-and-white Send icon to send the message via the Internet to its intended recipient.

> **NOTE**   To use the Messages app to send and receive text messages via Apple's iMessage service, your iPad 2 must have access to the Internet via a Wi-Fi or 3G connection.

When the recipient of your message responds, her incoming message is displayed in the window on the right side of the screen if her conversation is open. Otherwise, an incoming message alert displays on the left side of the screen (as well as within the Notification Center window). You can tap each conversation listed on the left side of the screen, one at a time, to read incoming messages from different people and respond to them.

If you send a message to someone who isn't currently online, the message is received when he again accesses his Messages app or uses his iOS device to access the Web. Likewise, when you turn on your iPad and reconnect it to the Web, your missed incoming messages are displayed in the Notification Center window and on the left side of the Messages app screen when you relaunch the app.

iMessage offers a free way for you to communicate with friends, co-workers, or relatives via text message who also use iOS devices. At this point, however, iMessage is not compatible with other text messaging services offered by AT&T Wireless, Verizon, or other cell phone service providers, or with the Instant Messaging functionality offered by AIM, Windows Live Messenger, or Facebook.

> **NOTE**   For more information about the new Notification Center in iOS 5, see Chapter 5, "Using the Calendar App and Notification Center."

PARTICIPATING IN VIRTUAL MEETINGS FROM ANYWHERE

If your company uses virtual meeting software, such as GoToMeeting or WebEx, there are apps that enable you to participate in these meetings using your iPad from anywhere an Internet connection is available (such as from your home, hotel room, poolside at a resort, or from a client's office.)

Web conferences or virtual meetings involve using the Internet to connect people at different locations, enabling them to talk while simultaneously sharing information on their computer screens in real time. This capability has changed the way many companies do business.

This extremely affordable technology is actively being used by companies of all sizes and in many different industries for a wide range of purposes, such as the following:

- Boosting employee productivity by keeping people connected.
- Encouraging people to collaborate on projects, even if they're located in different locations.
- Increasing sales by transforming traditional sales calls into highly engaging interactive presentations.
- Reducing training costs by hosting live, interactive training sessions (or webinars) via the Web rather than in person.
- Cutting travel expenses and travel time and enabling people to see and hear each other while sharing content on their computers (such as a PowerPoint presentation) without having to meet in person.
- Providing technical support. Clients can share their computer desktops, which enables your support team to efficiently resolve technical issues remotely.

GOTOMEETING OFFERS VIRTUAL MEETING CAPABILITIES FOR iPAD USERS

One of the pioneers in the virtual meeting field is Citrix Systems, Inc., with its GoToMeeting software for PCs and Macs. However, the company more recently launched a free iPad app that enables people to attend online-based virtual meetings that are hosted by others using GoToMeeting.

Virtual meetings that are hosted by a company using GoToMeeting or GoToWebinar are free to attend. All an attendee needs is a high-speed Internet connection and the GoToMeeting software or app running on a PC, Mac, iPad, or other device.

> **TIP** The host of a virtual meeting that utilizes GoToMeeting or GoToWebinar pays a flat monthly fee, starting at $49.00 USD per month, to host an unlimited number of meetings with up to 15 attendees each. Virtual meetings cannot be hosted from an iPad.

Attendees using a PC or Mac to participate in a meeting can utilize audioconferencing via Voice over IP (VoIP) service—using their computers' microphones and speakers—while simultaneously being able to view whatever the meeting host is showcasing on his computer screen, such as a PowerPoint presentation or a spreadsheet report. People can also collaborate on Word documents, for example.

Thanks to the GoToMeeting app for iPad, tablet users can do everything a meeting attendee using a PC or Mac can do, such as see who is presenting, who's talking at any given moment, and who else is attending the meeting.

Using the GoToMeeting app, meeting attendees can view exactly what is on the presenter's screen and simultaneously join a voice conversation via a VoIP connection (using the iPad's built-in microphone and speaker or a headset that's connected to the tablet).

> **TIP** iPad users report getting the best results when using a headset with the VoIP feature of the GoToMeeting app. However, to ensure a clear voice connection, attendees can also dial in to the meeting using a regular phone (or cell phone) while simultaneously using their iPads to view the onscreen presentation aspects of the meeting and to see who's attending. With this setup, you might experience a lag between seeing someone speak on your iPad and then hearing the voice on your phone, or vice versa. Whether the lag is scarcely noticeable or quite annoying depends on the speed and clarity of your phone and Internet connections.

The GoToMeeting app was designed to utilize some of the tablet's key features, such as its touch-screen interface, so you can zoom in on content being showcased during a meeting.

This app is ideal for mobile executives who want or need to "attend" meetings or webinars from a location outside their offices. When an attendee gets invited to a virtual meeting via email, from the iPad the user simply taps the link embedded within the invitation email to connect to a meeting and automatically launches the GoToMeeting app. From within the app the user can manually enter a meeting ID and her username to be connected to a meeting within seconds.

The GoToMeeting app is available from the App Store. However, to view a free demo on how GoToMeeting works on an iPad, visit www.gotomeeting.com/iPad. This app enables the user to attend an unlimited number of meetings with anyone, anytime.

If you're a business owner, entrepreneur, or consultant and you're interested in hosting virtual meetings that can be attended by others using an iPad, PC, Mac, or another device, a free 30-day trial of the GoToMeeting service is available. After the initial trial period, your business can sign up for a fee-based month-to-month or annual contract.

ANOTHER VIRTUAL MEETING OPTION: THE WEBEX PLATFORM

In addition to utilizing Citrix's GoToMeeting software and iPad app, similar functionality is provided by Cisco Systems via its popular WebEx virtual meeting solution (www.webex.com). For businesses, consultants, or entrepreneurs who already use WebEx to host meetings, the company offers a free iPad app that enables people to attend virtual meetings from their Apple mobile devices. Users connect via a Wi-Fi hotspot or through a 3G web connection (provided by a wireless data provider).

> **CAUTION** Participating in a virtual meeting requires a significant amount of wireless data use and quickly uses your monthly wireless data allocation from your wireless data provider. To avoid surcharges for additional wireless data use, consider using a Wi-Fi connection to participate in virtual meetings using the WebEx app.

To schedule and host a meeting using Cisco's WebEx, the host must be using the WebEx software from a Mac or PC and be a paid subscriber to the service. Pricing starts at $49.00 USD per month to host an unlimited number of meetings that can be attended by up to 25 people. A free 14-day trial of the service (for hosting purposes) is available.

Attending meetings, however, is free and does not require a WebEx membership (but the free WebEx software for the PC, Mac, iPhone, or iPad is required). You can download WebEx for iPad free from the App Store.

> **NOTE** For a company that already uses GoToMeeting or WebEx in-house, allowing employees, customers, and/or clients to attend virtual meetings or web-inars from an iPad means attendees don't need to be tied to a desk or office to participate. This makes it much easier to schedule meetings with groups of people and avoid timing conflicts, plus it reduces the number of absentees because the attendees can participate from wherever they happen to be.
>
> To find other apps that work with other web-based virtual meeting platforms, visit the App Store. In the search field enter "web meetings" as the search phrase. Alternatively, you can enter the name of the virtual meeting software or service your company uses, such as Fuze Meeting.

MAKING AND RECEIVING PHONE CALLS FROM YOUR iPAD WITH SKYPE

Skype is a VoIP phone service that enables you to make and receive calls over the Web (as opposed to a cellular phone network or traditional telephone landline). The Skype service is available for PCs and Macs and requires special software to transform a computer into a virtual speakerphone. With the Skype software, users can make and receive calls that originate from the Internet.

The free iPad-specific Skype app enables your tablet to act as a speakerphone to make or receive calls whenever it's connected to the Internet. The Skype app uses your iPad's built-in microphone and speaker (or headphone jack) to enable you to hear and be heard during calls.

Making unlimited Skype-to-Skype calls is always free. However, there is a very low per-minute fee to make calls to a landline or cellular telephone from your iPad using Skype. This per-minute fee is typically only pennies per minute, even if you're traveling overseas and make a call back to the United States. You can also save a fortune on international calling from the United States when making calls to any other country.

The new iPad-specific Skype app also enables the tablet to be used for videoconferencing via the Web, and it enables you to communicate with any other Skype user, regardless of what wireless mobile device or computer they're using (including PCs running Windows), as long as it's running Skype software. Skype-to-Skype videoconference calls via the Web are always free.

NOTE Although Skype calls originate from the Internet, you can make calls to (or receive calls from) any landline or cell phone. Thus, your iPad 2, when connected to the Internet via a 3G or Wi-Fi connection, is transformed into a full-featured speakerphone, complete with caller ID, conference calling, a mute button, and one-touch dialing.

Skype works much better (and with no limitations) when used with a high-speed Wi-Fi Internet connection. Using Skype with a 3G connection requires a significant amount of wireless data usage, which quickly depletes your monthly wireless data allocation from your wireless data provider or results in high international wireless data roaming fees if you use it abroad.

Through Skype, you can obtain your own unique telephone number (for an additional fee of $6.00 USD per month), which comes with call forwarding, voice mail, and other features. With your own number you can manage incoming calls whether or not Skype is activated and your iPad is connected to the Web. Thus, people are able to reach you inexpensively by dialing a local phone number regardless of where you're traveling. However, you can initiate calls without paying for a unique local phone number.

When traveling abroad, making and receiving calls on a cell phone (such as an iPhone or BlackBerry) costs anywhere from $.50 USD to $3.00 USD per minute because international roaming fees apply. With Skype, though, that same call costs just a little more than $.02 USD per minute. Alternatively, you can pay a flat fee of less than $20.00 USD per month to make and receive unlimited domestic and international calls from your iPad.

In terms of call quality, as long as you're within a 3G coverage area or Wi-Fi hotspot and your iPad has a strong Web connection, calls are crystal clear. The Skype app is easy to use, and it enables you to maintain a contact list of frequently called people; dial out using a familiar telephone touchpad display (see Figure 13.5); and maintain a detailed call history that lists incoming, outgoing, and missed calls.

If you opt to establish a paid Skype account (to have your own unique phone number or make non-Skype-to-Skype calls), setting up the account takes just minutes when you visit www.Skype.com. All charges are billed to a major credit card or debit card.

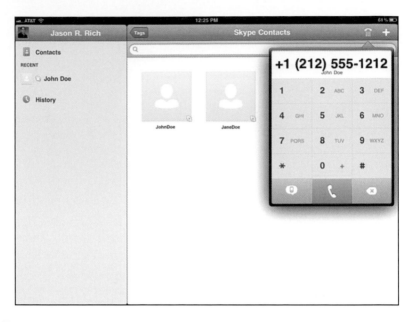

FIGURE 13.5

The Skype app offers a ton of calling features, but the app is easier to use than most smartphones or cell phones.

TIP   For added privacy when using Skype on your iPad (so people around you can't listen in on your conversations), connect wired headphones to the tablet's headset jack. You still use the tablet's built-in microphone, so the intended people hear what you're saying during calls.

Currently, the app does not work with traditional wireless Bluetooth headsets, but a special Skype wireless headset is available ($44.99 USD at http://shop.skype.com/headsets/wireless/itech-easychat-306).

FINDING AND USING NEWS AND INFORMATION APPS

It wasn't long ago that the majority of working Americans woke up, had their morning newspaper waiting at their front door, and got up to speed on current events while enjoying their morning coffee or commute to work. That same evening, they'd be home in time to watch the evening edition of the network television news.

For most people, those days are gone. The Internet now plays a prominent role in how people stay up to date on current events and major news stories. With an iPad 2 in hand, going beyond just reading text-based news headlines is easy and in-depth, but personalized, news coverage is always just a few screen taps away.

Every major television and radio news organization now has a proprietary app designed to stream content directly to iPads, whenever and wherever the tablet user happens to be. In

addition, newspaper and magazine publishers are making digital editions of their printed publications available to tablet users. Some of the Internet's own news services have begun formatting content specifically for the iPad.

So, whether you prefer to watch, listen to, or read up-to-the-minute news coverage, with specialized apps, your Internet-connected iPad can serve up the personalized news and timely information you want or need.

TELEVISION NEWS APPS

All the major U.S. television news organizations, including CNN, Fox News, ABC News, *NBC Nightly News* and *The Today Show*, CBS News, MSNBC, and even the BBC, have proprietary, iPad-specific apps that not only stream content from live or previously broadcasted news programs but also offer personalization and interactive elements, which enable you to quickly access and watch only the news stories that are of interest or relevant to you on an on-demand basis.

> TIP   To learn more about video content that can be streamed to your iPad for viewing (as opposed to being downloaded and stored on your tablet), see Chapter 15, "Downloading Versus Streaming Online Content."

Television news apps are free of charge because most of them are advertiser supported (which means you view ads, just like when watching television).

WEATHER CHANNEL MAX+ FOR IPAD

The Weather Channel offers its own free app that enables you to watch on-demand weather reports directly from the cable television network and view graphic-based weather forecasts for any city or region in the world. Whether you're tracking a major storm, deciding what to pack for a business trip, or want to know what the weather will be like in your home city later in the week, this app offers the features, functions, and weather coverage you need. See Chapter 11, "Using Travel-Related Apps," for more on iPad apps that provide information on the great outdoors.

NETWORK NEWS ON THE GO: ABC NEWS, CBS NEWS, AND *NBC NIGHTLY NEWS* APPS

The news divisions of three major U.S. television networks each has their own proprietary iPad app that is designed to offer video-based local, national, and international news reports on-demand.

The ABC News for iPad app (see Figure 14.1), for example, combines text-based articles with video footage from news stories. You can literally scan the globe as you select only the stories and headlines that are of interest to you.

FIGURE 14.1

The ABC News app enables you to choose the news stories that interest you.

The CBS News for iPad app (see Figure 14.2) offers real-time video reports broadcast throughout the day, as well as on-demand video stories from *CBS Evening News* and other news-oriented programs, such as *The Early Show*, *CBS MoneyWatch*, and *48 Hours*.

This app also enables you to select from U.S. news, world news, politics, science/technology, health, entertainment, MoneyWatch, sports, crime, and opinion-oriented content, which are all presented by the network's top journalists, reporters, and producers.

The *NBC Nightly News* app (featuring Brian Williams as of this writing) enables you to watch news segments from the past 15 days, browse video news stories by topic, and then watch segments or entire news broadcasts directly from the app. At a glance, you can also see the most popular news stories.

FIGURE 14.2

The CBS News for iPad app enables you to watch programming from CBS News anytime it's convenient. You can focus only on the news stories you're interested in.

INTERNATIONAL NEWS AGENCIES: ASSOCIATED PRESS AND REUTERS

When it comes to news, few organizations have the experience, reputation, and resources as The Associated Press. Using a vast selection of multimedia content, this app offers a highly personalized and customizable experience, as you access only the news that's of interest to you. What's offered from the AP News app, however, includes local, national, and global news coverage.

Reuters News Pro for iPad is another free, news-oriented app that combines breaking news stories with an emphasis on global financial news coverage. Although you can stream content from the Web, this app enables you to save content on the iPad for later offline viewing. Global and national news, financial news, sports, entertainment, science, health, and business are among the news categories offered. Financial reporting, financial data and charts, and a currency converter (featuring current exchange rates) are among this app's offerings.

CNN FOR iPAD AND FOX NEWS FOR iPAD

You can use your iPad to stay up to date with the latest live news reports from CNN, so there's no need to sit in front of a television to be informed about breaking news stories. (Your iPad must have access to the Internet to watch live, streaming broadcasts.)

The CNN for iPad app (see Figure 14.3) also enables you to scan news headlines using a colorful slideshow format, from which you can access stories, articles, and news coverage. You can post comments of your own that pertain to the news stories you access from the app.

Not to be left out of the iPad news-related app mix, in June 2011 the FOX News Network launched its own free app, called Fox News for iPad. In addition to being able to watch video news clips and clips from FOX News programming, this app features a live Fox News Channel ticker, live coverage of major news events, the ability to watch FoxNews.com Live on weekdays (between 9:00am and 3:00pm EST), and the ability to listen to FOX News Radio anytime.

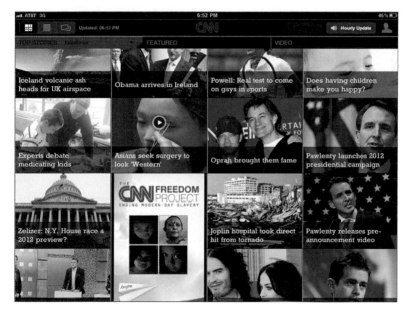

FIGURE 14.3

The CNN for iPad app enables you to access live CNN broadcasts and recently aired stories, and you can obtain additional coverage through text, photos, and other multimedia content.

TIP In addition to the national television networks and major cable stations that have their own news-oriented apps, a growing number of local network affiliate TV stations in many cities across America have their own iPad apps that enable users to access local news coverage.

To determine whether your local ABC, CBS, NBC, FOX, or CW affiliate has its own iPad app, visit the App Store. In the Search field enter the station name or ID letters, such as NBC 4 (New York), WBZ News (CBS Boston), CBS 2 (Chicago), or KGAN (CBS Cedar Rapids, Iowa).

STREAMING RADIO NEWS APPS

Throughout the country, many news/talk radio stations have begun broadcasting live on the Internet, allowing listeners to hear local coverage from their hometown stations regardless of where they're listening from. To make these streaming broadcasts available to iPad users, many stations and radio networks have released proprietary apps. You can find these apps in the App Store. Using the Search field, enter the name or call letters for your favorite radio station or network.

SIRIUSXM SATELLITE RADIO APP

SiriusXM Satellite Radio has its own SiriusXM app that, for a monthly fee, enables iPad users to stream radio broadcasts from the majority of the stations that are part of this subscription-based satellite radio service. News-related stations available through the SiriusXM app include BBC Radio, ESPN Radio, CNBC, MSNBC, CNN, HLN, and NPR.

NOTE If you're already a SiriusXM subscriber, adding the ability to stream programming from the Internet on a computer or iPad costs an additional $2.99 USD per month.

Because this app requires a large amount of data to be transferred wirelessly to your tablet, it's best to use a Wi-Fi connection, or you'll quickly use your monthly 3G wireless data allocation.

NPR FOR iPAD

Instead of reading or watching television, NPR for iPad (see Figure 14.4) enables you to obtain your news by hearing the unique voice and approach of National

Public Radio. This interactive app has a magazine-style format but enables you to access past radio broadcasts on demand or listen to programming that is being broadcast live on NPR stations around the country. Accompanying these audio-based broadcasts and reports are informative articles and photos, as well as other relevant multimedia content.

FIGURE 14.4

The NPR for iPad app combines streaming audio broadcasts with other news-oriented multimedia content.

From this free app, you can quickly find the local NPR radio station wherever you happen to be visiting or, when you're away from home, you can tune into familiar voices from your home city's NPR station.

NEWSPAPER AND MAGAZINE NEWS APPS

Many local, regional, and national newspapers now have digital editions to accompany their print editions. Subscription prices vary and, in some cases, depend on whether you're a current subscriber to the print edition of the newspaper. Just a few of the major daily newspapers with a digital edition include *The New York Times, The Washington Post, The New York Daily News, The Los Angeles Times,* and *The Chicago Tribune.*

WORKING WITH THE NEWSSTAND IN iOS 5

With the introduction of iOS 5, Apple created and launched its proprietary Newsstand app, which now is preinstalled on all iPads. Not to be confused with the iBooks app (which is used for finding, purchasing, downloading, and reading eBooks), the Newsstand app is used to manage and access all of your digital newspaper and magazine subscriptions in one place.

After you launch Newsstand, tap the Store icon and browse through the ever-growing collection of digital newspapers and magazines that are available for the iPad. With the tap of an icon, you can subscribe to any publication or, in some instances, purchase a single current or back issue.

All purchases made are automatically billed to the credit card you have on file with your Apple ID account, or you can pay using iTunes gift cards. When you opt to purchase a single issue of a publication or an ongoing subscription, you need to confirm your Apple ID and enter your password to initiate the purchase, just like when you purchase an app, iTunes content, or eBook.

> **TIP** To entice you to become a paid subscriber, some publishers offer free issues of their digital newspaper or magazine that you can download and read before actually paying for a subscription.

After you purchase a digital newspaper or magazine subscription (or a single issue of a publication), it appears on your Newsstand shelf in the Newsstand app. Tap the publication's cover thumbnail to access the available issue(s).

If you've subscribed to a digital publication, Newsstand automatically downloads the most current issue as soon as it's published, so when you wake up your tablet from Sleep Mode each morning, your favorite newspaper can be waiting for you.

Using a Home screen icon badge and the Notification Center, you are notified immediately whenever a new issue of a digital publication is automatically downloaded to your iPad and is ready for reading. When you access Newsstand, you also see a thumbnail of that publication's cover on the main Newsstand shelf screen.

You can shop for digital newspapers or magazines from within the Newsstand app by tapping the Store icon. Alternatively, you can find and purchase digital newspapers and magazines from within the App Store. However, all new purchases are sent directly to your tablet's Newsstand folder for easy access within the Newsstand app.

Some newspaper and magazine publishers make the digital edition of their publication freely available if you're already a paid subscriber to the traditional print edition of that publication. In addition to mainstream newspapers and magazines now being made available in digital form, there is a growing selection of industry-specific and special interest publications also available through the App Store and Newsstand app.

THE NEW YORK TIMES FOR iPAD APP

The New York Times, a world-renowned major daily newspaper, has been a pioneer in transforming a traditional print newspaper into an interactive experience, without losing the print edition's format or compromising on its coverage.

The *NYTimes for iPad* app reproduces each edition of the printed newspaper, including all articles and photos. This is a free app, but to access all the news coverage and content, you must have a paid subscription (via an in-app purchase).

THE DAILY: iPAD-EXCLUSIVE DAILY DIGITAL NEWS

The Daily, which is published by News Corp., is a first-of-its-kind, daily digital "newspaper" available exclusively to iPad subscribers. Each issue of *The Daily* (see Figure 14.5) contains seven sections, including News, Business, Gossip, Opinion, Arts & Life, Apps & Games, and Sports. This equates to at least 100 pages of new and original content being published 365 days per year.

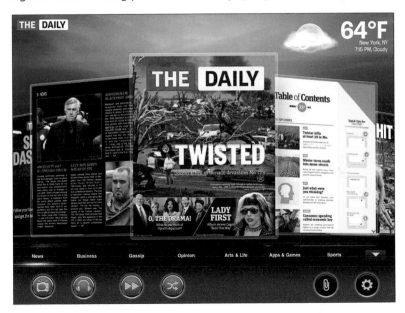

FIGURE 14.5
The Daily is the first digital newspaper published exclusively for the iPad.

Because this publication is created every day exclusively for the iPad, it offers a unique user interface that's extremely interactive. The publication makes full use of the tablet's touch screen and vibrant HD display. So, your experience reading this digital-only publication is a cross between reading a newspaper, perusing a magazine, and surfing around a website. All the articles, photos, related videos, and interactive content are displayed in full color for easy reading on your iPad 2.

Priced at $.99 USD per week, or $39.99 USD per year, each daily issue of this digital-only publication is automatically downloaded to your iPad 2 through the publication's proprietary app.

This digital publication is loaded with full-color graphics and photos, and it offers an interactive element, which includes streaming videos, links to websites, and other unique content (including a daily crossword puzzle). Much of the content within each issue can be downloaded and read offline.

In terms of content, *The Daily* is very much like *USA Today* in that it's a general-interest, full-color publication that offers news and plenty of other articles of interest to the reader. The publication is created by a dedicated staff of veteran news reporters, editors, and journalists. It is not simply a collection of news headlines with links to wire service stories.

A free, two-week trial subscription to *The Daily* is provided upon downloading the publication's free app from the App Store (visit www.thedaily.com, the App Store, or the Newsstand app for details).

USA TODAY FOR IPAD APP

Every Monday through Friday, *USA Today* covers the highlights of what's happening in America and throughout the world. The *USA Today* for iPad (shown in Figure 14.6) is a free app that does not require a paid subscription for content, but it does offer the same content and colorful format as the printed newspaper.

After you install the app on your tablet, the iPad must have access to the Internet to download up-to-the-minute content in each of the newspaper's sections, which include the main section, Money, Sports, Life, Tech, and Travel.

The *USA Today* for iPad app is somewhat customizable; for example, it displays a local weather forecast for your present location. After you scan the headlines, you tap links to access the entire stories, which appear just as they do in the printed newspaper.

There's even a daily, interactive crossword puzzle that you can freely access within the app from the Life section.

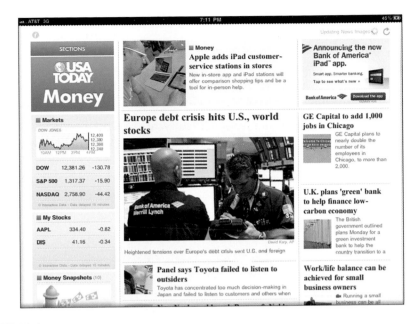

FIGURE 14.6

The USA Today *app offers a similar on-screen design to the printed newspaper.*

THE WALL STREET JOURNAL DIGITAL EDITION

Many business and financial professionals refer to *The Wall Street Journal* as the most important information they read each day. With a paid subscription to *The Wall Street Journal*'s digital edition, every issue is delivered directly to your iPad in time for your morning coffee or daily commute to work.

You can purchase single issues of *The Wall Street Journal* digital edition for $1.99 USD each. Discounted subscriptions are available at different price points based on whether you're a subscriber to the printed newspaper and the duration of the digital subscription you purchase.

Each digital edition of *The Wall Street Journal* is identical to the printed edition; however, the app also grants you access to extra content, including videos and archival information. Plus, throughout the day, updated content is published and accessible from your iPad as part of the ever-changing "Now Edition."

You can store articles or the entire newspaper, so you can read it anywhere and anytime, even if an Internet connection is not available at the time you want to read the digital publication.

OFFICIAL *DRUDGE REPORT* APP

If you're web-savvy and enjoy getting your ongoing "fix" of breaking news in quick tidbits by quickly scanning headlines to pick and choose which news stories are of interest, check out *The Drudge Report*'s website, which has become a news-gathering solution for busy people.

The free Official *Drudge Report* app is linked directly to DrudgeReport.com and offers everything you love about *The Drudge Report*, but the content is formatted for your iPad as opposed to your computer screen. There are other apps that utilize content from the *Drudge Report*, but the Official *Drudge Report* app is the only one directly affiliated with the popular Internet site.

> **NOTE** The publishers of many popular national magazines, including *Time* and *Newsweek,* as well as business, financial, and industry-oriented publications, now offer digital editions. Most digital editions of magazines require either a paid subscription for the digital content, or you need to be a paid subscriber to the print edition of the publication to get free access the digital content.
>
> To determine whether your favorite magazines have digital editions, visit the App Store. In the Search field enter the titles of the magazines you're interested in downloading and reading on your iPad.
>
> To read a digital edition of a magazine, you first need to download a free, propri-etary app for each publication and then potentially make an in-app purchase to download past or current issues.

CREATING A NEWS FOLDER ON YOUR iPAD

If you rely on several news-oriented apps and websites to stay informed, create a folder on your iPad 2's Home screen that contains your most frequented news apps. You can also include Home screen bookmark icons that link directly to news-oriented sites you frequent on the Web. The Introduction to this book covers how to create custom folders on your iPad's Home screen, and Chapter 4, "Surfing the Web," discusses how to create Home screen bookmarks linked to web pages.

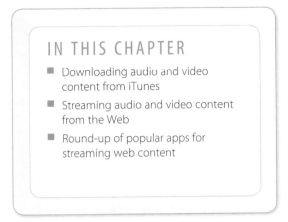

15

DOWNLOADING VERSUS STREAMING ONLINE CONTENT

When it comes to enjoying audio or video content, whether it's music, audiobooks, episodes of your favorite TV shows, blockbuster movies, or something else, you have a variety of options for procuring content to enjoy on your iPad.

The first thing you need to understand, however, is that there are three ways to enjoy audio or video content on your iPad:

1. Using the iTunes app, you can download and store music, movies, TV shows, or audiobooks on your tablet. Although iTunes offers some free content, you must purchase or rent the majority of what's available. After you download and save content on your iPad, you no longer need an Internet connection, and you can enjoy the content as often as you wish.

2. You can transfer audio or video content from your primary computer to your iPad using the iTunes sync process or iCloud. This can include content acquired from iTunes or from other sources. When you transfer content to your iPad, it is stored on your tablet, and you don't need an Internet connection to enjoy it.

3. You can stream content directly from the Web. When you stream content, you must have either an audio or video player app. The content you stream is sent to your iPad but isn't stored. This means that to listen to or watch streaming web content, your tablet needs to maintain a constant 3G or Wi-Fi Internet connection. Thus, if you're using a Wi-Fi connection, you cannot leave the coverage area of the Wi-Fi hotspot your tablet is connected to as you're streaming content from the Web.

CAUTION   The ability to stream content from the Web and experience it on your iPad gives you free access to a wide range of programming. However, whenever you stream audio or video content from the Web you are transferring a tremendous amount of data to your tablet. Thus, if you use a 3G connection, you quickly use your monthly wireless data allocation. So, when streaming web content, it's best to use a Wi-Fi connection.

Not only does a Wi-Fi connection allow data to be transferred to your tablet at much faster speeds, there's also no limit as to how much data you can send or receive. Plus, when streaming video content, you are often able to view it at a higher resolution when you use a Wi-Fi connection.

One of the new features Apple's online-based iCloud service offers is the ability to store multimedia content—including your entire music library—on the Web and download it to your tablet.

The iCloud service is described in detail in Chapter 8, "Syncing to Your Computer via iTunes or iCloud." However, if you're interested in simultaneously making your entire music library available to your primary computer and all of your iOS devices, including your iPad, you might want to invest in the premium iTunes Match service that's available through iCloud for $24.95 USD per year. This service makes all your digital music, including content not purchased from iTunes, available to you via the iCloud service, anytime and anywhere there's an Internet connection.

NOTE   Although you still need to purchase most iTunes content, including music, you can now store that content either on your iPad or on iCloud and access it with your iPad.

DOWNLOADING CONTENT FROM iTUNES

Apple's own online-based iTunes Store offers one of the world's largest collections of music, television shows, movies, audiobooks, and other video content that you can purchase, download, and experience on your iPad using the newly designed Music app for audio content or the Videos app to play video content.

To purchase content from iTunes, launch the iTunes app on your iPad, and then tap one of the command buttons at the bottom of the screen, based on the type of content you're looking for. As you can see from Figure 15.1, you can select Music, Movies, TV Shows, Podcasts, Audiobooks, or educational content from iTunes U.

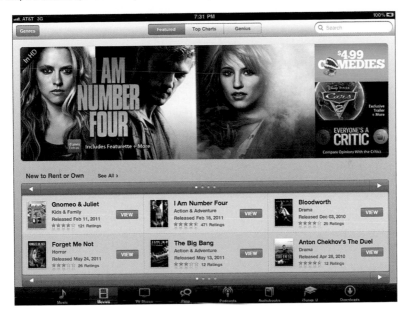

FIGURE 15.1

Directly from your iPad, use the iTunes app to find, purchase, and download a wide range of entertaining content, including music, TV shows, and movies.

When you tap the Music button, you'll have instant access to millions of songs from nearly every major recording artist or band in existence. You can purchase and download individual songs, or you can purchase and download entire albums, often with a single tap on the screen.

> **NOTE** The interface for finding, purchasing, and downloading content from iTunes using the iTunes app is extremely similar to finding and purchasing apps from the App Store.

To find exactly what you're looking for when visiting the iTunes store with the iTunes app, use the Search field in the upper-right corner of the screen and enter a singer's name, the name of a recording artist, or a band's name. Alternatively, you can use the virtual keyboard to enter a song title, an actor's name (from a TV series or movie), a movie title, or a TV show title (see Figure 15.2). In the Search field, you can also enter any other keyword or search phrase, based on what you're looking for.

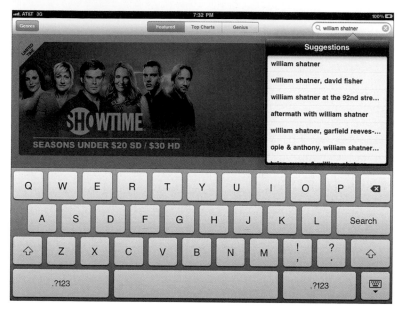

FIGURE 15.2

Use the iTunes Search field to find exactly what you're looking for in the iTunes Store.

After you tap the Music, Movies, TV Shows, Podcasts, Audiobooks, or iTunes U command icon, within that category of content you'll be able to see what's New and Noteworthy, or you can tap one of the buttons located near the top-center of the screen to see various Top Charts.

You can use Apple's proprietary Genius feature to help you select content to purchase and download from iTunes. This feature keeps track of all your past iTunes purchases and makes suggestions for future purchases or downloads based on what you enjoy.

Any time you purchase and download content from the iTunes Store using the iTunes app on your iPad (or use iTunes on your computer, and then transfer the content to your iPad), you own the content. It is stored on your iPad so you can view or listen to it as often as you want.

However, if you rent a TV show episode or movie from the iTunes Store, that content is saved on your tablet (or stored on your computer's hard drive) for up to 30 days; after that time it is automatically deleted. From the moment you begin watching the rented TV episode or movie, the file remains available to you for a 24-hour period, after which time it is automatically deleted. During those 24 hours, you can watch the TV episode or movie as often as you want without having to rent it again.

> **TIP** The benefits to purchasing TV shows from iTunes are that you own them and can watch them as often as you want—plus they are commercial-free.

ACQUIRING iTUNES CONTENT FROM YOUR COMPUTER

Using the same iTunes software on your primary computer that can be used for syncing data with your iPad (as opposed to using iCloud), you can click the iTunes Store option on the left side of the iTunes screen (see Figure 15.3) and access the online-based iTunes Store to purchase (or in some cases, rent) and download music, music videos, television shows, movies, audiobooks, and other content.

FIGURE 15.3

Find, purchase, and download content from the iTunes Store on your computer, and then transfer it to your iPad using the iTunes sync process.

With the iTunes software on your computer, you can also access the App Store to purchase and download apps for your iPad. If you're using your iPad, you use the App Store app, not the iTunes app, to purchase apps and use the iTunes app to purchase (or rent) television show episodes, movies, music videos, audiobooks, and other types of content.

> **NOTE** When you access the iTunes store from your primary computer, you can also find and purchase eBooks that you can transfer to your iPad (via iTunes sync or iCloud) and read using the iBooks app. Or you can find, purchase, and download digital editions of newspapers and magazines, which you can transfer to your iPad and access from the Newsstand app.

After acquiring content from the iTunes Store using your computer, you must transfer that content to your tablet using iCloud or the iTunes sync process before you can enjoy it on your iPad. Chapter 8 covers how to transfer content between your primary computer and iPad using the iTunes sync process or wireless iCloud service.

> **TIP** An iPad that's connected to the Internet using a Wi-Fi connection can download any content from the iTunes Store directly to the tablet. However, if you're using a 3G Internet connection, you cannot download TV show episodes and movies directly to the iPad because these files are too large. Therefore, you must use a Wi-Fi connection with your iPad or acquire that content using the iTunes software on your primary computer and then transfer it to your iPad.

COST OF ACQUIRING CONTENT FROM iTUNES

Although some iTunes content is free (including all podcasts and iTunes U programming), you must purchase the majority of music, TV show episodes, movies, and audiobooks. In the case of TV episodes or movies, you can purchase or rent them.

When it comes to video content, the iTunes Store often offers TV show episodes and movies in two formats—standard definition and high definition (see Figure 15.4). Either format will work fine on your iPad. However, because the iPad has an HD screen, the quality of the video will be significantly better if you download and watch HD-formatted video, especially if the TV show or movie is special effects–intensive. Storing HD video on your iPad, however, does take up more space.

FIGURE 15.4

When downloading video content from iTunes, you can often choose between standard and high-definition format.

The cost associated with acquiring content from iTunes is as follows (all prices are in U.S. dollars):

Content Type	Standard Definition	High Definition
Purchase Music Single (One Song)	$.99 to $1.29	N/A
Purchase Music Album	$7.99 to $15.99	N/A
Purchase Music Video	$1.99	N/A
Purchase TV Show Episode	$1.99	$2.99
Purchase Made-for-TV Movie	$3.99	$4.99
Rent TV Show Episode	$.99	$.99
Purchase Entire Season of a TV Show	Price varies, based on TV series and number of episodes. It's always cheaper to purchase an entire season, as opposed to separately purchasing all episodes in a season.	Price varies, based on TV series and number of episodes. It's always cheaper to purchase an entire season, as opposed to all episodes in a season separately.

Content Type	Standard Definition	High Definition
Purchase Movie	$.99 to $14.99	$.99 to $19.99
Rent Movie	$.99 to $3.99	$1.99 to $4.99
	(New releases start at $3.99, with library titles available for as little as $.99 per rental.)	
	(New releases start at $4.99, with library titles available for as little as $1.99 per rental.)	
Audiobooks	$.95 to $41.95	N/A
	(Unabridged audiobooks of current bestsellers tend to be among the higher priced titles. These tend to range from $14.95 to $26.95.)	

STREAMING VIDEO ON YOUR iPAD

To stream video content to your iPad from the Internet, you need to use a specialized app based on where the content is originating from on the Web. Whenever you're streaming video content from the Web, you can pause the video at any time. Depending on the app, you can also exit the app partway through a video, and resume watching the video from where you left off when you later relaunch the app.

ABC PLAYER

The ABC Player is a free app from the ABC Television Network that enables you to freely watch full-length episodes of your favorite ABC-TV dramas, reality shows, sitcoms, game shows, and soap operas. The episodes are streamed to your iPad, and you watch them using this app. The shows are advertiser supported, so you have to watch ads during the programs you stream.

The ABC Player app is separate from the free ABC News app (featured in Chapter 14, "Finding and Using News and Information Apps"), which enables you to watch news coverage from the network. The other network news organizations, including *NBC Nightly News* and CBS News, along with each network's respective morning program (*Today* and so on) also have their own, separate apps for streaming that programming to watch on your iPad.

TV.COM

The free TV.com iPhone app (which also works perfectly on an iPad) enables you to watch full episodes of your favorite TV shows from the CBS Television Network, The CW Network, Showtime, CNET TV, and a few other television networks. The app works with a 3G Internet connection, but a Wi-Fi connection is recommended to experience the highest quality video possible.

With the TV.com app, you can pause the show you're watching and resume watching it later. All content is free of charge, but it is advertiser supported, so you must watch ads while you stream programs.

YOUTUBE

The YouTube app (see Figure 15.5) comes preinstalled on your iPad 2. With it, you can watch streaming videos produced and uploaded by everyday people, companies, television networks, and other organizations. In addition to millions of entertaining videos and video blogs, YouTube features free educational content and how-to videos. All YouTube content is free of charge to watch. Some of it is advertiser supported.

FIGURE 15.5

Millions of free videos are available for viewing on YouTube. Stream from the Internet directly to your iPad using the YouTube app that comes preinstalled on your tablet.

NETFLIX

The Netflix video service is subscription-based, and enables you to have movie and TV show DVDs shipped right to your door. Netflix also has an Internet-based streaming service that enables you to watch thousands of movies and TV show episodes via the Internet on your television, computer screen, or directly on your iPad (when you use the free Netflix app, shown in Figure 15.6). The subscription fee for Netflix's content streaming service starts at $7.99 USD per month.

FIGURE 15.6

Netflix offers thousands of movies and TV show episodes that you can stream to your iPad with a paid subscription and the free Netflix app.

Included with a Netflix unlimited membership is the ability to watch as much streaming content as you'd like per month. Simply browse the Netflix Instant Watch library, and tap the Play button when you find the movie or TV show episode you want to watch. You can also create and manage an Instant Queue.

As you're watching a movie on your iPad, you can tap the pause button and then resume watching it on your computer screen or on another Netflix-compatible device, including your television set that's equipped with the proper equipment, such as a Nintendo Wii, Xbox 360, PlayStation 3, Apple TV, Roku Streaming Player, many Internet compatible Blu-ray players, or a DVR (such as a TiVo system). Some newer TVs also have Internet connectivity and access to Netflix built in.

HULU PLUS

Full-length episodes from thousands of current and classic TV series are available on your iPad using the free Hulu Plus app. However, the majority of the content offered from this service requires you to pay a monthly subscription fee of $7.99 USD to access and view it.

Hulu Plus members can access season passes to current TV shows airing on ABC, FOX, and NBC or pick and choose from thousands of episodes from classic TV series. All video is streamed at 720p HD resolution to your iPad, so a Wi-Fi connection is recommended, although the app does work with a 3G Internet connection.

The Hulu Plus app enables you to pause programs and resume them later, plus you can create a queue of shows to watch on your tablet. Visit www.hulu.com/plus to subscribe to the Hulu service and browse available programming.

HBO GO

If you're already a paid subscriber to the HBO cable television network, you can download the free HBO Go app (see Figure 15.7) and watch every episode of every HBO original series on-demand, as well as an ever-changing line-up of movies, comedy specials, sports programs, and documentaries that are currently airing on HBO.

FIGURE 15.7

Watch HBO TV series, movies, documentaries, and specials on-demand using the free HBO Go app.

After you set up a free online account with your local cable or satellite television provider, you can sign in to the HBO Go app and select programming you want to watch. Begin playing a TV episode or movie with the tap of a finger, or create a queue of shows to watch at your leisure. You can pause movies and TV episodes and resume them later.

One great feature of the HBO Go app is that HBO sometimes releases episodes on this app one week before it airs on television. Plus, you can access behind-the-scenes content of popular HBO series, such as *Game of Thrones*.

> TIP   With the HBO Go app, or any other app that's used for streaming TV shows and/or movies, you can watch your favorite programming on-demand, as long as your iPad has access to the Web. You never have to worry about missing the scheduled air time for a show or movie on TV again because you decide what to watch and when it begins.
>
> Plus, instead of paying $15.00 USD or more for a pay-per-view movie while staying at a hotel while you're traveling, you can simply stream a movie on your iPad and enjoy a high-definition video experience, with amazing sound quality (if you attach optional headphones to the tablet's headphones jack). See Chapter 19, "Must-Have Accessories," for information about top-quality headphones that are perfect for use with the iPad 2.

STREAMING AUDIO ON YOUR iPAD

In addition to streaming videos, TV shows, and movies to watch on your iPad, you can stream audio programming from AM, FM, and satellite-based radio stations and radio networks, as well as Internet-based radio stations. The apps described in this section are just a few of the many options available from the App Store.

PANDORA RADIO

The free Pandora Radio app enables you to create a custom-programmed Internet radio station that features all your favorite songs, recording artists, and bands. After you choose your favorite artists, for example, the app can also automatically select and play similar music based on your tastes and preferences.

SIRIUSXM

Available to subscribers of SiriusXM satellite radio, the free SiriusXM app enables you to stream broadcasts from virtually all the 120+ channels offered through this subscription-based service, including commercial-free music stations, news/talk stations, comedy, sports, and others special-interest stations and programming. For more information, visit www.siriusxm.com.

If you're already a subscriber to SiriusXM, you can add the ability to stream pro-gramming to your iPad for an extra $2.99 USD per month. A free, seven-day trial, giving you full access to all programming from your iPad using the SiriusXM app, is available.

TUNEIN RADIO PRO

The TuneIn Radio Pro app ($.99 USD) enables you to listen to or actually record thousands of AM and FM radio stations on your iPad. The app helps you find sta-tions of interest that originate from all over the world.

Listen to music, news/talk, sports, and more at your leisure, as long as your iPad has access to the Web. With the iPad's multitasking capabilities, you can choose a station to stream and listen to, and then proceed to use your tablet with other apps as radio programming plays in the background.

The recording feature of this app enables you to pick a station, as well as a start and stop date and time to record. You can then listen to those recorded broad-casts any time you want. The app's built-in RadioTime directory features more than 40,000 radio station and program listings.

As you're listening to music being broadcast on a radio station via this app, you can tap an icon to automatically purchase that music from iTunes. The app works with a 3G or Wi-Fi Internet connection and has a user-friendly interface that makes finding radio stations or specific programs very easy.

Using the GPS feature of the app, you can instantly find local radio stations wherever you happen to be, or you can be away from home, yet still listen to your favorite hometown stations, talk radio personalities, or DJs.

16

RELAXING WITH GAMES

By reading about many different types of work-related apps, you've had the opportunity to preview just some of the ways business professionals, small business operators, entrepreneurs, consultants, and others working in many different industries are currently using the iPad 2 in today's competitive business world.

Your iPad 2 is capable of more than just being a tool for work, however. It can be used to compete against others (human or computer-controlled opponents) in a wide range of challenging, exhilarating, fun, and unique games.

Its slim and compact design, combined with its stunning 9.7-inch, high-resolution touch screen display, along with its capability to access the Web, its built-in three-axis gyro sensor, and built-in speaker (plus headphone jack), enable your iPad to be used as a state-of-the-art mobile gaming device.

Available from the App Store are literally thousands of challenging, visually stunning, and highly innovative single and multiplayer games. So, if you need a quick diversion from important business matters, you're looking to lose yourself for a few hours at a time within a simulated world that's filled with action and adventure, or you want to challenge others in a game of skill, you have the right device. The iPad 2 has emerged in the video game industry as the leading portable gaming machine—and incredible new gaming experiences are constantly being introduced.

> TIP   In the App Store, every week Apple reviews all the latest games available for the iPad and chooses one to be named Game of the Week. These games tend to be the most advanced in terms of graphics, sound, and game play and make the best use of the iPad 2's built-in features.
>
> From the iPad, tap the App Store app icon that's displayed on your Home Screen. Tap the Features command icon that's displayed at the bottom of the screen. The Game of the Week is promoted in the large graphic displayed near the top of the App Store screen or in the three smaller graphic banners displayed near the top-right of the screen.
>
> Alternatively, you can tap the Categories button at the bottom of the App Store screen, and then select the Games category. The Game of the Week is promoted in a graphic banner near the top of the screen. (You can also find, purchase, and download Apple's the Game of the Week for iPad by accessing the App Store from iTunes on your primary computer.)

You might think that video games are just for kids. Well, think again. Many of the most popular games for the iPad are actually designed with intelligent adults in mind. You'll find many different card games (such as blackjack and poker), puzzle games, casino games, crossword puzzles, Sudoku, sports games, and realistic simulations, for example.

A VARIETY OF GAMING EXPERIENCES

As you're about to discover, the thousands of games available from the App Store are divided into different categories. Some of the different types of gaming experiences you can experience on your iPad 2 include the following:

- **Action and Adventure:** From character-based games to high-action shoot'em ups, you can find iPad games that feature highly detailed graphics, realistic sound effects, and plenty of fast-paced challenges.

- **Action and Puzzle Challenges:** Games such as Tetris, the massively popular Angry Birds, and Flight Control are among the many different types of action-based puzzle games that can make you think and test your reflexes simultaneously. The best puzzle games are very easy to learn, very difficult to master, and extremely addictive.

- **Casino and Card Games:** These games faithfully re-create the casino experience (slot machines, roulette, craps, and so on). Some games enable you to compete against real players or computer controlled opponents as you play popular card games, such as blackjack, many variations of poker, or solitaire.

- **Classic Arcade and Video Games:** Pac-Man, Sonic the Hedgehog, Space Invaders, Asteroid, Centipede, and many others have been faithfully re-created for play on the iPad, complete with their original graphics and sound effects.

> **TIP** To make classic arcade games, as well as action and adventure games more realistic, a company called ThinkGeek (www.thinkgeek.com/gadgets/cellphone/e75a/?itm=ipad_joystick) offers a removable joystick attachment that sticks onto your iPad's screen, giving you more arcade-like control over the on-screen action. It's priced at $24.99 USD for one or $39.99 USD for two.
>
> The Fling for iPad, from Ten 1 ($17.96 USD, http://tenonedesign.com/fling.php) offers similar game controller functionality but uses a totally different design. This is more of a removable thumb pad that attaches to the iPad 2's screen.
>
> The iCade accessory for iPad from Ion Audio ($99.99 USD, www.ionaudio.com/products/details/icade) is actually a wooden housing into which you insert your iPad 2 . iCade transforms the tablet into what looks like a tabletop coin-op arcade machine, complete with a full-size joystick controller and eight arcade-style buttons. You can use it to play more than 100 classic arcade games from Atari (like Asteroids, Centipede, and Battlezone), which are sold separately from the App Store.

- **Classic Board Games:** Faithful adaptations of classic board games, such as Monopoly, Chess, Checkers, Backgammon, Life, Dominos, Boggle, Scrabble, Uno, Risk, and Yahtzee, are all available for the iPad as single- or multi-player games.

- **Crossword Puzzles:** If you're looking for crossword puzzle challenges, the options are extensive. There's the subscription-based NY Times Crosswords app that re-creates each day's *New York Times* crossword puzzle that's published, plus the app offers a massive archive of 4,000+ past puzzles. You can also find dozens of other crossword puzzle apps available from the App Store.

- **Simulations:** These games enable you to immerse yourself in a computer-generated, virtual world that can re-create a real-life environment or enable you to experience the most imaginative of scenarios. You can build and manage the city of your dreams with SimCity Deluxe for iPad, wield a mighty sword in a game like Infinity Blade, become a sniper in Super Sniper 2 HD, or help Papa Smurf build and manage a colorful Smurf village in Smurfs' Village. There are also flight simulators, where you can pilot all sorts of aircraft, or you can become the lead keeper of your own virtual zoo (when you play Tap Zoo).

- **Sports Simulations:** These are games based on real-life sports, such as golf, baseball, basketball, football, and NASCAR. In many cases, the games re-create real-life professional athletes or teams using actual stats and faithfully re-create the arenas, stadiums, courses, or tracks where the real-life sports take place. In fact, the more you know about the real-life sport when playing some of these simulations, the better you'll be at playing these video games. There are also sports games that are less realistic, such as NBA Jam by EA Sports for iPad, that focus more on arcade-style action as opposed to realism.

- **Sudoku Puzzles:** Challenge your mind with the many different versions of Sudoku available from the App Store. Also available are other types of word- and number-based puzzle challenges, such as many different word search games.

Within each of these game categories, you can find many different game-play experiences—some created by the most talented and imaginative designers in the video game industry.

Although some of the games are adaptations of popular video games originally designed for Nintendo, Sony, Microsoft, Sega, or Atari gaming systems, for example, the iPad editions of these games often take full advantage of the features and functionality that are unique to the iPad.

Because your iPad can connect to the Web, you're able to experience real-time, multiplayer games and compete against friends, co-workers, your kids, or total strangers. In fact, Apple's own online-based Game Center (accessible through Game Center compatible games or the Game Center app that comes preinstalled on your iPad 2) offers a free online forum in which you can meet and compete against others as you experience a growing number of popular multiplayer iPad games.

Thousands of free games are available from the App Store. Some are advertiser supported; others offer optional in-app purchase options so you can access extra levels or gain special power-ups, tools for the game, or added functionality within a game. Many games are paid apps, ranging in price from $.99 USD to $4.99 USD (although occasionally you might find a game priced a bit higher).

> **TIP** To further enhance your game-play experience, consider investing in high-quality, noise-reduction headphones that you can use with your iPad. This enables you to truly experience the stereo sound effects and music that often add realism and intensity to a game. See Chapter 19, "Must-Have Accessories," for information about optional headphones that can connect to your iPad 2's headphones jack or that can work wirelessly via a Bluetooth connection.

TWELVE AWESOME iPAD 2 GAMES

Based on your personal taste, you'll easily find many different games that appeal to you as you browse the App Store. This section features a cross-section of 15 extremely popular or truly innovative games that are well worth experiencing on your tablet.

ANGRY BIRDS HD

This is a whimsical, puzzle-challenge-style game that has quickly taken the world by storm. The Angry Birds franchise has become the most popular game on mobile devices (including cell phones and tablets) throughout the world.

For the iPad 2, there's a free version of Angry Birds HD that offers limited levels. However, after you get hooked on this game (and you will), you'll quickly want to upgrade to the paid version of the game, which is priced at $4.99 USD. Version 1.6.1 of Angry Birds HD now features 255 challenging levels that require logic, skill, perfect timing, creativity, and patience to master.

The concept of the game involves shooting different species of cartoon-style birds from a slingshot positioned on the left side of the screen. The goal is to destroy structures on the right side of the screen and squash the green pigs that occupy the structures. The structures take into account real-life physics, which you need to consider as you plan their destruction.

The birds serve as cannonballs, which you must aim at your targets. However, each species of bird has different capabilities as it flies through the air and then (hopefully) hits its target. For each level, you're given a specific number of birds— sometimes from the same species and sometimes from multiple species—to accomplish your objectives. Each level offers a totally different structure design with different obstacles and challenges to overcome (see Figure 16.1).

FIGURE 16.1

Every level of Angry Birds HD offers an entirely different challenge, so you need to develop a new strategy, yet utilize perfect timing and logic to prevail.

Angry Birds HD takes just minutes to learn, but it can keep you challenged and entertained for hours on end. When you've completed this game, you might want to find Angry Birds Rio and Angry Birds Seasons, which are two fun-filled sequels.

> **CAUTION**   This is a highly addictive and fun game. There are separate versions of Angry Birds for the iPad 2 and iPhone, so be sure to download the iPad-specific (HD) version to experience the best graphics on your tablet.
>
> Due to its popularity, there are many knock-off games that try to capitalize on the popularity of the Angry Birds games. Your best bet, however, is to stick to the original!

One of the great things about Angry Birds HD is that you can play it for just a few minutes at a time, during a coffee break or between meetings, or you can literally spend hours at a time working your way through multiple levels. Long flights, for example, will literally fly by when you immerse yourself in this game.

Angry Birds HD is one of many iPad 2-specific games that's compatible with Apple's Game Center online service and app.

CONTRACT KILLER

Angry Birds offers a fun, whimsical, but challenging way to pass the time, whereas Contract Killer is a much more intense game in which you take on the role of an assassin. Using a variety of weapons, you perfect your sniper skills as you hunt down and kill mobsters, criminals, and other human targets.

Contract Killer (see Figure 16.2) features five realistic, three-dimensional locations that you visit as you experience the game's 17 story-based missions. Each time you kill a target, your skill level and experience increases, which grants you access to a larger selection of weapons. In all, the game includes 20 distinct weapons, from basic handguns to deadly sniper rifles.

Contract Killer is a free game; however, there are in-app purchases available (priced between $1.99 USD and $49.99 USD) that enhance your experience. The game is also compatible with Apple's online-based Game Center.

Unlike some first-person shooting games, this one is more about taking your time and strategizing the best way to kill your adversary or target. It's not a fast-paced shooting game, but it does require precision, perfect timing, and skill.

FIGURE 16.2

Contract Killer is a rather realistic and challenging shooting game.

FLIGHTCONTROL HD

The concept behind Flight Control HD ($4.99 USD) is fairly straightforward. You take on the role of an air traffic controller, whose job it is to safely land an endless lineup of aircrafts onto one, two, or three runways and a heliport. The incoming aircrafts approach at different speeds, must land on specific runways, and come from all directions. Your job is to keep the aircraft from crashing.

As each incoming aircraft appears on the game screen, you use your finger to quickly create a flight path for it to the appropriate runway. The trick, however, is lining up aircrafts that need the same runway but that are approaching at different speeds and from different directions. If you cause a mid-air collision, the game ends.

Flight Control HD (see Figure 16.3) features rather simplistic graphics, but this is more a game involving perfect timing and strategy. It can also be a real-time multiplayer game, so you can compete against other human opponents via a local area network or through Game Center.

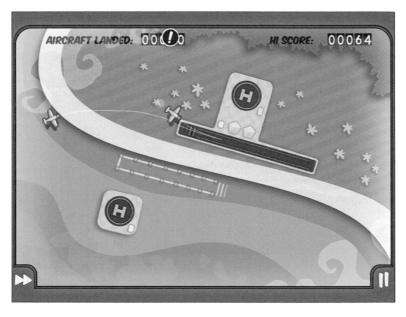

FIGURE 16.3

Flight Control is easy to learn but very difficult to master. You can spend five minutes or five hours at a time playing this addictive, fun, and challenging game.

The iPad-specific version of the game features eight different airports (another of which is shown in Figure 16.4), each of which offers a unique set of increasingly more difficult challenges. Between the iPhone and iPad editions of Flight Control, more than three million copies have been sold of this truly fun and addictive game.

Like many good action-based puzzle challenges, you can play Flight Control HD for just a few minutes at a time, or it can keep you entertained for hour after hour of continuous play.

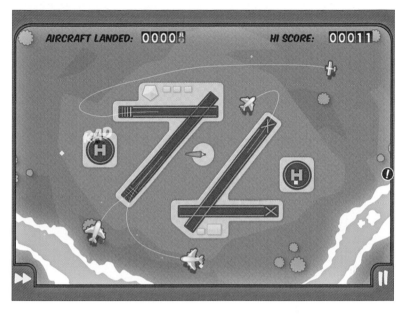

FIGURE 16.4
Each different airport within Flight Control offers a new set of challenges that become increasingly more difficult.

MADDEN NFL 11 BY EA SPORTS FOR iPAD

From EA Sports—which has been creating Madden NFL football simulations for all the popular gaming consoles since the 1980s—this iPad-specific edition of the Madden NFL game franchise ($.99 USD) offers authentic NFL football action, featuring faithful re-creations of real-life teams and players.

Match up all 32 NFL teams that feature up-to-date rosters (encompassing more than 2,000 real-life NFL players). You can play through a 16-game schedule in Season Mode or skip right to Playoffs mode to experience last season's playoffs.

Madden NFL 11 by EA Sports for iPad features cutting-edge, extremely detailed, and photo-realistic graphics. It's almost like watching an NFL game on television, only you're in control of the action. One great feature of this game is that two iPad users can link their tablets via a Bluetooth connection and play head-to-head. If you're a football fan, this is one game you won't want to miss.

Each year, EA Sports releases a new version of Madden NFL, which includes the latest team rosters and stats.

NEED FOR SPEED HOT PURSUIT FOR iPAD

Need For Speed Hot Pursuit for iPad is a somewhat realistic, high-action racing simulation game that features 20 faithful re-creations of real-world production cars, including 15 cop versions. Although you can spend time picking and choosing your vehicle and then upgrading it over time, you can also jumpstart this game and begin racing in just seconds, taking on the role of cop or racer in high-speed pursuits through varying terrain.

Like all of the Need For Speed games from Electronic Arts, this one (shown in Figure 16.5) features awesome graphics and extremely realistic and fast-paced, arcade-style action. This iPad-specific edition, however, makes full use of the tablet's built-in gyro sensor and touch-screen display.

FIGURE 16.5

This Need For Speed game feature highly detailed and fast-moving graphics.

As you make your way through this game's various challenges, you earn vehicle upgrades. However, you can also pay for extras through in-app purchases ($.99 USD to $2.99 USD each). The game requires quick thinking and faster reflexes.

NY TIMES CROSSWORDS

Every day, millions of people challenge their minds by attempting to complete the crossword puzzle that appears in the *New York Times* newspaper. Now, with a paid subscription, this same puzzle can automatically be downloaded daily to your iPad, so that you can experience it through an interactive app.

NOTE The NY Times Crosswords app is separate from the subscription-based NY Times for iPad app that offers a digital edition of the entire major daily newspaper.

As a paid subscriber to this service, you also get unlimited access to an online archive of more than 4,000 past *New York Times* crossword puzzles. The NY Times Crosswords app (see Figure 16.6) offers a unique interface that fully utilizes the tablet's virtual keyboard and touch-screen display. You can even choose to complete the puzzle using a virtual pencil (which is erasable) or virtual pen (which is not), and then communicate with fellow puzzle solvers and crossword enthusiasts online.

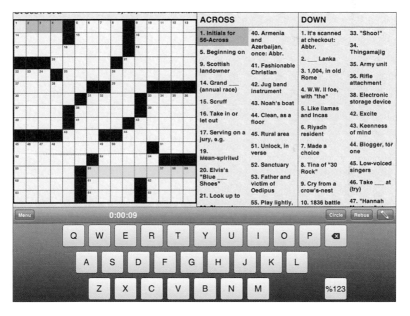

FIGURE 16.6

Enjoy the latest crossword puzzle from the New York Times anywhere and anytime on your iPad.

The NY Times Crosswords app is free; however, to acquire the puzzles, you need to subscribe to the service, which costs $1.99 USD per month, $9.99 USD for six months, or $16.99 USD per year. A subscription includes access to the puzzle archive, which you can search by entering a specific issue date. As you're solving the daily crossword puzzle, you can also listen to music from your iTunes library or enjoy the music that comes with the app.

> **TIP** You can access the daily crossword puzzle that appears in *USA Today* by loading and launching the free USA Today iPad app, tapping the blue-and-white USA Today logo in the upper-left corner of the screen, and then tapping the purple-and-white USA Today Life section logo. Next, tap the Crossword option on the left side of the tablet's screen to access the interactive crossword puzzle.
>
> A unique, daily crossword puzzle is also featured in each edition of *The Daily*, which is available via a paid subscription from the App Store (see Chapter 14, "Finding and Using News and Information Apps," for details). Plus, you can find dozens of different free and paid crossword puzzle apps featured in the App Store.

PAC-MAN FOR iPAD

The classic arcade game Pac-Man has been faithfully adapted to the iPad. All the familiar graphics and sound effects are featured. The iPad edition of Pac-Man is priced at $1.99 USD; however, a scaled-down "lite" version is freely available (see Figure 16.7). A faithful adaptation of Ms. Pac-Man for iPad is sold separately.

There are many Pac-Man knock-off games available for the iPad. However, if you want to experience the true arcade classic, be sure to purchase and download Namco's Pac-Man for iPad.

Get ready to reunite with Blinky, Pinky, Inky, and Clyde (the ghosts from Pac-Man) who chase their nemesis (Pac-Man) through a bunch of different mazes. To date, this is one of the best classic arcade game adaptations available for the iPad.

SCRABBLE FOR iPAD

Compete against computer-controlled opponents or human players as you put your vocabulary and spelling skills to the test in this faithful adaptation of Hasbro's Scrabble board game. One unique feature of this iPad-specific edition is that you can participate in up to 25 multiplayer games (against separate opponents) at a time, and view the game board in stunning 3D graphics.

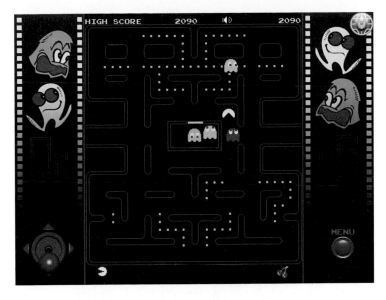

FIGURE 16.7

Pac-Man, which is one of the most popular classic arcade games of all time, has been faithfully adapted to the iPad.

Up to four players per game can experience Scrabble for iPad ($4.99 USD), which offers a very easy-to-understand user interface. You can play the game with others over a local area network, or you can pass around the same iPad. The different game-play modes adapt the screen accordingly to keep each player's letter tiles confidential.

Electronic Arts has done an amazing job adapting Scrabble and a handful of other classic Hasbro board games to the iPad.

SOCIAL SUDOKU

As you browse the App Store, you'll discover many different Sudoku apps. Social Sudoku was developed by the team that creates Sudoku puzzles for the *Los Angeles Times*, *Chicago Tribune*, and many other major daily newspapers. The organization also operates the world's largest online Sudoku community (www.sudoku.org.uk).

Social Sudoku ($1.99 USD) is a single- or multiplayer Sudoku puzzle game (see Figure 16.8) that offers many different levels of difficulty and six different game-play variations built in to the app. This game is Game Center-compatible. For more information, visit www.socialpuzzler.com.

FIGURE 16.8

Social Sudoku enables you to solve Sudoku puzzles alone, or you can challenge others.

SOLITAIRE

There are many versions of this classic card game available from the App Store, and some of them are free. The Solitaire app from MobilityWare ($.99 USD) offers many features you might already be familiar with if you play the version of Solitaire that comes with Microsoft Windows on a PC.

In addition to fully utilizing the iPad's touch-screen display, this app has a handful of different game-play variations and options, and it enables you to choose a custom background and custom-create your own card decks by featuring your own photos on the card backs.

Although Solitaire is the perfect one-player game to help you pass the time, there are a handful of other card games, such as poker and blackjack, that enable you to compete against computer-controlled opponents or human players. Use the App Store's Search field to find these games.

TETRIS FOR iPAD

This puzzle game first became popular worldwide in the early 1980s, when it was released for the IBM PC in 1986. There was a resurgence in its popularity in 1989 when it was bundled with the original Nintendo Game Boy handheld video gaming system. Today, this classic puzzle challenge lives on and is playable on just about every gaming system, as well as on cell phones, tablets, and other devices.

The goal of Tetris is to arrange different shaped blocks that fall from the top of the screen into solid rows and columns, which causes them to disappear. If the rows and columns are not solid, the blocks stack up higher and higher until they reach the top of the screen and the game ends.

Learning to play Tetris takes just a minute or two, but you can play it for years before you'll truly master it. Tetris for iPad ($7.99 USD) is a faithful adaptation of the classic game (see Figure 16.9), but one that makes full use of the iPad's touch-screen display. This version also offers several new game-play modes.

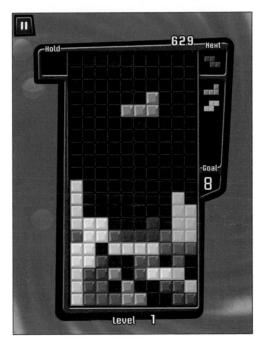

FIGURE 16.9

One of the best puzzle games of all time—for any video game system—is Tetris, and it's now offered on the iPad. It's challenging; addicting; and requires fast-thinking, fast reflexes, and strategy to master.

TEXAS POKER PRO

If you enjoy playing card games, there is no shortage of single- and multiplayer versions of popular card games for your iPad. For example, you can find many different versions of poker, including the casino-style Texas Poker Pro ($.99 USD).

Texas Poker Pro enables you to utilize the Web to play against real people (including strangers from around the world). This app links to an online community for poker enthusiasts and enables you to interact with others (via text-based, real-time chats), day or night, while also playing against them. This app is suitable for all levels of poker players.

The Texas Poker Pro app offers a realistic casino simulation that involves gambling with virtual chips. As you experience this game, you have the option of purchasing additional virtual chips via in-app purchases, starting at $.99 USD for $10,000 worth of chips.

CAUTION Due to the simulated gambling nature of this app, and the fact you can chat with strangers, it's not suitable for kids. So, if your kids tend to borrow your iPad, be sure to keep them away from this otherwise entertaining and challenging app.

GAME CENTER: MEETING AND COMPETING WITH FELLOW GAMERS

Playing single-player games on your iPad 2 is certainly fun and challenging; however, many games designed specifically for your tablet also offer multiplayer capabilities. This means you can challenge other human (noncomputer-controlled) players when experiencing your favorite games via the Web, by passing a single iPad among multiple players or by linking multiple iPads wirelessly, depending on the game.

To make finding players to compete against easier, and to offer an online forum where you can boast about your latest high score achievements, Apple has created Game Center, which is an app that comes preinstalled on your iPad and works with the Game Center online service.

From within Game Center, you can find third-party games (available from the App Store) that are compatible with this service. Plus, you can create your own online profile and have it include details about your high score achievements in the various games you play.

Game Center makes it easy to meet up with friends online to compete in multi-player games, or you can use the player match feature to safely find total strangers to compete against via the Web.

You can also enjoy all the various Game Center–compatible games without becom-ing active on the Game Center service. However, this service and its related app add a fun and social element to many popular, third-party, iPad-specific games.

Game Center is compatible with hundreds of games, some of which are free to download, whereas others are paid games available from the App Store. Regardless of what game(s) you experience Game Center with, using this online service and the Game Center app is always free.

You can use your Apple ID to set up a free Game Center account. To find Game Center–compatible games, launch the Game Center app from your iPad's Home Screen; tap the Games button near the bottom-center of the screen; and then, while your iPad is connected to the Internet, tap the Find Game Center Games graphic banner. You are transferred to the Game Center section of the App Store (shown in Figure 16.10).

FIGURE 16.10

Browse through hundreds of Game Center–compatible games in a special section of the App Store.

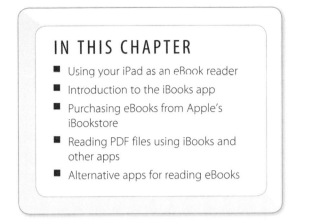

USING iBOOKS

By downloading the free iBooks app from the App Store, you can transform your iPad 2 into a powerful eBook reader, purchase eBooks from Apple's online-based iBookstore, and read PDF files imported via email to your iPad.

However, if you already have an eBook reader, such as Amazon's Kindle or Barnes & Noble's NOOK, in addition to the iBooks app, you can download the free Kindle or NOOK app from the App Store and then find, purchase, and download eBooks formatted for the Kindle or NOOK, respectively, and access your personal library of eBooks you've already acquired for your Kindle or NOOK.

Each eBook reader, such as the iPad, Kindle, or NOOK, formats eBook files differently and features a different interface for reading eBooks. In addition, each of the different online-based eBook stores offers a different selection of eBooks title, and charges different prices to purchase eBooks. What's available from Apple's own iBookstore via the iBooks app is only one option when it comes to shopping for, purchasing, and adding eBooks to your iPad.

Regardless of which eBook reader you use with your iPad, you have access to millions of eBook titles published by the world's leading publishers. You have access to electronically published works from self-published authors, as well as free eBook content that's in the public domain.

From your iPad, you can easily read full-length business, self-improvement, and how-to books, or you can find books in any category, such as the latest fiction from your favorite author. Perhaps you're reading this book in eBook format right now!

NOTE   To read a full-length eBook, you use the iBooks app, the Kindle app, or the NOOK app, for example. To download and read a digital edition of a magazine or newspaper on your iPad and manage your digital subscriptions, use the Newsstand app, described in Chapter 14, "Finding and Using News and Information Apps." For many digital publications, a proprietary app will also be needed, but this will be downloadable from within Newsstand and/or the App Store.

SELECTING AND DOWNLOADING eBOOKS

The free iBooks app has two distinct, but related, purposes. It serves as a conduit for accessing the online-based iBookstore, from which you can find, purchase, and download eBooks from publishers, as well as download free eBooks that are in the public domain.

After you have used iBooks to load eBook content onto your iPad, you can use this app to read your eBooks (see Figure 17.1) using a customizable user interface that enables you to personalize how the pages of your eBook appear on your screen.

ACCESSING THE iBOOKSTORE

When your iPad is connected to the Internet, you can use the iBooks app to shop for eBook titles from the iBookstore. From the main iBooks Bookshelf screen (see Figure 17.2), tap the Store icon near the upper-left corner of the screen to access the online-based iBookstore.

Your tablet must have access to the Internet to find, download, and purchase eBooks from iBookstore or any other online-based bookstore. However, you don't need Internet access to read eBooks after you've loaded them into your iPad.

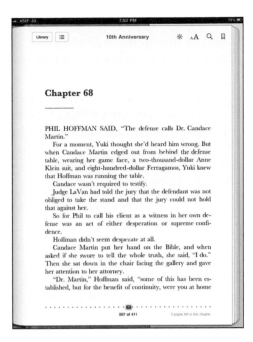

FIGURE 17.1

As you read an eBook, your iPad's screen looks like the pages of traditionally printed hardcover or paperback books. However, you can adjust the appearance of the text on the screen, making it larger or smaller, for example.

FIGURE 17.2

The main Bookshelf screen of iBooks. From here, you can access iBookstore or read an eBook.

Just as when you use iTunes or the App Store to make purchases, iBookstore charges your eBook purchases to your Apple ID account, which is linked to your major credit card. You can also pay for eBooks using prepaid iTunes gift cards offered by Apple.

When you tap the Store icon, your iPad connects to the Web and accesses iBookstore. At the bottom of the screen are five command buttons: Featured, NY Times, Top Charts, Browse, and Purchases. These five buttons, the Search field, the Categories button in the upper-left corner of the screen, and the Featured and Release Date tabs enable you to quickly search the iBookstore's multimillion-title eBook selection to find exactly the titles you are looking for.

Here's a rundown of how you can use these iBookstore command buttons and tabs:

- **Featured:** Titles in this category are eBooks featured by Apple that include new titles by bestselling authors. When you select this search option, you see two tabs near the top-center of the screen: Featured and Release Date. When you select the Featured tab, a listing of Apple-recommended eBook titles displays. When you select the Release Date tab, the recommended eBooks are sorted based on their release date, with the newest eBooks listed first.

- **NY Times:** Taken from the weekly *New York Times* bestsellers list, these are the books from the newspaper's Fiction and Non-Fiction lists that are available in eBook form from iBookstore. Keep in mind that not all books that appear on the published *New York Times* bestseller lists are available in eBook form or are sold through Apple's iBookstore.

- **Top Charts:** Based on sales of eBooks through iBookstore, the Top Charts category lists the current most popular titles. Here, you find a master list of popular books from all categories, plus individual Top Charts lists within specific categories, such as Business & Personal Finance, Fiction & Literature, Professional & Technical, and Reference. These lists change frequently.

> **TIP** As you browse iBookstore, you'll find a large selection of business and how-to books that you can read at your leisure and then refer to at any time. Your iPad can store hundreds of full-length books simultaneously. Using the Search feature of iBooks, you can find specific content within individual books easily and quickly.

- **Browse:** This search feature enables you to find eBook titles based on keywords, an author's name, a publisher, a subject matter, or other search criteria.

- **Purchases:** iBookstore automatically keeps track of all your eBook purchases and downloads. Thus, if you delete an eBook from your tablet's memory, you can download it again later at no charge. All of your online purchases are tracked by iBookstore and also stored on iCloud, so you never have to worry about accidentally purchasing the same eBook twice.

- **Categories:** The Categories button enables you to browse eBook titles based on category or subject matter. The eBooks are divided into 24 different categories.

UNDERSTANDING iBOOKSTORE'S eBOOK LISTINGS

While browsing iBookstore, you will see individual eBook listings for titles that relate to what you are looking for. As you can see in Figure 17.3, a typical eBook listing includes a graphic of the eBook's title, author, category, star-based rating, and price icon.

FIGURE 17.3

An eBook listing offers a quick summary of a book title. As you're browsing iBookstore, you can simultaneously view many eBook listings.

Tap a book's title or cover artwork to access a detailed description of that eBook, which includes the capability to download and read a free sample of most eBook titles. Alternatively, to quickly purchase and download an eBook, tap the Price button within its listing or its Description window. When you tap a Price button, it changes to a Purchase button. Tap the Purchase button to confirm your purchase decision. You then need to enter your Apple ID password to begin the download process.

It takes between 5 and 20 seconds to download a full-length eBook to your iPad. As soon as it's downloaded and ready to read, the book's front cover artwork displays as part of the Bookshelf screen.

> **NOTE** Some eBooks are freely available from iBookstore. In this case, the Price button displays the word Free. When you tap this button, it is replaced by a Download button. You still need to enter your Apple ID password to confirm your download request, but you are not charged to download free eBook content.

REVIEWING eBOOK DESCRIPTIONS

When you're looking at an eBook listing, if you tap the book's title or cover thumbnail image, a new and detailed eBook Description window displays. The window is divided into several sections.

Displayed near the top-left corner of a typical eBook Description window, which is shown in Figure 17.4, is the book's front cover artwork. To the right of this is a summary of the book, including its title, author, publication date, publisher, star-based rating, language it's published in, category, and length.

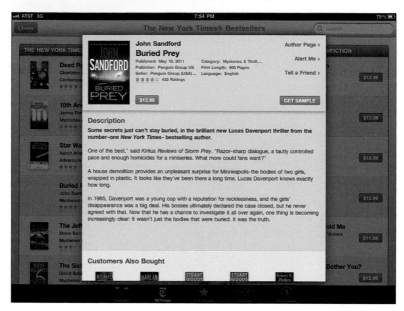

FIGURE 17.4

Read a detailed description of an eBook before making your purchase or downloading it.

> **TIP** From the iBookstore, you can return to the main bookshelf screen of iBooks by tapping the Library button near the upper-left corner of the screen.

In the upper-right corner of the Description window are links for visiting the author's web page and for sharing details about the book with someone else via email. There's also a Get Sample button, which you can tap to download a free sample of the eBook. The length of the sample varies (it's determined by the eBook's publisher); it will be between a few pages to a full chapter of the book.

Below the cover thumbnail is the eBook's Price button. Tap this button to purchase the book and download it. When you tap this button, it changes to a Download button. Tap the Download button, and then enter your Apple ID to confirm your book purchase and download it. (Once again, if the eBook is free, the Price button is a Free button instead, as shown in Figure 17.5).

FIGURE 17.5
If an eBook is free, its price icon says Free; however, you still need to enter your Apple ID to confirm the download request.

The next section of the Description window is the eBook's star-based rating. Here, you can view an overall average rating for the eBook. Five stars is the highest rating possible. You can also see how many ratings the book has received from other iBookstore customers, and you can view a chart that depicts how many one-, two-, three-, four-, and five-star ratings the eBook has received.

Scroll down the Description window to read reviews written by others who have purchased, downloaded, and presumably read the eBook. To exit an eBook Description window, tap anywhere on the iPad's screen that is outside the window.

CUSTOMIZING iBOOKS SETTINGS

From the bookshelf screen of iBooks, tap a book cover thumbnail to open that eBook and start reading it. While you're reading eBooks, you can hold the iPad in portrait or landscape mode. If you're reading a digital edition of a traditional paperback or hardcover book, your reading experience is more authentic if you hold the iPad in portrait mode (vertically).

As you're reading an eBook, tap anywhere near the top of the screen to make the various buttons and options appear. The Library button is displayed near the upper-left corner of the screen. Tap it to return to iBook's Bookshelf screen.

To the right of the Library button is the Table of Contents button (see Figure 17.6). Tap it to display an interactive Table of Contents for the eBook you're reading. As you're looking at a Table of Contents, tap any chapter number or chapter title to immediately jump to that location in the book. Alternatively, you can tap the Bookmarks button to see a list of bookmarks you have previously set as you were reading that eBook (see Figure 17.7). You'll find out how to set a bookmark later in this section.

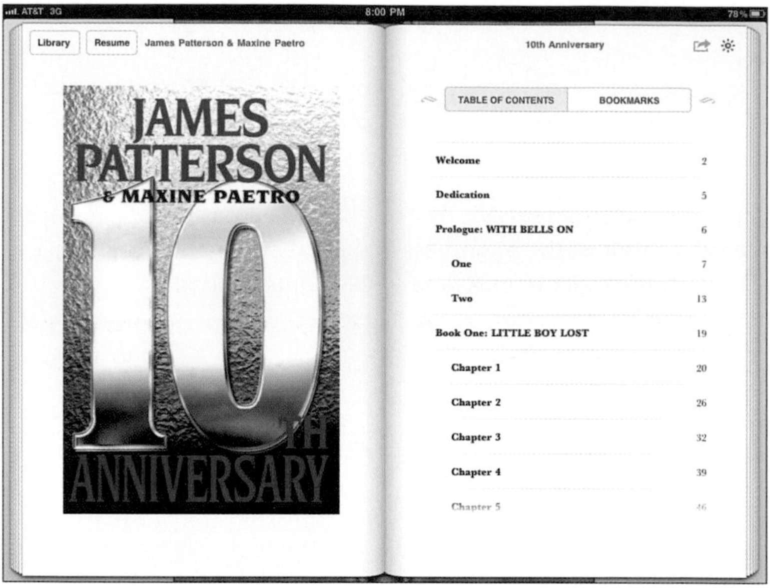

FIGURE 17.6

The Table of Contents screen for every eBook is interactive. Tap the chapter number or chapter title to jump to the appropriate page.

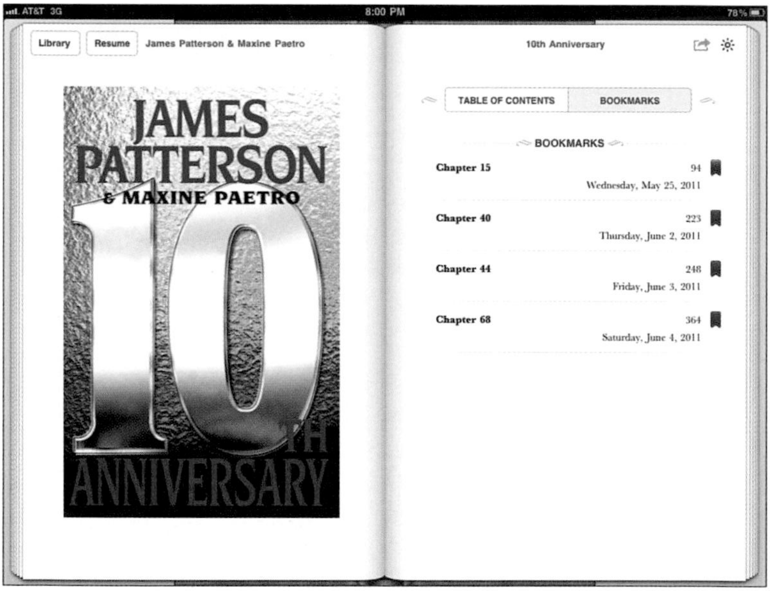

FIGURE 17.7

As you're reading, you can set bookmarks within an eBook and quickly return to those pages anytime later from the Bookmarks screen.

> **TIP** To exit the Table of Contents screen and return to reading your eBook, tap the Resume button that is displayed near the top-left corner of the screen.

As you're reading an eBook, you might notice several additional command buttons and options near the upper-right corner of the screen. The button with the sun on it enables you to adjust the brightness of the screen as you're reading. Use your finger to adjust the slider to make the screen lighter or darker.

Tap the aA button to change the font size or font style of the text on the page. You can also turn on or off the onscreen sepia effect (see Figure 17.8). By default, this effect is turned off.

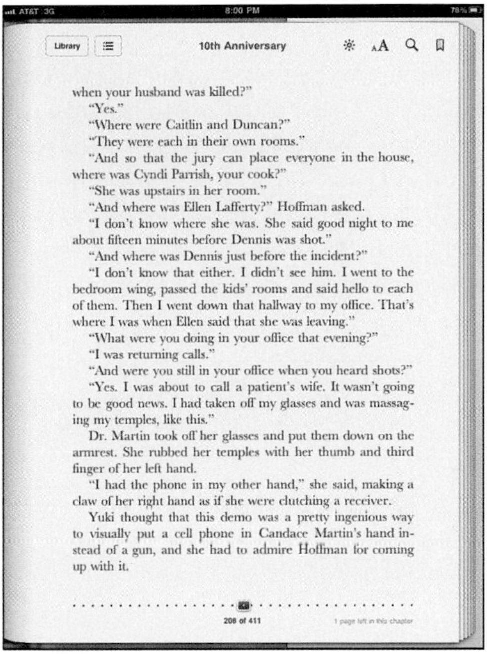

FIGURE 17.8

Some people prefer to read with the sepia effect turned on.

When you tap the small a button, the font size of the text shrinks. Tap the A button to increase the font size. The changes take effect immediately. Choose a font size and font that is the most visually appealing to you.

Also near the top-right corner of the screen is a magnifying glass button. Tap this to access a Search field and quickly locate any keyword or search phrase that appears in the eBook you are currently reading.

The bookmark button is near the extreme upper-right corner. When you tap this button, you add a red bookmark to the page you're reading. Any time you exit out of iBooks, the page number you're currently on is automatically saved, so when you return to reading the eBook later, you can immediately pick up where you left off. Adding a red bookmark to a page also stores that page. You can later access your list of bookmarks from the Table of Contents page and then instantly jump to any bookmarked page.

> **TIP** To access your list of bookmarks, tap the Table of Contents button. Near the top-center of the screen, tap the Bookmarks icon to display the list of book-marks that you've saved in the eBook you are currently reading. Tap any bookmark listing to jump to that page.

Turn pages while you're reading by swiping your finger from right to left across the screen to move one page forward. You can also back up a page by swiping your finger from left to right. Near the bottom-center of the screen is the page number in the eBook you're currently reading, as well as the total number of pages in the eBook (see Figure 17.9). The number of pages remaining in the current chapter is displayed to the right of the page number. You can't use this feature to "scroll through" a bunch of pages at a time, but you can access the Table of Contents and jump around that way.

FIGURE 17.9

View the page number you're on, and how many pages remain in the chapter, by looking at the bottom of the screen as you're reading an eBook.

READING PDF FILES

You can also use the iBooks app to read PDF files you download or transfer to your iPad. This can include a wide range of business-related documents that vary in length from a single page to a book-length manuscript. Keep in mind that PDF files can be protected by the creator, making it so that you can't edit, annotate, or print it. However, in most cases, you do have the ability to read, print, and/or annotate the PDF files you access on your iPad.

When you receive an email with a PDF file as an attachment, tap and hold your finger on the email's PDF file attachment thumbnail for a few seconds to download and open it.

When a menu window appears, you have several options, based on what PDF reader apps you have installed on your iPad. In Figure 17.10, the available options are Quick Look, Open in "iBooks," and Open In. If you also have other PDF reader apps installed on your iPad, such as Evernote or GoodReader for iPad, those apps are listed here as well because they can be used to open and read (as well as edit or annotate) PDF files.

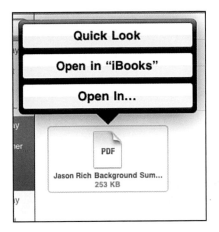

FIGURE 17.10

You can open and read a PDF file that is an attachment in an incoming email using the iBooks app.

Quick Look enables you to view a PDF document on your iPad's screen. Using the buttons in the upper-right corner of the document preview window, you can then open the PDF file in iBooks or print the file if you have your iPad 2 configured to work with a wireless printer.

The Open in iBooks command automatically launches the iBooks app and enables you to read the PDF document as if you're reading an eBook you downloaded from iBookstore.

> **NOTE** The Open In command enables you to open a PDF file using another third-party app. When you tap this menu option, you see a list of compatible apps for viewing, printing, sharing, and annotating PDFs. These apps might include PDF Reader, GoodReader, UPad, and Dropbox, for example.

When a PDF file opens in iBooks, you see command buttons displayed along the top of the screen and small thumbnails of the PDF document's pages displayed along the bottom of the screen.

Tap the Library button to return to iBook's main Bookshelf screen. Notice when you do this that the Bookshelf displays all the PDF files stored on your iPad—not only eBooks you downloaded from iBookstore. To access your eBooks, tap the Collections button in the upper-left corner of the iBooks Bookshelf screen (see Figure 17.11) and tap the Books option. (In this figure, the PDFs option is selected.) From this screen, tap the Store icon to return to iBookstore.

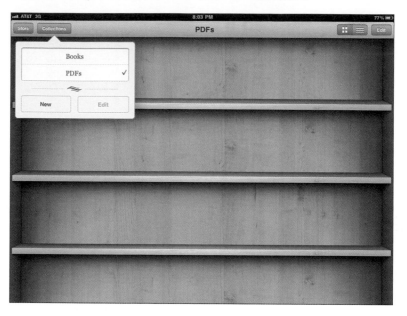

FIGURE 17.11

From the Bookshelf screen in iBooks, you can view your collection of eBooks or thumbnails for the PDF files that are stored and accessible using iBooks.

As you're viewing a PDF file from within iBooks, next to the Library button is the Table of Contents button. Tap it to display larger thumbnails of each page in your PDF document, and then tap any of the thumbnails to jump to that page. Alternatively, tap the Resume button to return to the main view of your PDF file.

To the immediate right of the Table of Contents button is a button that enables you to Email or Print the document you're currently viewing.

There are three additional command buttons in the upper-right corner of this screen. The button with the sun on it enables you to adjust the brightness of the screen. The magnifying glass button enables you to search a PDF file for specific text within the document, and the Bookmark icon enables you to bookmark specific pages in the PDF file for later reference. These buttons should seem familiar; they're used the same way when reading eBook files.

Also as you're reading a PDF file, you can hold the iPad either in a vertical or horizontal position. If you tap anywhere on the screen (except for on a command button or page thumbnail), the icons and thumbnails on the top and bottom of the screen disappear, giving you more onscreen real estate to view your PDF document. Tap near the top or bottom of the screen to make these icons and thumbnails reappear at any time.

> **NOTE** If you need to annotate your PDF files as you read them, instead of using the iBooks app, you need a separate app, such as GoodReader or UPad, both of which are available from the App Store.

READING eBOOKS FORMATTED FOR OTHER eBOOK READERS

Although Apple has worked out distribution deals with many major publishers and authors, the iBookstore does not offer every book in publication. In some cases, eBook titles are available from Amazon.com or Barnes & Noble (BN.com), but not from iBookstore. It might be the case that you owned a Kindle or NOOK eBook reader before you purchased your iPad, which means you might have already acquired a personal library of eBooks. You cannot access Kindle- or Nook-formatted eBooks using the iBooks app.

If you want to shop for eBooks from Amazon.com, or access your current Kindle eBook library from your iPad, you need to download the free Kindle app from the App Store. This app gives you access to Amazon.com and enables you to download and read Kindle-formatted eBooks.

Likewise, if you want to shop for eBooks from BN.com or access your current NOOK eBook library from your iPad, you need to download and use the free NOOK app from the App Store. The NOOK app gives you access to BN.com and enables you to read NOOK-formatted eBooks.

> **TIP** As competition between iBookstore, Amazon.com, and BN.com heats up, prices for eBook titles will likely become more competitive. So, not only will you discover variations on eBook title offerings between these online eBook stores, you will notice different prices for popular book titles.

Initially, the concept of reading an eBook on your tablet's screen might seem strange because you've probably grown up reading traditionally printed books. However, after spending a few hours reading your first eBook or two, reading on your iPad will become a comfortable experience.

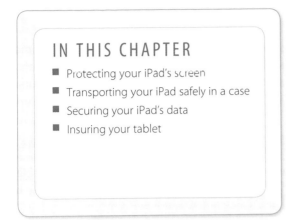

IN THIS CHAPTER

- Protecting your iPad's screen
- Transporting your iPad safely in a case
- Securing your iPad's data
- Insuring your tablet

18

PROTECTING YOUR iPAD 2 AND ITS DATA

Your iPad 2 is designed to be taken with you and used throughout your day in a variety of conditions. However, you need to make sure to protect and maintain the tablet as you carry it with you. In addition to keeping the battery charged throughout the day, which is a topic covered in Chapter 19, "Must-Have Accessories," it's also important to protect the iPad's screen against accidental scratches and to protect the entire tablet from accidents, such as being dropped or having some type of liquid spilled on it.

After you have made sure the iPad itself is well protected, you should focus on your important and potentially confidential data to make sure it too is safe. Finally, you might also consider purchasing optional insurance for your tablet in case it does get damaged, lost, or stolen.

Apple offers its AppleCare program, which covers the tablet against certain types of problems and grants you unlimited access to Apple's superior technical support for two years.

- **RadTech's ClearCal:** www.radtech.us/Products/clearcal-ipad-display-film. aspx ($19.95 USD for screen-only coverage)
- **Speck Products' ShieldView Screen Film for iPad:** www.speckproducts. com/tablet-ipad-cases.html ($24.95 USD for screen-only coverage, available in clear or matte forms)

It'll take you about 15 to 20 minutes to apply the InvisibleSHIELD from Zagg, and most protective film products like it, to the iPad. Make sure you follow the supplied directions carefully.

In many shopping malls across the United States, you'll find specialized kiosks that sell similar protective film products for your iPad (and other devices). In some cases, these companies will apply the protective film to your device for you. Removing the protective film, however, takes just seconds, and it leaves no sticky residue.

> **TIP**   3M offers a special Screen Protector film for the iPad 2 that also includes the company's patented Privacy Screen feature. When installed over your tablet's screen, if you're looking at the screen head-on, you see everything with complete clarity. However, if someone attempts to look over your shoulder, all he sees on your iPad is a dark, blank screen.
>
> This microlouver Privacy Screen technology can help you keep your data or whatever you're working on private, and it also protects your screen against scratches. To purchase an optional 3M Privacy Screen protector film for your iPad 2 ($39.99 USD), visit www.Shop3M.com.

SCREEN COVERS AND CASES

Adding a clear protective film to your iPad is certainly a good strategy to help protect your tablet when it's being used or transported. In addition to this optional protection, however, seriously consider investing in a screen cover for your iPad. A screen cover is used to protect the screen when the device is not in use—when you're transporting it, for example.

While designing the iPad 2, Apple created a special screen cover for it, called the Smart Cover, which protects the tablet's screen when it's not in use. In addition, as you're using the iPad, the Smart Cover also doubles as a stand (adjustable into two different positions).

Made from either leather ($69.00 USD) or polyurethane ($39.00 USD), these interchangeable Apple Smart Covers quickly attach and detach from your tablet using magnets. When placed over the screen, a Smart Cover automatically places your iPad 2 into sleep mode. When removed, it wakes the device.

When you fold back the Smart Cover, it can serve as a stand that enables you to position your tablet horizontally on a flat surface, which is ideal for watching a movie. You can also arrange the Smart Cover into a position that's more suitable for typing.

CAUTION You cannot use Apple's Smart Cover as a stand to hold your iPad 2 in a portrait (vertical) position.

Apple's Smart Covers come in 10 colors. The leather versions offer a more conservative color selection and have a classier look that's more suited to business professionals.

NOTE Smart Covers are available wherever Apple products are sold, including from Apple Stores and Apple.com. For more information, visit www.apple.com/ipad/accessories.

Several companies that manufacture cases and accessories for the iPad 2 have also released their own versions of the Smart Cover. Some of these also offer full-body protection for your tablet, a different color selection, or additional stand positions.

The iPad 2 Smart Case from BoxWave ($89.95 USD, www.boxwave.com/accessories/apple-ipad-2-cases_4284.htm) is an example of a hybrid screen cover that offers the features and functionality of Apple's Smart Cover, but it also offers full-body protection to the tablet. These cases are made from animal-friendly synthetic leather and come in a variety of colors.

Another variation of the Smart Cover is the Ultra Thin Smarty Complete ($59.99 USD, www.ipadcasefinder.com/featured/the-ultra-thin-smarty-complete.html), available from iPad Case Finder. This cover offers the features and functionality of an Apple Smart Cover but also offers full-body protection in a thin, sleek, and stylish design. Six color choices are available.

When choosing any type of screen cover or case for your iPad, make sure that it offers ample protection but also keeps all of the tablet's buttons and ports easily accessible without having to remove the iPad from the case. Depending on your needs, you might also want a case that looks stylish but also easily fits in your briefcase, purse, backpack, or messenger bag.

Keep in mind that how much you pay for a "designer" iPad 2 screen cover or case often has little relevance to its quality, functionality, or stylish design. Be sure to choose a screen cover or case for your tablet that's well made.

padded case, sleeve, or pouch) into a briefcase, purse, backpack, or messenger bag, you'll know the entire tablet is well protected.

Many companies offer iPad 2 slip covers, sleeves, and pouches in a wide range of colors and styles, including the following:

- **WaterField Designs** (http://sfbags.com/products/ipad-cases/ipad-cases.php): This company offers multiple iPad 2-specific cases and covers, each of which comes in a variety of colors. The company also offers messenger-style bags with built-in, padded compartments designed for the iPad.

- **Timbuk2** (www.timbuk2.com): This San Francisco–based company's large selection of messenger bags and backpacks are made from extremely durable ballistic nylon and have strong hook-and-loop closures. The bags offer compartments for an iPad, as well as custom-fitted padded slip cases for the iPad 2. All the products are made in the United States, are affordable and are available in a wide range of colors.

  For example, the Timbuk2 Plush Sleeve for iPad 2 ($40.00 USD) offers a ballistic nylon exterior, has a faux fur lining, and is well padded with high-density foam for added protection.

- **BoxWave** (www.boxwave.com): In addition to offering a handful of different cases and covers for the iPad 2, the company offers the Manila iPad Leather Envelope (from $29.95 USD), which looks like a traditional manila envelope. In reality, it's a well-made, custom-fit, padded slipcover for your iPad. This is a slim and lightweight slipcover that also offers a soft interior to keep your tablet from getting scuffed during transport.

SECURING YOUR DATA

Throughout *Your iPad 2 at Work*, you've read about a handful of ways to protect the data stored on your tablet. For example, you can use the passcode protection feature that's built in to the iOS. When activated, an iPad 2 user must enter the correct passcode (which you preset) before she can get past the iPad's Lock Screen whenever the tablet is turned on or awakened from sleep mode.

To recap, you can activate the iPad's Passcode option by tapping the Settings app icon from the Home screen and then selecting the General option from the left side of the Settings screen.

With the General option highlighted, select the Passcode Lock feature that's displayed on the right side of the screen. When the Passcode Lock window appears, tap the Turn Passcode On button, and then enter a four-digit numeric passcode.

After it's activated, you need to enter this passcode whenever the iPad 2 is turned on or awakened from sleep mode. For added protection, you can turn on the Erase

Data option (also found in the Passcode Lock screen of the Settings app). When this additional feature is active, if someone enters the wrong passcode 10 times, all data on your tablet is deleted.

If you're concerned that a four-digit passcode doesn't offer ample protection, you can turn off the Simple Passcode option (also found in the Passcode Lock window of the Settings app). This enables you to create and use a longer, alphanumeric password.

> **TIP** If you're using your iPad to access your company's network, your company can implement additional security software onto the network itself that ensures a secure wireless connection whenever you access it with an iPad. Based on the type of network you'll be accessing, the steps for establishing this secure connection vary. To learn more, visit www.apple.com/ipad/business/integration.

> **NOTE** If you use your iPad to connect to a corporate intranet, Juniper Networks offers its proprietary Junos Pulse Mobile Security Suite (888-586-4737, www.juniper.net/pulse). It provides instant and secure connectivity to your corporate intranet from anywhere. This includes secure remote access to corporate email, applications, and intranet resources providing that the corporate intranet itself utilizes the Juniper Networks Secure Access SSL VPN Appliance.

PROTECTING YOUR iPAD FROM THEFT OR LOSS

If your iPad is lost or stolen, Apple offers its powerful Find My iPad feature, which enables you to pinpoint the tablet's exact location on a map as long as it's turned on and able to connect to the Internet. If the tablet is turned off, you can set the Find My iPad feature to keep trying to locate the iPad if it is later turned on.

To utilize Find My iPad, you must set up your device in advance (prior to it being lost or stolen). To do this on an iPad running iOS 4.2 or later, access the Home screen and tap the Settings icon.

Next, select Mail, Contacts, Calendars and either create a free MobileMe/iCloud account (using your Apple ID) or access your existing MobileMe/iCloud account. If you're creating a new MobileMe/iCloud account, it must be verified before the Find My iPad service can work.

From the MobileMe/iCloud account screen, scroll down and turn on the Find My iPad feature. Confirm this option by tapping the Allow button when prompted. This enables Apple to locate your iPad whenever it's turned on (and not in Airplane mode).

After Find My iPad is activated, if you misplace your iPad or the device is stolen, you can access the Me.com website (https://me.com/find) from any computer or wireless Internet device and have the Find My iPad service quickly pinpoint the exact location of your device.

From this website, you can also type a message that displays on your device's screen (asking for the device to be returned), or you can force the device to emit a sound (so you can more easily find it if it's lost in the same location where you are—such as if it's under the sofa cushion).

You can also lock the device using a password or wipe out and delete the contents of your iPad remotely, which ensures that your sensitive data doesn't fall into the wrong hands. You can always restore your data from an iTunes or iCloud backup after the unit has been retrieved.

Although this is a useful tool for securing your iPad, it's not foolproof. If the iPad is not turned on or is in Airplane mode, for example, the Find My iPad features won't work. However, when this tool is used with the tablet's Passcode feature, it does provide an added level of security that helps keep your data safe if your iPad gets lost or stolen.

INSURING YOUR iPAD

If something were to go wrong with your iPad, you would either have to pay to replace the unit outright because it's been lost or stolen, or you might have to pay a hefty repair bill for damages that aren't covered by the warrantee.

The four most common mishaps people have with their iPads are that the unit gets lost, stolen, damaged by liquid, or accidentally dropped. Unfortunately, none of these problems are covered by Apple's warranty or AppleCare.

You can gamble on the fact that you won't encounter any of these problems. If you do have problems, you could potentially purchase a used or refurbished iPad 2 as a replacement for your original device instead of buying a new one.

To guard against troubles, the optional AppleCare extended warranty plan ($99.00 USD) for the iPad 2 has a few advantages, especially for non-tech-savvy people. For two years, AppleCare offers unlimited and extemporary technical support, in person at any Apple Store or by telephone. Plus, the optional AppleCare plan offers hardware coverage of the iPad itself, as well as its battery, earphones, and included accessories.

However, this coverage protects only against manufacturing defects and workman-ship. According to the AppleCare Protection Plan for iPad 2 Terms and Conditions, the coverage does not protect against problems that are "caused by accident, abuse, neglect, misuse (including faulty installation, repair or maintenance by anyone other than Apple or an Apple Authorized Service Provider), unauthorized modification, extreme environment (including extreme temperature or humidity), extreme physical or electrical stress or interference, fluctuation or surges of electrical power, lightning, static electricity, fire, acts of God or other external causes."

The coverage also does not offer protection against loss or theft. For full insurance coverage for an iPad 2 against loss, theft, or accidental damage, you can acquire third-party insurance, which is offered by a handful of companies.

> **TIP** Enter the search phrase "iPad insurance" in a search engine to find insurance companies that offer optional coverage for Apple mobile devices.

Two companies that offer comprehensive iPad 2 insurance coverage are Square-Trade (www.squaretrade.com) and Worth Ave. Group (www.worthavegroup.com). Both of these companies offer two-year insurance coverage for between $79.00 USD and $100.00 USD. However, what's covered under each policy varies. In many cases, a $50.00 USD deductible applies per claim.

As you evaluate the various insurance policies and extended warranty programs, determine what's covered and what's not, how much of a deductible you'll be charged per claim, and how repairs or product replacements are handled. Ideally, you want a policy that offers next-day equipment replacement.

Purchasing insurance or an extended warrantee for your iPad 2 is optional. Like any type of insurance, it offers you peace of mind and financial protection should something go wrong. If you're a person who is extremely reliant on your Apple tablet, having this added protection could save a lot of frustration and stress, and it can provide you with quick equipment replacement.

> **TIP** Regardless of whether you opt to protect your Apple hardware, it's essential that you regularly back up your apps and data. Using iOS 5, you can do this in a variety of ways using the iTunes sync process or wirelessly via iCloud. See Chapter 8, "Syncing to Your Computer via iTunes or iCloud," for details on backing up your data.

19

MUST-HAVE ACCESSORIES

From external keyboards to high-end headphones, battery packs and chargers that will keep your tablet running, wireless printers, desktop stands, and cables for connecting your iPad 2 to other devices, you can connect a variety of optional accessories to your iPad 2 to enhance its functionality.

Apple offers its own selection of iPad 2 accessories (some of which are discussed in this chapter). However, you can also find an ever-growing lineup of powerful and useful accessories from third-party companies.

> **TIP** To learn more about or order Apple's iPad 2 accessories, visit www.apple.com/ipad/accessories.

you place it on a flat surface, such as a desk or airplane seatback tray table. You can keep the iPad 2 in the case at all times because it's designed to offer full access to all of the tablet's buttons and ports. You can only use the iPad 2 in landscape position with this keyboard/case combo.

Brookstone offers a growing selection of iPad 2 accessories, including cases, keyboards, external speakers, headphones, desktop stands, external battery packs, and chargers. These accessories are available from the company's chain of retail stores, via mail order, or from Brookstone's website.

> **TIP**   When shopping for accessories, be sure you order the iPad 2 version of the product, as some accessories also have separate iPad versions available that won't work properly with the iPad 2.

BATTERY OPTIONS

Depending on how it's being used, your iPad 2 has an average battery life of 10 hours (less if you're doing a lot of web surfing via a 3G connection). Unfortunately, it's not always convenient to recharge your iPad by connecting it to your primary computer (via the supplied USB cable) or by plugging it into an electrical outlet. Fortunately, you can purchase option battery packs and battery chargers to help you keep your iPad sufficiently powered.

BATTERY PACKS

A handful of companies offer external, rechargeable battery packs for the iPad that plug into the tablet via a cable that connects to its docking port. These optional battery packs come in different configurations and sizes, but most of them are smaller than a deck of cards.

The RichardSolo 9000 mAh Universal Mobile Charger ($69.95 USD, www.RichardSolo.com) connects to your iPad 2 via the supplied USB cable. It can dramatically extend the life of your tablet's battery power in between charges. This particular external rechargeable battery pack measures 3.76" × 1.57" × 1.57" and doubles the battery life of your tablet to about 20 hours per charge.

If you don't always have access to an electrical outlet for recharging your iPad's batteries, Revolve's xeMilo battery pack ($99.99 USD, http://revolveusa.com/index.php?p=1_55_xeMilo) has a built-in solar panel, which enables it to be recharged using sunlight. (You can also recharge it from a traditional AC outlet.) The unit (see Figure 19.2) measures 5.75" × 3.5" × .69" and weighs 10 ounces.

FIGURE 19.2

The Revolve xeMilo is a solar-powered external battery pack for your iPad.

BATTERY CHARGERS

Your iPad comes with a white USB cable that you use to connect the tablet to your primary computer (unless you have an older computer that doesn't have a USB outlet). The tablet uses the USB connection to charge its batteries while it's connected to the computer.

You can attach the AC adapter that comes with your iPad 2 to the USB cable and charge your iPad by plugging the adapter into an electrical outlet. For those times when neither your primary computer nor an electrical outlet is available, you can purchase and use an optional car charger to plug the iPad into your car's 12v power outlet/cigarette lighter.

These accessories are readily available from consumer electronics stores, mass market retailers, and office supply stores (such as Best Buy, Radio Shack, Staples, Wal-Mart, and Target), as well as Apple stores and Brookstone.

The 2-amp USB Car Charger for iPad 2 from Brookstone (www.brookstone.com) is priced at $24.99 USD. Similar car charger products include the Griffin PowerDuo for iPad 2 ($39.95 USD, www.griffintechnology.com/ipad) and the Kensington PowerBolt Duo Car Charger for iPad 2 ($29.99 USD, http://us.kensington.com/html/17729.html).

When choosing a car charger adapter, make sure that it's been approved to work with an iPad 2, as opposed to an iPhone (which uses the same 30-pin dock connector).

> **TIP** While driving in your car, a car charger adapter can be used to keep your iPad 2 running when the tablet's internal battery goes dead, and it can be used to simultaneously recharge the tablet's battery. Depending on your vehicle, however, the engine might need to be running for its 12v power outlet to operate.

DESKTOP STANDS FOR EASIER iPAD ACCESS

While you're sitting at your desk, there are a variety of ways to prop up your iPad 2 for easy access and viewing. These desktop stands come in a wide range of styles. Some are designed exclusively to hold up your tablet in only a portrait or landscape direction, whereas others are more flexible. Ideally, you want a stand that's stylish and sturdy. It should also be able to hold your iPad in portrait or landscape mode and potentially in a position that's conducive to typing.

Twelve South offers its metal Compass iPad stand ($39.99 USD, www.twelvesouth.com/products/compass). It looks like a small metal easel that is adjustable into several positions, which enables it to hold your iPad at several different angles. The Compass offers a contemporary look on a desktop, but it folds up into a compact package that fits in a pocket or purse, so you can use it while on the go. You can set it up in seconds, and it works great on an airplane seatback table.

Brookstone offers the modern-looking X-Stand for iPad ($49.99 USD, www.brookstone.com), which is designed to stay on your desk- or tabletop. The stand—which is available in black, silver, or red—pivots, which enables you to quickly switch between portrait and landscape mode. Your tablet is held firmly in place using silicon corner pads, but you can easily remove it from the stand.

Levenger offers its Thai Pad iPad stand ($39.00 USD, www.levenger.com) that looks like a strange-shaped pillow made with 100% silk upholstery and hypoallergenic polyfiber stuffing. The Thai Pad offers sturdy back support for your tablet and an ergonomic wrist support. You can use it on a tabletop or desk, or you can position it on your lap. Because it's not portable, this stand is more suitable for use at home than in the office, and it's great when you're using your tablet while sitting on a couch.

> **NOTE** Levenger (www.Levenger.com) also offers a handful of wooden desktop iPad stands and lap desks, ranging in price from $39.00 USD to $179.00 USD. Visit the company's website; call (800) 544-0880 to request a full-color catalog; or visit one of the company's retail locations in Boston, Chicago, and Washington, D.C.

Griffin offers several different iPad 2 desktop stands, including its contemporary-looking Arrowhead ($19.99 USD, https://store.griffintechnology.com/arrowhead). This stand is comprised of two weighted "feet" that, when used together, create a sturdy platform for your tablet in both portrait and landscape positions. Rubber pads on the bottom of the feet keep the stand from sliding around on the tabletop or desk, and rubber coating in the cradle for the iPad also keep your tablet firmly in place.

iPAD CAMERA CONNECTION KIT

Although your iPad 2 has two built-in cameras, neither of them offer the resolution of most mid- to high-end digital SLR or digital point-and-shoot cameras. If you have a separate digital camera, you can connect it directly to your iPad via a USB cable and Apple's iPad Camera Connection kit ($29.00 USD). With the connection kit, you can quickly transfer your digital images from the camera's memory card to your tablet for viewing, editing, and sharing your photos.

Available from Apple Stores, Apple.com, or wherever Apple products are sold, the iPad Camera Connection Kit comes with two adapters that connect to the bottom of your iPad via the 30-pin Dock Connector port.

One of the adapters serves as an SD memory card reader. If your digital camera uses an SD memory card, you can insert the card directly into this memory card reader when it's attached to your iPad, and then quickly transfer its digital photo contents to your tablet. The second adapter is a standard USB port connector. You can use it to connect your digital camera (via its USB port) to your iPad (via this connection adapter and the USB cable that's supplied with your digital camera).

> **NOTE** If your digital camera also shoots digital video, you can also transfer videos to your iPad 2 using the iPad Camera Connection Kit.

After your photos are transferred from your digital camera, you can view and share them using the Photos app. You can edit the photos using a third-party app, such as Photogene or CameraBag. You can view videos you transfer from your digital camera to your iPad using the Videos app, or you can view, edit, and share them with the iMovie app.

HEADPHONES AND EXTERNAL SPEAKERS

Whether you're listening to music, watching TV shows or movies, recording and then listening to important meetings, or streaming content from the Web, the speaker built in to your iPad has decent quality, but it's not good enough to satisfy a true audiophile. It's possible to dramatically improve the sound output of your tablet simply by plugging decent-quality stereo headphones into the iPad's headphone jack or by using good-quality external speakers.

When it comes to adding external speakers to your iPad, the choices are plentiful, and the price range is dramatic. You can spend between $50.00 USD and $100.00 USD for some decent external speakers, or you can invest hundreds in some top-of-the-line speakers from companies such as Bose (www.bose.com) or Bang & Olufsen (www.bang-olufsen.com).

NOTE External speakers can connect to your iPad in a variety of ways: via the headphone jack, the 30-pin Dock Connector port, or a wireless Bluetooth connection (so no cables are required).

If you want awesome quality sound from an external speaker but portability is important, Jawbone's Jambox Wireless Speaker ($199.99 USD, www.jawbone.com) is the perfect companion for your tablet. This battery-powered speaker has an output capacity of 85 decibels and measures 6" × 1.5" × 2.25". It truly offers the power and sound quality you'd expect from an expensive home theater system. Because it's portable, battery-powered, and wireless (see Figure 19.3), you can use it virtually anywhere.

FIGURE 19.3
The Jawbone Jambox is the ideal portable speaker for the iPad.

iHome (www.ihomeaudio.com, from SDI Technologies) also offers a complete line of external speakers with built-in connectors or docks for an iPad. These speakers are mid-priced and are ideal for at-home use. The iHome iA100 ($199.00 USD), for example, is a feature-packed clock radio with a built-in iPad dock. It also offers wireless Bluetooth connectivity and a built-in AM/FM radio and clock display.

If you prefer to listen to high-quality audio in private, such as when you're on an airplane, for example, consider investing in a pair of high-quality, noise-reduction stereo headphones. These range in price from $100.00 USD to $300.00 USD and are available from companies such as Bose, Monster Beats, Audio-Technica, Sony, and JVC.

In addition to full-size headphones that fit over your ears, you can achieve true portability and convenience without compromising sound quality with a pair of in-ear headphones. The Bose MIE2i mobile headset ($129.95 USD, www.bose.com) is ideal for listening to audio or watching TV shows or movies on airplanes.

> **NOTE** As you discover later in this chapter, if you've already invested in a high-quality home theater system, there are multiple ways to connect your iPad 2 to it, either using cables or a wireless connection. Connecting to your home theater system enables you to view content stored on your tablet on a large-screen HD television or listen to audio on your stereo surround-sound speakers.
>
> Built in to iOS 5 are enhanced AirPlay features that support video mirroring, which enables you to wirelessly stream whatever audio or video content (as well as photos) that is stored on your tablet directly to your HDTV when an Apple TV device ($99.00 USD) is utilized.

CONNECTION OPTIONS: HD, VGA, HOME THEATER

It's almost impossible to rave too much about the big output possibilities from this single handheld tablet. When you connect your iPad to your office (or home office) equipment, the machine on which you do your research and prep work becomes a production device that increases the impressiveness of your digital output. Let's consider some of the possibilities.

CONNECTING TO AN HD MONITOR OR A TV

If you have a high-definition television (HDTV) or monitor with an HDMI input, you can use Apple's Digital AV Adapter ($39.00 USD) to connect your iPad to that monitor. After connecting, you use the iOS's Video Mirroring feature so everything you see on your iPad's screen is displayed on the monitor or television set.

This is a great way to showcase your Keynote presentations to groups of people in a meeting situation or display your digital photos on your television at home. In addition to this adapter, you need a standard HDMI cable (sold separately) that's long enough to connect your iPad to your monitor.

> CAUTION   The Apple Digital Video Adapter enables you to display whatever appears on your tablet's screen simultaneously on an HD monitor or television set that has an HDMI input.
>
> Keep in mind, however, that certain apps that play copyrighted video content, such as television episodes or movies downloaded from iTunes, or content streamed using the Netflix or HBO Go apps cannot be displayed on a monitor using this adapter. For this, you must use the AirPlay feature of the iPad's iOS along with an Apple TV unit that's connected to your home theater system.

CONNECTING TO A VGA MONITOR

The Apple VGA Adapter ($29.00 USD) connects from your iPad's 30-pin Dock Connector port to a monitor cable (sold separately) that then attaches to a standard VGA computer monitor. This enables you to display content from your tablet on a computer monitor as you give presentations or demonstrations using content, data, drawings, or animations from your iPad, for example. This type of connection works with most LCD projectors as well.

CONNECTING TO A SOUND SYSTEM OR HOME THEATER SYSTEM

There are several ways to give your iPad a louder voice. The method that gives you the most flexibility to wirelessly stream audio and video content, as well as photos between your tablet and television set, is to connect an Apple TV device ($99.00 USD) to your home theater system and to have a Wi-Fi hotspot set up in your home. With this equipment, you can fully use your iPad's AirPlay feature.

Keep in mind, however, that Apple TV and other home theatre equipment can just as easily be used in a work environment, office, conference room, or auditorium, allowing you to stream content from your tablet and share it with others on large-screen TVs and monitors that are connected to high-end audio systems, for example.

You can also connect your iPad directly to your home theater system using the Apple Composite AV Cable ($39.00 USD), which enables you to watch iPad video on a big screen with stereo sound. Depending on the input connections available as part of your system, the Apple Component AV cable (which serves the same purpose as the Apple Composite AV cable but offers different connectors) is also available.

> **TIP** The Apple Digital AV Adapter, Apple VGA Adapter, Apple Composite AV Cable, Apple Component AV Cable, and Apple TV device are all sold separately and available wherever Apple products are sold, including Apple Stores and Apple.com.

If you want to give a presentation or transform a blank wall in your home or office into a 60-inch diagonal screen, the Cinemin Swivel Video Project ($299.99 USD, www.wowwee.com/en/products/tech/projection/cinemin/swivel) or the Cinemin Slice Projector ($429.99 USD, www.wowwee.com/en/products/tech/projection/cinemin/slice) are extremely portable, battery-powered projectors that connect directly to your iPad. Both devices enable you to give presentations, watch video media, or project digital photos on any wall or screen without needing a television, speaker system, or cables.

You can set up either projector in minutes, and you can use them virtually anywhere with your iPad. These projectors offer WVGA resolution and project an image up to 60 inches diagonal from about 8 feet away from a wall or screen.

ACCESSORIES FOR TRAVELING ABROAD

When you travel overseas with your iPad, being able to access the 3G wireless web and recharging your tablet are relatively straightforward processes regardless of whether you travel with a laptop computer.

> **TIP** See Chapter 11, "Using Travel-Related Apps," for information about apps you might find useful when traveling outside the United States, such as a currency converter and the Flight Track Pro app.

USING INTERNATIONAL POWER ADAPTERS

When traveling abroad, you need to be able to recharge your iPad's battery. If you'll want to recharge your tablet using an electric outlet overseas, you must attach a special adapter to the end of the white USB cable that came with your iPad.

Available from Apple Stores and Apple.com, the Apple World Travel Adapter Kit ($39.00 USD) comes with six international power adapters that connect to the power adapter that came with your iPad 2. This kit enables you to plug in your tablet just about anywhere in the world.

REPLACING YOUR iPAD'S MICRO SIM CARD FOR WIRELESS WEB ACCESS

If you have an iPad 2 Wi-Fi Only model, your tablet is able to connect to the Internet via a Wi-Fi connection anywhere in the world you travel that has a public Wi-Fi hotspot available (this includes many hotels, cafés, and airports).

iPAD 2 WI-FI + 3G (AT&T WIRELESS)

When you leave the United States, your 3G wireless service through AT&T Wireless is not available. However, you can visit any Apple Store or Apple Authorized Reseller while you're overseas (or many cellular service providers) to obtain a micro SIM chip for your iPad 2, which temporarily replaces your AT&T micro SIM chip while you're traveling.

Because you can purchase 3G wireless data service on a month-to-month basis or, in some cases, on a predetermined amount of wireless data usage, you can easily obtain a new micro SIM chip that works in the country or countries you're visiting, insert it into your iPad, and be able to access 3G wireless data service in almost any country you're visiting.

If there's an Apple Store where you're going, an Apple Genius can offer you a micro SIM chip from a local 3G data service provider, help you swap the chip in your iPad 2, and activate the 3G wireless data account using a major credit card within 10 or fewer minutes. Alternatively, you can visit a retail location for a wireless service provider and swap out the micro SIM chips yourself.

After you set up 3G data service in a specific country, any time you return to that country, you can use the same micro SIM chip and purchase additional access. However, when you replace your AT&T Wireless micro SIM chip with the micro SIM chip for the local 3G wireless data provider in the country you're visiting, make sure you do not misplace the tiny AT&T micro SIM chip that you need when you return home.

While traveling, the price for 3G wireless data access varies based on the country you're visiting and the wireless data service provider you need to use. You will probably find the prices to be reasonable in most countries.

Throughout Europe, one of the leading wireless 3G data service providers that supports the iPad 2 is O2 (www.o2.co.uk). Upon arriving in any European country, you can visit an O2 retail location (which are as commonplace as AT&T Wireless locations in the U.S.) or visit any Apple Store and obtain a free O2 micro SIM chip.

With the O2 micro SIM chip installed in your iPad 2, you can sign up for 3G wireless data service for £2.04 per day for up to 200MB of data usage, or you can sign up for 1GB of wireless data usage, which you can use within a 30-day period for £10.21.

Through O2, there's also a plan that offers 2GB of wireless data usage over a 30-day period for £15.32. These last two plans are recurring, meaning you will be auto-matically billed for the plan every 30 days until you cancel it. However, you can easily cancel the plan at the conclusion of your trip with no penalties or extra fees incurred. When you install the O2 micro SIM chip, you can activate it and choose a wireless data plan directly from your tablet.

> **TIP** If you know you need to swap micro SIM chips in and out of your iPad while traveling abroad, make sure you bring along the small metal SIM chip ejector tool that came with your tablet. For information about what this tool actually looks like and how to use it properly, visit this page of Apple's website: http://support.apple.com/kb/HT4577.

iPAD 2 WI-FI + 3G (VERIZON WIRELESS)

Because your iPad Wi-Fi + 3G that's registered with Verizon uses CDMA technology, before leaving for your trip overseas, contact Verizon Wireless and activate a CDMA Global Data Roaming plan.

Wireless data roaming is available in many countries for a flat fee of $30.00 USD for 75MB or $100.00 USD for 200MB. For more information, contact Verizon directly at (800) 922-0204.

WIRELESS PRINTING

The easiest solution if you want to take advantage of the Print command that's now built in to many apps, including Safari, Mail, Pages, and countless others, is to invest in an AirPrint-compatible printer. You can also print PDF files from within iBooks and other PDF reader apps.

> **TIP** To learn more about the AirPrint functionality built in to iOS 5, visit http://support.apple.com/kb/HT4356.

Currently, Hewlett-Packard (www.hp.com/eprint) offers a full line-up of about 20 ePrint-compatible printers, which range in price from less than $100.00 USD to about $500.00 USD and that offer what the company calls HP ePrint.

Any ePrint-compatible printer is fully AirPrint compatible, which means the printer can be easily configured to wirelessly print from your iPad 2 as long as the iPad and printer are connected to the same Wi-Fi network.

HP Printers with ePrint functionality include several PhotoSmart printers (capable of printing professional-quality photo prints), several all-in-one printers, and some higher-end OfficeJet Pro and LaserJet Pro laser printers, which are ideal for home office or corporate use.

One of the great things about ePrint-compatible printers that are connected to the Web is that you can use them when you're within a few feet of the printer, or you can be absolutely anywhere in the world with your iPad and still print, as long as the printer is also connected to the Web. You send files to the printer, and they'll be waiting for you when you return to the printer's location.

If you have an ePrint-compatible printer, you do not need any specialized software or apps to print directly from your iPad. Any app with a built-in Print command sends the content, file, photo, or document that you're viewing on your tablet directly to the printer.

WHAT IF YOUR PRINTER ISN'T EPRINT- OR AIRPRINT-COMPATIBLE?

Many printers offer wireless or web connectivity, but they do not offer the ePrint feature or direct AirPrint compatibility. In this case, there are optional third-party apps you can use with many of these printers to wirelessly print from your iPad. This solution, however, typically requires some configuration of settings on your printer and within the third-party printing app you utilize.

Some of the apps you might want to investigate if you want or need to print wire-lessly from your iPad to a printer without ePrint or AirPrint compatibility include Print n Share ($8.99 USD), DocPrinter ($5.99 USD), PrintCentral Pro for iPad ($9.99 USD), Print Magic HD ($4.99 USD), or Print Agent Pro for iPad ($5.99 USD). These and other apps like them are available from the App Store.

Many of these apps enable you to print from your iPad to any printer if you go through your PC or Mac, or you can print wirelessly directly to the printer if the printer has Wi-Fi functionality.

If you're planning to create prints of photos you've shot using your iPad or that are stored on your tablet, you might want to edit them a bit first. Although the upgraded Camera and Photos apps that come preinstalled with iOS 5 offer new photo-editing capabilities, these editing tools are still limited compared to what you can do with specialized photo-editing apps, such as Snapseed, Photogene, and CameraBag, for example, which are available from the App Store. These optional apps are relatively easy to use but offer professional-quality photo editing and enhancement tools directly on your iPad. After you edit them, you can use iOS 5's AirPrint functionality to send the photos to a compatible photoprinter.

CREATING PRINTS FROM YOUR PHOTOS

If you want to quickly create full-color prints from either photos you've shot using your iPad's built-in camera or from digital images that you've imported and potentially edited on your iPad, there are a few quick and easy ways to do this that do not require connecting your tablet to a computer.

USING A PHOTO PRINTER

Several companies make photo printers that you can connect to your iPad 2 using a cable and the iPad's 30-pin Dock Connector port, wireless Wi-Fi, or Bluetooth.

For example, the Photo Cube from VuPoint Solutions ($149.00 USD, www.vupointsolutions.com) is a small desktop printer that attaches to your iPad's Dock Connector port via a USB cable. This printer can create 4" × 6" prints straight from your iPad in less than 45 seconds each. The printer itself weights 3.1 pounds and measures just 7" × 4" × 6". It does not require the use of a computer to operate. Each replaceable printer cartridge for the Photo Cube has a 36-print capacity and costs about $36.00 USD, which means each print costs about $1.00 USD.

HP also offers a line of full-size photo printers that you can use with your iPad 2 via a wireless connection. These printers enable you to create full-color prints up to 8.5" × 11" directly from any app that has a print feature, including Photos, Snapseed, and Photogene. For information about HP's ePrint printers, visit www. HP.com/eprint or any Hewlett-Packard printer authorized dealer.

PROFESSIONAL PRINTING

Many one-hour photo processing services and professional photo labs enable you to email digital image files to be transformed into full-color prints. You can email your photo files directly from your iPad.

There are also a handful of free apps available from the App Store that enable you to choose digital images stored on your tablet and directly email them to a one-hour photo processing lab. You can pick up prints at the store, or you can have them shipped directly to your door.

The free Walgreens for iPad app enables you to upload multiple photos to your local Walgreens location and then pick up your prints within an hour (or have them shipped to you). The app even helps you find the nearest Walgreens location, which is ideal when you're traveling. A per-print fee applies, which varies by location and print size.

Similar functionality is also offered by the free RitzPix for iPhone app (which works perfectly with an iPad). Using this app, you can upload multiple images to the closest Ritz Camera location and then have prints in a variety of sizes created from those digital files within an hour. A per-print fee applies, which varies by location and print size.

> **NOTE** To create prints from your digital images, you also have the option of transferring the images from your iPad to your primary computer and then printing them from photo editing/printing software that's installed on that computer.

THE FUTURE LOOKS BRIGHT FOR THE iPAD

With the introduction of iOS 5 for the iPad 2, hundreds of new features were added to the tablet's operating system, making it an even more powerful and versatile tool for business users. No other tablet in existence offers such a robust operating system and vast collection of third-party apps, and the improvements just keep coming.

New editions of the most popular business-related apps are constantly being released. As these apps evolve, they get closer and closer to offering all of the functionality you'd expect from a full-featured software application on a desktop or laptop computer.

Meanwhile, all kinds of new content is continuously being made available via the Web, or in the form of eBooks and digital publications, to give you access to vast amounts of information that's literally at your fingertips wherever you happen to be using your iPad 2.

Combine this content with your hand-picked collection of power-packed apps, and the capabilities of the latest optional accessories released for the iPad, and the tablet's potential is limitless. As your iPad becomes more powerful, the need to also use a laptop computer or even a desktop computer diminishes.

At this point, even the most prolific and visionary science-fiction writers would be hard pressed to come up with ways to dramatically improve upon the iPad 2. Yet, you can bet that the hardware designers and software engineers at Apple are hard at work on developing the iPad 3 and the iOS 6 operating system.

The future looks bright for the future of iPad. The ways in which business professionals can utilize this incredible device either alone, with Apple's iCloud online-based service, or with a primary computer or network will continue to grow with the iPad.

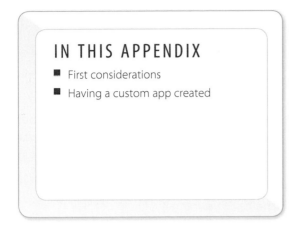
DOES YOUR COMPANY NEED A CUSTOM APP?

When Apple's CEO Steve Jobs announced the iOS 5 upgrade for the iPad in early June 2011, he also stated that, to date, more than 25 million iPads had been sold and that the App Store currently contained more than 90,000 iPad-specific apps (plus many iPhone apps that work on the iPad). The number of iPad-specific apps is now well in excess of 100,000.

Some of these 100,000+ apps were created by midsize to large companies in an effort to better cater to the needs of their customers or to serve as a marketing tool to increase business. Another portion of these apps were custom-designed for specific companies to be used in-house by employees in an effort to streamline or automate specific tasks or give people access to company resources while they're in the field.

Every day companies in all different industries are discovering innovative ways to utilize the iPad 2. Some of these uses, however, require that a custom app be created.

FIRST CONSIDERATIONS

If you're thinking about having a custom app developed for the iPad 2, first carefully define the purpose for the app and determine exactly what you want it to do.

Next, sketch out or create a detailed outline for the app. For example, figure out what options should appear on the various screens and decide what features and functions the app needs to include. This includes determining your target audience for the app. For this step, absolutely no programming knowledge is required, but considering these things gives you, and the programmers you ultimately hire to develop your app, a clear understanding of your goals.

> **TIP**   Based on your company's needs, determine whether an iPad-specific app is more appropriate or if your app development budget is best spent on an app that runs on all iOS devices, including the various models of iPhones, iPads, and iPods. Making an app available to all users of iOS devices dramatically increases the potential audience for the app, which is important if the app caters to your customers or clients.

Before proceeding further, visit the App Store to determine whether an iOS app already exists that meets your needs. If similar apps already exist, determine whether you can use one or what your intended app needs to do differently or better. It's essential that you understand, from day one, how the app will be used and how it will fit into your company's established workflow and overall business objectives.

> **CAUTION**   If you hire an app developer to begin work on a custom app but you have only a vague idea about what the app should do, how it will be used, and who it will be used by, this will result in a variety of potentially costly problems.
>
> At the very least, having a clearly defined one- or two-page summary of what you want the iOS app to do helps a developer dramatically when it comes to designing and programming the app you envision.
>
> Remember, the app developer you hire is most likely an expert at designing apps and programming, but he probably does not understand your business, industry, customers, or unique needs for the app. Thus, it's your company's responsibility to bring this knowledge to the table and stay active in the development process for your app. If your app developer doesn't understand your needs or isn't listening to you during development meetings, find a new developer. Otherwise, you'll wind up paying a fortune for a custom app that doesn't meet your needs or expectations, that is confusing to use, and that is actually detrimental to your business because the end result will be an app that does not achieve its objectives.

Next, invest $99.00 USD (per year) and join Apple's iOS Development Program (http://developer.apple.com) to learn more about what's possible in terms of having a custom app created and to gain access to the resources and tools available to you.

HAVING A CUSTOM APP CREATED

After determining that your company does want to pursue developing a custom app, you need to hire experienced and knowledgeable app designers and programmers (unless you already have someone on staff). It's important to understand that developing a custom app is a time-consuming and potentially costly process that requires a clear understanding of what's possible and what you're trying to accomplish.

By hiring an independent iOS app developer, companies are creating innovative, proprietary, and highly specialized apps for use in-house. An app that gives a sales force a streamlined method for entering and processing orders while on the road and grants them full access to an online inventory database or catalog from their mobile devices is an example of a custom app.

In some situations, cutting-edge companies are developing custom apps for their customers and clients as a way to boost sales, distribute marketing or promotional content, improve customer service, increase brand awareness, or build customer loyalty.

Thanks to the GPS capabilities and Maps app that is built in to the iPad, a custom app can determine where a customer is located at any given moment and direct her to a company's nearest retail location. This same customized app can enable a customer to place an order online from her mobile device and have it waiting for her upon her arrival at her destination. In the case of Pizza Hut or GrubHub, for example, a customer can arrange for food delivery with a few taps on her mobile device's screen.

The cost of developing a custom app is becoming far more economical than it was just a year or two ago, in part due to increased competition among independent software and app developers.

One of the biggest challenges you face after you decide to have a custom app developed is not determining what the app should do or how it will be used; it's finding and hiring an independent app developer that's capable of creating an app that perfectly caters to the intended audience by offering the end user value, simplicity, security, and intuitive functionality.

It's important to realize up front that having a custom iOS app created is very much like having customized software developed for any other platform. Having a well-designed, highly functional, and bug-free app developed that includes a slick user interface and the back-end functionality you need is going to be a costly and time-consuming endeavor that should include involvement from various departments within your company.

One problem that many companies encounter is that they hire a low-cost app development company or team of programmers. Companies that do this wind up with an inferior result that is riddled with problems. It's important to choose an app development company that's stable because you want the same company to be around in the future to support the app and make enhancements or bug fixes.

Speaking of app development problems, to save money some businesses opt to outsource their work to small, overseas app development companies. Common problems with this solution include dealing with time zone differences, which causes delays in communication, and significant language barriers. If you're unable to easily communicate with your app developer, explain your needs, and closely follow the app's development, the end result is often not what you anticipated.

Ultimately, your goal should be to establish a long-term relationship with the app developer you hire. Even if you choose not to add new features or functions to the app down the road, as Apple releases new versions of the iOS operating system, you might need to have the app updated to keep it functional.

> **NOTE** As a general rule, when it comes to hiring an app development company, you generally get what you pay for. A single freelancer or a small development company might be able to create the initial app for you, but if you want or need the app to be updated or expanded with new features in the future, that same freelancer or small development company might not be available or might have gone out of business.

Before hiring an app developer, look at the company's portfolio of work. Carefully evaluate the quality of its apps, including the user interfaces and functionality. Also, keep in mind that many different factors go into calculating development costs and the amount of time the development process will take.

Development costs for most good-quality apps, created by an experienced and competent development company, run between $5,000 and $50,000 USD. Realistically the development, programming, and testing process typically take between 12 and 16 weeks.

The more detailed your company's initial outline or plan for the app is, the easier it is for the app development company you hire to offer you a reliable price quote. How much you wind up paying for the app's development is in part based on the complexity of the app itself.

> TIP As you're sketching your app on paper and brainstorming about what the app should be able to do, start with what you envision the app's home screen and main menu will look like. Then work your way out from there, focusing on one page or screen of the proposed app at a time. This helps you create a more comprehensive plan for your app.
>
> To help you sketch a map or detailed plan for your app, consider using easy-to-use flowcharting or diagramming software on your primary computer, such as Microsoft Visio (www.microsoft.com), SmartDraw (www.smartdraw.com), or OmniGraffle (www.omnigroup.com/products/omnigraffle).
>
> To keep things simple, start by developing an app with the core features and functionality you want or need. Work with your app development team to get the core app up and running so you can release it to your workforce or customers. You can later revise the app to add new features and functions after the initial app has proven itself to be a success. After launching your app, solicit feedback from its audience to discover ways to improve upon its interface, its features, and its functionality.

Hiring a freelance programmer, as opposed to a full-service app development company, is a low-cost option for small to mid-size businesses. You can find iOS app programmers using an online service, such as eLance.com or guru.com. Alternatively, use a search engine to enter the search phrase "iOS app developer" to find links to app developer websites.

Another method for finding a well-qualified developer is to search the App Store for apps you like, and then make contact with those developers. Part of every app's description in the App Store includes the developer's name and a link to the developer's website.

> TIP It's a good idea to have a lawyer who represents your company create a contract between your organization and the app developer. The contract should clearly state who will ultimately own the programming code and indicate that your company will also receive the source code associated with the app, not just the finished app.
>
> In addition to indicating who owns the code, the contract should give you the right to modify the code as needed in the future and ensure that the code contains no backdoor access that could later be used by the app developer for unauthorized purposes.
>
> Also, if your company will own the code, by purchasing it outright from the developer, the contract should stipulate what rights the developer has to reuse or resell the source code (or portions of it) to develop future applications.

POTENTIAL LOW-COST CUSTOM APP SOLUTION

If you're thinking about having a proprietary app developed for in-house use to handle specialized tasks, determine whether it would be less expensive to have a developer create a mobile website that your iPad-using employees could access. Another alternative might be to have a custom database application created using FileMaker Pro and then use the FileMaker Go app for iPad to allow for remote access to that custom database.

Often, having a custom FileMaker Pro database created is significantly less expensive and much faster than having a iOS custom app developed, yet the functionality could be very similar, depending on your company's needs. To learn more about the FileMaker Pro and FileMaker Go options, visit www.filemaker.com/products/filemaker-go.

TIP   To learn more about having a custom iOS app developed for your business, visit Apple's iOS In Business website (www.apple.com/iphone/business/apps).

Index

C

H

I

N

O

P

Sudoku community, 305
ThinkGeek, 295
Timbuk2, 332
Trip Advisor, 225
TripIt, 225-226
Twelve South Compass stand, 342
Twitter business resources, 94
Ultra Thin Smarty Complete, 329
viewing, 92-93
Voice Recorder HD, 213
VuPoint Solutions, 351
WaterField Designs, 332
Weather Channel Max, 227
World Clock app, 224
Worth Ave. Group, 335
Yahoo! mail accounts, 52
Zagat To Go app, 227
Zagg, 326
Week view (Calendar), 100
what's hot apps, 138
Wi-Fi
benefits over 3G connections, 31
connecting, 30-31
FaceTime, 253-255
iCloud, accessing, 175
setting up, 19
Skype, 265
wireless
printing, 349-350
ePrint-compatible printers, 349
photos, 351
third-party apps, 350
setup, 17
Apple ID accounts, 20
country, 18
Find My iPad service, 21
iCloud services, 21
iOS 5 versus iOS 4.3.3, 18
language, 18
upgrading from original iPad, 19
Wi-Fi networks, 19
syncing third-party apps, 175-176
word processing, 151
Pages app, 178
command buttons, 181
creating documents, 181
deleting documents, 180
exporting documents, 189-190
font compatibility, 183

formatting, 183, 187
full-screen mode, 187
graphics, 185
landscape/portrait modes, 181
opening screen, 179
printing, 186
renaming documents, 179
ruler, 189
settings, 186-187
viewing documents, 180
Penultimate, 210-211
World Clock app, 224
Worth Ave. Group, 335

X

X-Stand, 342

Y

Yahoo!
calendars, syncing, 113
mail accounts, 52
Year view (Calendar), 102
Yelp app, 215
YouTube app, 23, 287

Z

Zagat To Go app, 227
Zagg InvisibleSHIELD, 326
zooming in/out (Safari), 92